Expanded Praise for *Waking Up*

"Brendan's book is your light at the end of the tunnel. If you are feeling lost – whether it be in your professional or personal life – this book will help you find what you've been missing. Whether you feel passion-less, direction-less, or out of focus, let Brendan's journey to find himself help *you* find *your* way to becoming someone you love."

—Jimmy Valiant, wrestling legend, WWE Hall of Famer

"After reading *Waking Up*, you may have the urge to reach out to Brendan and become his friend. I get it—there's something electric about him. He's a former wrestler, covered in tattoos and loves rock music…he just screams 'badass.' But once you dive into his book, you'll see there's so much more to him. Brendan takes a no bullsh*t approach to life and tells his story the same way. He takes you through the good, the bad, and the ugly—it's a refreshing take on the 'personal growth' story you so often read about."

—Rusty Brown, lead singer, Electric Mary

"Known as Knuckles Nelson in the ring, Brendan was the 'bad guy' who everybody loved to hate. Brendan's new book gives us a new side of him as he takes the reader on a colorful and engaging trip through the ups and downs of professional wrestling and his honest pursuit of personal peace and redemption thereafter. It's a trip you'll be glad you went on."

—Sheldon Goldberg, Wrestling Promoter and Historian

WAKING UP

From the Wrestling Ring to the Yoga Mat

BRENDAN HIGGINS

Redwood Publishing, LLC

Copyright © 2021 Brendan Higgins

All rights reserved. No part of this publication may be reproduced, distributed, or transmitted in any form or by any means, including photocopying, recording, or other electronic or mechanical methods, without the prior written permission of the publisher, except in the case of brief quotations embodied in critical reviews and certain other noncommercial uses permitted by copyright law. All photographs in the book are part of the Brendan Higgins personal collection, unless otherwise stated, and are covered under the same copyrights and may not be reproduced without permission from the author.

Published by Redwood Publishing, LLC
Orange County, California
www.redwooddigitalpublishing.com
First Printing, 2021
Printed in the United States of America

ISBN: 978-1-952106-75-0 (paperback)
ISBN: 978-1-952106-76-7 (ebook)

Library of Congress Control Number: 2020925902

Disclaimer: The author has tried to recreate events, locations, and conversations from his memories of them. Although the author and publisher have made every effort to ensure that the information in this book was correct at press time, the author and publisher do not assume and hereby disclaim any liability to any party for any loss, damage, or disruption caused by errors or omissions, whether such errors or omissions result from negligence, accident, or any other cause. Separately, the reader should regularly consult a physician in matters relating to his/her health and particularly with respect to any symptoms that may require diagnosis or medical attention. To contact the author, reach him at www.yogibiker.net.

10 9 8 7 6 5 4 3 2 1

Contents

Foreword xiii
Introduction xv

Chapter 1   As Long as It Doesn't Rain 1
Chapter 2   Chasing a Childhood Dream. 27
Chapter 3   The "Boston Bad Boy" 65
Chapter 4   Japan 81
Chapter 5   Salisbury Beach 99
Chapter 6   Courage to Change the Things I Can 125
Chapter 7   Welcome to My Nightmare 145
Chapter 8   Goodbye, Mom; Hello, Yoga. 163
Chapter 9   A Visit to Old Dominion: The Boogie
                Man Is Real. 183
Chapter 10 River City 223
Chapter 11 Righteously Reborn 241
Chapter 12 What a Difference a Year Makes. 253
Chapter 13 Of the Electric Mary Persuasion 267
Chapter 14 Pomp and Extenuating Circumstance . . . 311
Chapter 15 The Universe Speaks 325

Acknowledgments 363
2018 Boogieland Motorcycle Playlist 367

This book is dedicated to my mother,

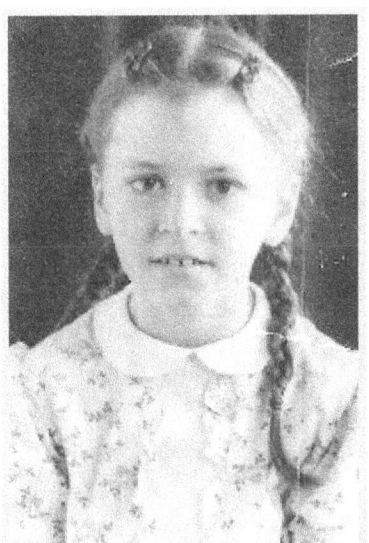 

Barbara Jean Branch Higgins
February 11, 1938–November 17, 2014

I'm gonna move you onto Knuckles
Gonna see what he can do for me

———

—Electric Mary, "The Way You Make Me Feel"

Foreword

"Katzman, Knuckles is different, he's not like everyone else."

That's how the late Tony Rumble introduced me to Knuckles Nelson more than twenty years ago. Tony had started the Century Wrestling Alliance and I was a talk show host for WRKO in Boston. Tony had become somewhat of a regular on my show and our shared love for professional wrestling solidified a friendship.

When Tony asked me to consider an on-camera role for his show, I was intrigued. I accepted but told Tony that in order to properly fill these shoes, I needed to be educated on each wrestler's storyline and background. Through Tony, I learned enough about each wrestler like they were my own family member. When he started talking about Knuckles Nelson, I perked up. Tony, known as the Boston Bad Boy, was the one who'd set wrestlers straight. He was a pleasure to be around but tough to impress. His insight on Knuckles Nelson was beyond the wrestler—he wasn't telling me about Knuckles Nelson, he was telling me about Brendan Higgins. The man behind the Knuckles Nelson persona.

Knuckles was a determined but angry guy. Part of the perpetually evil group known as "The Brotherhood" whose members would do anything to win, Knuckles was known for his vicious behavior in the ring and taunting pattern outside of it.

Brendan Higgins was different. Over the years, Brendan and I developed a friendship and today, he is somebody I count as my best friend. He is my brother from another mother. And Tony was right—he's not like everyone else.

The life that Brendan has lived can only be described as "one wild ride." This isn't a book about what it's like to be a wrestler, but rather a collection of personal discoveries, as Brendan finds himself.

Whether you are one of the legions of pro wrestling fans, devotees of rock music, practitioners of yoga or one who walks with Bill W., Brendan's story is your story. As he searches for answers, often on his own, you'll find your own answers to your own problems. You'll hurt when Brendan is hurting, cry when Brendan is crying, smile when he smiles, and laugh when Brendan laughs.

Buckle up. You're about to go on a ride that will take you from small town Rhode Island to Australia, Japan, wrestling rings, locker rooms shared with superstars, hot yoga studios and the bottom of too many empty bottles. More than anything else though, you'll look at the life of Brendan Higgins and understand just what Tony meant over twenty years ago when he first introduced me to Brendan Higgins, aka Knuckles Nelson.

—Jeff Katz

Introduction

In August of 2018, I found myself searching for answers. My personal and professional life had come off the rails. I watched myself make one bad decision after another. I had been living through failed relationships, health issues, disappointment, and loss at every turn. The pieces to the puzzle of life remained scattered, and I felt compelled to piece them together once and for all. I decided to confide in key people who I felt had been placed in my path to help me find the answers: a childhood friend, a rock 'n' roll singer in Australia, a radio talk show host (who also happens to be my best friend), a unique collection of yoga teachers, a WWE Hall of Famer known as "Boogie," and a florist all helped me on my quest for answers.

This is one man's story of his search for redemption. *My* story. The story of how I found the untapped courage to face my past and develop and embrace the idea of asking for help. How I put one foot in front of the other while learning to process my feelings and while believing in doing the next right thing, no matter what, and allowing life to unfold, accepting what is. I learned to trust myself for the first time; I changed a pattern of living in fear and relinquished long-standing beliefs. I let go of the need to control everything.

Some of the work took place in the comfort of my own home. Additional growth and change occurred in a yoga studio in North Kingstown, Rhode Island. A long journey on my Harley-Davidson became necessary for the ghosts of my past to be faced. An epic adventure to the land Down Under changed my perspective in ways I never could have predicted. Countless hours with a spiritual mentor in a flower shop in East Greenwich, Rhode Island, triggered the process of finding the *raw truth* I was looking for. My desire and desperation for answers whizzed like a trail of dominoes with changing speeds.

Writing this book felt like piloting an airplane without having taken flying lessons. With limited formal education and no prior writing experience, I checked my ego at the door and let my soul guide me. I felt determined to face my demons. During the process of writing this book, my personal spiritual awakening unfolded. *When the student is ready, the teacher will appear.* One of my teachers turned out to be my childhood hero, the professional wrestling legend "Handsome" Jimmy Valiant a.k.a. "The Boogie Woogie Man." Operating on faith, I traveled from Rhode Island to his home in Shawsville, Virginia, by motorcycle. My goal was to meet and hopefully spend time with the man known as "Boogie"—and to personally ask him about his philosophy of life. What he shared with me provided me with the motivation to dig deeper within myself for answers and inspired me to write this book. For months, I sat at my kitchen table writing with a pen in composition notebooks. One night I lost electricity and wrote by candlelight.

My goals in this undertaking are the following: To leave behind a book after I am gone. To share my experience while taking a stroll down memory lane. To provide an example of a willingness and ability to change. I want to share with the universe what I found out along the way.

—Brendan Higgins

CHAPTER 1

As Long as It Doesn't Rain

Sat on my hands for as long as I can
Now I'm stacked up and ready to go
I look at the sun for the answer to questions
I probably already know
Drop the ball, thank you all
One more chance to play
I'm back on the horse that I fell from
Back on the horse that I rode here on
Oh yeah, oh yeah
Let me out

Electric Mary, "Let Me Out"

I PLANNED THE TRIP MONTHS IN ADVANCE. THE BUILDUP grew with each passing day. It consumed my thoughts. Itinerary: From my driveway in Middletown, Rhode Island, to my ultimate destination, Shawsville, Virginia. Departure date: August 4, 2018. Purpose: To pay a visit to my childhood hero, professional wrestling legend and WWE Hall of Famer "Handsome" Jimmy "The Boogie Woogie Man" Valiant. Depending on your age, you probably remember "Handsome" Jimmy during the '60s and '70s. Along with his in-ring brothers, "Luscious" Johnny and, later, "Gentleman" Jerry, the Valiant Brothers trailblazed across the country and around the world as a highly decorated and internationally known tag team. They created quite a stir on their way to capturing several major tag-team championships, including two World Wide Wrestling Federation (WWWF) tag-team titles. In the Northeast, Jimmy is still known as "Handsome," and in the South, he's known simply as "Boogie." Throughout the '80s and beyond, Jimmy completely transformed himself into "The Boogie Woogie Man"—going from a *heel,* or bad guy, to a beloved *babyface,* or good guy.

Several months prior to the trip, I learned Boogie would be making a rare appearance in my home state of Rhode Island for his induction into the New England Pro Wrestling Hall of Fame, an annual event created by my friend Joe Bruen.

Joe owns All Axxess Entertainment, a company showcasing celebrity interviews and wrestling matches spanning the past two decades. He created a hall of fame for the New England wrestling territory. I made a point to attend the ceremony at the Brightridge Club in East Providence. It would be a great thrill to meet my all-time favorite wrestler. Growing up, I had idolized Boogie.

The ceremony included a long list of inductees into the New England Pro Wrestling Hall of Fame. Brian Fury, Aaron Morrison, Beau Douglas, Jonny Idol, Ricky Sexton, Dylan Kage, Fred "The Rocket" Curry Jr., Nikki Roxx, and Paul Roma were all honored. Jimmy Valiant was last. The room was filled to capacity, with hundreds in attendance. Right before his induction, I moved to an empty seat closer to the front of the room. I wanted to listen to what this man had to say. After all, he had given his entire adult life to the wrestling profession. Right after I'd settled into my new seat, Perry Saturn sat down next to me. The two of us have strong ties to the New England wrestling scene and had competed against each other in the ring nearly twenty years earlier. We shared how much Jimmy had meant to us in our youth.

Jimmy was inducted into the Hall of Fame by Sheldon Goldberg. When he was introduced, he stood up and began to shuffle his feet, moving his shoulders and arms back and forth as he danced his way to the podium. His famous ring music, Manhattan Transfer's "Boy from New York City," played. He kept his back to the crowd before whipping his body around with perfect timing to address the audience. Without warning, he planted a kiss on the lips of Sheldon Goldberg. The crowd loved it! His first words were, "Woo! Mercy, daddy! The Boogie Man feels good tonight!" Keep in mind, by this time in the evening, the energy in the room had lost momentum. The long list of wrestlers and heartfelt speeches had left everyone in attendance tired. But that didn't matter. When Jimmy stepped up to the podium, the crowd erupted. Like a phone charger being plugged in, the energy returned to the room. I listened closely to the kind words he shared during his acceptance speech. He spoke warmly of his career. He expressed his love for his wife Angel, his children, and his grandchildren. He told the crowd that he enjoyed hearing from all the other inductees. He offered words of encouragement to fans, veteran wrestlers, and wide-eyed young wrestlers. He told everyone that Ric Flair and The Rock (both WWE Hall of Famers) put their pants on one leg at a time, same as we all do. The longer he spoke, the more inner peace I felt. In fact, it was the most peaceful I'd felt in a very long time.

Earlier that evening, I was able to speak briefly with my childhood hero, and during that short conversation, he suggested I visit Boogie's Wrestling Camp Hall of Fame and Museum—an offer he'd also extended to all in attendance during his acceptance speech. I knew very little about BWC, so I quickly got out my phone and did some research. Turns out, Jimmy and his wife, Angel Valiant, own and operate a campus for aspiring wrestlers to hone their skills and learn the art of professional wrestling. In addition, the public can observe practice and tour the five buildings filled with unique memorabilia and rich history from a sport I hold in very high regard. I decided at that moment that I would take him up on his offer.

I wanted to speak to him at greater length after the ceremony, but it was not meant to be; he left the building quickly that night.

Jimmy Valiant speaking to the crowd as Rich Palladino looks on

Meeting "Handsome" Jimmy Valiant, my childhood hero

The following morning, I told my best friend, Jeff Katz, about my plan to visit Boogie's Wrestling Camp. I extended an offer for Jeff to come along. He was quickly on board for the adventure. At the time, Jeff was living in Massachusetts with his wife, Heidi, and his children, Harry, Julia, and Joe. His job, however, was in Richmond, Virginia, as a well-known conservative talk-radio personality. It was one hell of a commute. (Jeff had an apartment in Virginia during the week and came home on weekends and holidays.) With Jeff working in Virginia, it felt like a golden opportunity to visit Boogie's historic wrestling camp together. We scheduled the trip for the weekend of August 12. That date fell through, but our second choice, August 5, turned out to be the same day as Jimmy Valiant's seventy-sixth birthday celebration. The shindig would be held right there at the camp. Fate was already casting her light on the idea. During my visit, I would come to learn firsthand just how popular Jeff is in the area. *The Jeff Katz Show* airs weekday afternoons on WRVA in Richmond. Countless celebrities from all walks of life make appearances on Jeff's radio show, including Jimmy Valiant—a fact I had not been aware of. Unbeknownst to me, Jeff had made a call to Boogie's wife, Angel, to let her know he would be paying a visit and bringing along one of her husband's longtime fans. The table was now set. My mode of transportation for the trip would be a 1998 Harley-Davidson Electra Glide Classic, black and green in color.

I was hopeful that the 1,500-mile trip would change the course of my life. Helping me to make these epic motorcycle journeys a reality was the most honest man I have ever known, my childhood friend of over fifty years, Bob Quattrocchi. A state representative in Rhode Island, Bob has always been in my corner. Once his political career took off, I began calling him "Rep." He smiles, as if to say, *OK, whatever.*

Bob was also my first wrestling opponent of record. During our grammar school days, we battled each other regularly in his parents' front yard. The Quattrocchi boys, Bob and his brother Alli, stayed ahead of the curve by exercising and lifting weights in grade school, before anyone else in the neighborhood. With good genetics and a natural athletic ability, Bob provided top-notch competition. I always played the part of "Handsome" Jimmy Valiant. Bob portrayed WWWF world champion Bruno Sammartino. On my walks home from his house, I prepared explanations for my mother for the bruises, ripped clothing, and bloody back. The wrestling bug had bitten me at an early age. I thought about wrestling constantly.

Bob also happens to be a Rhode Island Harley-Davidson legend. His family name is synonymous with the American motorcycle company. Going into the Quatro Harley-Davidson history would be a whole 'nother book. My friend also gave me the pleasure of riding a Harley for the very first time as a teenager.

One summer day—I think it was in 1982—we went to Misquamicut Beach on the Rhode Island–Connecticut border. In my youth, this was the home of beach nightclubs, restaurants, and outrageous beachgoers—a true see-and-be-seen landmark filled with bodybuilders, bikinis, and bikers. After one of many successful beach outings, we started the ride home. Bob pulled his bike into the breakdown lane. I pulled alongside him to see what was wrong. I was riding a Suzuki GS450 at the time.

"Ever ride a Harley?" he asked.

"No," I replied.

"Let's switch," he said, getting off his bike. "I want you to experience this for yourself."

He jumped on my bike, quickly familiarizing himself with the controls. He looked around in all directions, then looked at me and said, "I hope nobody I know sees me!" He then popped a wheelie back into traffic.

For the rest of the ride home, I had the pleasure of my first ride on a Harley-Davidson. This is a gesture he does not remember, but one I will never forget.

With my lifelong friend Bob Quattrocchi at Gators' Crossroad, Goodland, Florida

Bob working on my Glide

My '98 Electra Glide, the bike I would use for the Virginia trip, was previously owned by Bob. I considered it good karma to purchase his motorcycle. As a retired motorcycle mechanic, he makes sure my bike is in top condition for my epic journeys. Spending hours with him in his garage, with NewsTalk 630 WPRO in the background, we engage in thoughtful conversations about relationships, marriage, current events, the past, and (of course) motorcycles—all while he works on my bike. His wife, Edwina, drops in from time to time with a cold drink. I always feel better after hanging out with Bob. He is not afraid to talk about his feelings or life experiences. He never holds back, and openly discusses successes and failures. Bob was especially helpful to me as I stumbled through a divorce, helping me to keep my chin up. He offers valuable advice for the road too, reminding me to take my time and ride slowly. He cautions me to constantly watch other motorists—to anticipate their mistakes, because it's only a matter of time before someone makes one. He reminds me to have fun, to enjoy myself, to respect the road and the freedom we have in our great country. Evel Knievel and Steve McQueen have nothing on my friend Bob. The last of a dying breed. A true role model. Passionately standing up for his beliefs. Taking care of his family. A loyal friend to many. They broke the mold with Bob Quattrocchi.

The days leading up to my departure, I kept a close eye on the weather. For fourteen days straight, I checked the forecast faithfully. It was to be sunny and hot the entire duration of the trip—except for the day I was scheduled to leave; the forecast for August 4 called for rain.

Taking a flight or driving a car never entered my mind. Rain or shine, it felt necessary to arrive at Boogie's Wrestling Camp on two wheels. Boogie is a biker, and I needed to pay tribute to my childhood hero by making the journey on my bike. I wanted to wish him a happy birthday in person and have a conversation with him about life. After meeting Boogie briefly in Rhode Island, it occurred to me that I needed to ask him the fundamental questions my soul needed answers to:

*How do you determine the next right thing to do in life?
How do you know it's the right decision?*

It may sound crazy to most people, but it made perfect sense to me to jump on a motorcycle, look up my childhood hero, and ask him personal questions. The truth is, I had nothing to lose by trying. Inner peace had eluded me. I was living with a giant hole inside—an emptiness that affected every aspect of my life. A short temper had been a long-standing problem for me. My mother tells the story of watching me chase the neighborhood kids with a baseball bat and very bad intentions. I was four. As an adult, I would do my best to console her, explaining that I would need a good reason to go after someone with a baseball bat as an adult. She failed to see the humor in that.

Holding on to resentment was another character flaw that kept me in a headlock. My inner voice told me to ask Boogie his philosophy of life. Perhaps a little of his wisdom would rub off on me. It was worth a shot. Meeting Boogie at the New England Pro Wrestling Hall of Fame ceremony was not my first face-to-face encounter with my childhood idol, however. Our first meeting is a story worth telling: One cold winter day, my father came home from work (as he did every day) at 5:30 on the dot. He informed my younger brother Kevin and me of a work-related function that he needed to attend, and he told us we would be joining him for the evening. I had no interest in going. It was frigid outside. I'd already slipped into my flannel pajamas and heavy wool socks. The Jøtul wood stove was cranking out extreme heat. In front of the stove, our dog, Brownie, and our cat, Heidi, slept on their backs, sprawled out, their hind legs wide apart. The TV was on (mind you, these were still the days of black and white!), broadcasting what was to me, a very important episode of the 1960s program *Lost in Space*. A copy of *Pro Wrestling Illustrated* or *Inside*

Wrestling more than likely had my complete attention. Ideally, the conversation would have ended there. Unfortunately, my father's mind was made up.

My preferred reading material in my youth

Our home during the 1970s, in Scituate, Rhode Island

Before long, we were making our way down Tunk Hill Road to our destination: Mount Saint Charles Academy in Woonsocket, Rhode Island. I'd never been to the well-known, private Catholic school, but I did know of its reputation for producing high-level hockey players—some making it all the way to the National Hockey League. As we pulled into the parking lot, it reminded me of the Midland Mall around Christmastime: parking spots at a premium. Whatever this event was, a lot of people were attending. As we exited the station wagon, smoke-like breath billowed from my mouth and nostrils.

I expressed just how cold it was, stating, "Jesus Christ, it's cold!" An unfortunate choice of words.

My father grabbed me by the shoulders. He shook me, screaming just inches from my face, "Don't ever use that language around me!! Do you understand?!"

A combination of terror and embarrassment rippled through my body. I had no idea what I had done wrong, but my father quickly reminded me. People walked by as I adjusted my clothing, bent out of shape. I attempted to gather myself for the long walk to the school. At this point, I *really* didn't want to go. Luckily, I was used to this type of discipline from my father, and I walked it off.

When we got to the long row of doors in front of the building, my father pulled tickets out of his pocket. Once inside, I recognized the space as a school gymnasium. The basketball hoops above had been turned up for the evening, and there was a wrestling ring at center court. The ring ropes were wrapped in silver duct tape. A canvas covered the entire basketball court. Rows of white plastic folding chairs surrounded all four sides of the ring. The bleachers were pulled open on both sides of the court. Hundreds of people milled about the dimly lit building. Complete and utter confusion set in.

My father looked down, smiled, and said, "Happy Birthday, Bren."

I looked at my brother Kevin, who was equally surprised and excited. The so-called work-related function had been a complete hoax. Instead, we'd stepped directly into the World Wide Wrestling Federation.

My father and I have always enjoyed a bond through sports—the New England Patriots, Boston Celtics, Boston Red Sox, Boston Bruins, Rhode Island Reds, Providence College basketball, and professional boxing. We were a true New England sports household. However, my father is not a wrestling fan—not then, not now, not ever. Regardless, he attended many nights of wrestling action simply because I wanted to go. From Mount Saint Charles to Jack Witschi's Sports Arena; the Warwick Musical Theatre to the Rocky Hill State Fair; the West Warwick Civic Center to the Providence

Civic Center, we made the rounds. He would purchase tickets and take my friends from the neighborhood, including Bob and Alli Quattrocchi, Billy and Kevin Kennedy, and Bobby Boie. My father always came through. Once we became old enough, he'd drop us off and pick us up after the matches. Decades later, once I had laced up the boots, he'd return to wrestling venues. There would be no escaping the squared circle for Bob Higgins.

I have no recollection of the matches that night at Mount Saint Charles Academy. I do not recall the exact date, but the first match will be ingrained in my memory forever. Back then, wrestling offered a completely different experience for the fans than that of present-day wrestling matches. The interaction was much more personal. Barricades and security railings were nonexistent. The setting felt intimate in much smaller venues, like a high school gym or the local armory. The chairs were set up so close to the ring that you could extend your leg and touch the ring apron with your foot. There was no ramp leading to the ring and no curtain to come through. The wrestlers simply walked out of a locker room door. No pyrotechnics, no giant video screen, no ring music or colorful lights—in fact, there was nothing to enhance a wrestler's presence. It all fell squarely on the shoulders of the individual wrestler to make a connection with or an impact on the audience.

The ring announcer proudly approached the squared circle as the crowd settled in. Next, the referee jogged to the ring to a slight applause. Without warning, the locker room door burst open and out walked "Handsome" Jimmy Valiant. The crowd gasped. I sprang to my feet. Without realizing it, we'd taken seats in the section that the wrestlers used to go back and forth to the ring. The last several rows of this section were empty. I quickly ran to the last row, leaving my father and brother behind. I stood alone in front of the aisle seat. The distance from the locker room to where I stood was about fifty feet. Right away, I noticed "Handsome" Jimmy was standing alone, without his brothers or his manager, the great Captain Louis Albano. With his long, blond hair, "handsome" Jimmy Valiant was a magnificent sight. He stood over six feet tall and had an incredible physique. His ring attire was colorful and flashy, with stars covering his jacket and pants. Without a police escort or security of any kind, he began to strut toward the ring. He glided along with supreme confidence. Jimmy Valiant didn't need all the extras used today to get over with the audience; his natural charisma spoke for itself. My favorite human being on earth was heading straight toward me!

I stood proudly as he drew closer. And closer. I raised my hand for a high five. My admiration and support could not be mistaken. Surely, he would notice his biggest fan. He looked right at me, making eye contact. It felt like he and I were the only two people in the packed high school gym. Everything began to move in slow motion. Time stood still. And he continued walking to the ring, right past me. Yup, he left me hanging.

The crowd reacted with a loud chorus of boos. Jimmy smiled, loving every moment. My admiration would not be swayed. I knew he had a job to do—no pun intended. In wrestling, losing a match is known as doing the job for someone. "Handsome" Jimmy Valiant had my complete support. I would remain his biggest, if not *only*, fan for the evening. The boos turned to cheers as Tony Garea walked out the door next. At the time, Garea was one of the most popular wrestlers in the WWWF. I liked Garea, but he would not have my support against my favorite wrestler. (Little did I know then, as a young boy, that some twenty years later I would be working for Tony Garea in the World Wrestling Federation.)

I grew up a huge sports fan, with wrestling standing tall above everything else. "Handsome" Jimmy Valiant was head and shoulders above any athlete from any sport. To me, he was bigger than Carl Yastrzemski and Bobby Orr combined. I continued to follow Jimmy Valiant's career closely by attending live events in Rhode Island and through reading a variety of wrestling magazines. I would not be face-to-face with him for another forty years. I loved the bad-guy wrestlers, the *heels*—especially the Valiant Brothers, Adrian Adonis, Spiros Arion, Ric Flair, Bruiser Brody, and "Superstar" Billy Graham. I was drawn to the *I do as I please* attitudes that these wrestlers presented. I was so shy and afraid as a child, it was impressive to see athletes living lives on their own terms, not to mention doing it on television in front of large crowds. It gave me some measure of personal power to cheer for someone everyone else hated.

One night during the summer of '77, the WWWF returned to the Providence Civic Center. I'd lived and breathed for the day they would return to Rhode Island. I found myself at ringside, sitting in the second row. My brother Kevin and Bob Quattrocchi were seated next to me. We always seemed to sit next to or run into the same couple at the matches we'd attend: a middle-aged man and woman, fitting the mold of wrestling fans. They were always very kind to us, treating us to ice-cream sandwiches every time we crossed paths. While wrestling crowds from the '70s were filled with people from all walks of life, I never witnessed hostility among fans. They saved all those emotions for the wrestlers.

We had created a large sign on white construction paper, using a thick black Magic Marker. The sign read, *Superstar Billy Graham #1.* Billy was the most impressive-looking human I had ever seen—a bodybuilder with long blond hair, athletic agility, and a charismatic presence. And his impressive interview skills added to his superhuman aura. The WWWF champion noticed the sign as he walked around the ring before his title defense. He reached over the top rope, taking it from my brother, and circled the ring holding *our sign* over his head, his massive arms fully extended. Today, "Superstar" Billy Graham has gone on record with his belief that he would have made a great good guy, or *babyface,* during those years. We helped him prove his point that night. The three of us went bonkers in disbelief. The Superstar returned our sign, giving us a great childhood memory and a story that we're proud to tell.

Meanwhile, as my upcoming motorcycle trip grew closer, I created a killer music playlist. My bike is equipped with a kick-ass sound system. Bob Quattrocchi likes to jokingly remind me that he forgot to remove it before selling me the bike. Harley-Davidsons and rock 'n' roll—the two go hand in hand. The scenario rounds out perfectly with a beautiful woman on the back of the bike. My custom playlist consisted of some of my favorite songs, heavily dominated by the Australian rock band Electric Mary—a take-no-prisoners brand of music with a phenomenal lead singer, Rusty Brown. Both Rusty's voice and his lyrics touch my soul. It feels like he's singing directly to me. His songs mirror my life experiences, and they especially helped me as I was going through a terrible divorce. I had felt such a connection to Rusty and his music that I wrote him a letter and sent it to the Electric Mary Facebook fan page.

The summer of 2016 was the first time Electric Mary ever

hit my ears. It was the song "Gasoline & Guns" from the album *Alive in Hell Dorado*. I pulled my motorcycle to the side of the road to look up the information for the song on my phone. From that moment on, I started listening to Electric Mary faithfully, and at times, exclusively. I took the time to learn about the band and its members, past and present. I also did my homework on their songs, including "One in a Million," "Already Gone," "Stained," "Slave," "Lies," "Crashdown," "So Cruel," "Luv Me," "Sweet Mary C," "OIC," "My Best Friend," and, my anthem, "Let Me Out." These songs gave me strength and hope to get through each day.

The woman in my life at that time advised me not to bother writing to the fan page. She seemed to think if I expected a response of some kind, it would just be a waste of time. I ignored the advice, and a few days later, Rusty Brown responded personally. This sparked a friendship between two madmen living on opposite sides of the planet. In my correspondence, I thanked Rusty for making music that touched my soul. I told him of my previous life as the professional wrestler Knuckles Nelson. Thanks to YouTube, I felt like I already knew him. I had watched concert footage and interviews from years past and quickly brought myself up to speed on this phenomenal band and its history. Rusty's incredible acoustic version of "Mr. Big" by the English rock band Free also needed to be mentioned in my letter. Paul Rodgers of Free is another longtime favorite singer of mine. Rusty had no way of knowing his impact on my life, so it was very important to me to let him know.

"Fucking awesome, brother. This is why I make music," he replied.

Electric Mary—*Left to right:* Paul "Spyda" Marrett, Brett Wood, Rusty, Pete Robinson, Alex Raunjak (Photo courtesy of Chowie Photography)

Our frequent message exchanges led to video messages and FaceTime calls. Turns out, Rusty is a wrestling fan too. He started sending me videos from World Championship Wrestling in Australia from the early 1970s and shared stories of attending live matches at Festival Hall in West Melbourne. He was doing the same thing in Australia that I was doing here in America, watching the exact same wrestlers. The universe aligned perfectly when Rusty took the time to say hello to one of his biggest fans from thousands of miles away. I feel blessed to call him my friend. He took it upon himself to check in with me during my divorce. He reminded me to stay strong and told me stories of his adventures from the road while touring the world. His timing was excellent. He popped up on my phone in moments when I really needed a friend. We discussed favorite bands and favorite singers—a welcome distraction during a sad time in my life. One of my bucket list items was to introduce Electric Mary live in concert. I sent Rusty videos of my audition for the job. I kept myself ready by introducing my friends from the Boston-based band Movin' On at shows around New England.

Rusty once paid me the ultimate compliment. The 2019 release of Electric Mary's album *Mother* mentions Knuckles Nelson in a song titled "The Way You Make Me Feel." The opening line of the song: "I'm gonna move you onto Knuckles, gonna see what he can do for me." To be forever etched in Electric Mary lore is a tremendous honor.

The day of the trip, I woke up to a dark and dreary morning. My relentless weather checks did not disappoint. It was going to rain, and I was going to ride. I needed to leave on schedule in order to arrive in Richmond by nightfall. Upon my arrival in Virginia, I'd be able to get a good night's sleep, then, in the morning, ride another two hundred miles to Boogie's Wrestling Camp. The night before my trip, I kicked off my much-needed vacation with a rock concert in Boston. The "Stars Align Tour" featured Paul Rodgers, Jeff Beck, Ann Wilson, and Deborah Bonham (the sister of Led Zeppelin's drummer, the late John Bonham). A fabulous night of music! I didn't get home until after 1:00 a.m. For the next four weeks, I would be on vacation from my job in public transportation, placing my life on hold to travel and do as I please. My bike was already packed, and all I needed to do was get up and ride.

Before I left, I said a temporary goodbye to my cat, Friday. My neighbors Tyler and Anna, along with their two (soon to be three) daughters, had promised to feed and take care of my little buddy until I returned. I picked up Friday and hugged him, as I do every day. He purred, rubbing his head against mine. I always feel calm and safe holding my cat, and I believe the feeling is mutual. His name comes from his birthday, Good Friday. I put him down, said, "I'll be back," and walked out the door.

My cat, Friday (a.k.a. Esquire Fri Fri)

On several occasions leading up to the trip, I confided in my girlfriend at the time, Betsy, about a gut feeling I had that kept coming to the surface. It somehow seemed unlikely that I would return from my trip. She asked that I stop saying it. I was scaring her. It was not my intention to be dramatic or to frighten her. I had no way of knowing at the time, but in some ways, I *didn't* come back. A different person returned. But more on that later.

My trip began in Middletown, Rhode Island, located between Portsmouth and Newport, on Aquidneck Island in Narragansett Bay. At the time, I lived in a cottage on Oliphant Lane—a secluded property with a backyard the size of three football fields. The property line abutted a small airport.

Smaller size planes came and went during summer months. A red helicopter provided tours of the island. On the weekends, I could hear, off in the distance, faint screams from people as they enjoyed the adventure of skydiving. I liked the quiet takeoffs and landings of the aircraft.

I started the bike, probably waking my neighbor Katie (sorry about that, Katie). I turned on the music and headed for the Newport Bridge. Traffic was light, and temperatures were predicted to be in the high eighties. I crossed it, officially leaving the island, and then crossed the Jamestown Bridge. A short ride down Route 1 to Route 138, and finally to Interstate 95 South.

The sky was dark gray in all directions. The music, loud and clear. I could feel my bike purring beneath me. I started to entertain the idea of missing the rain altogether. I had barely finished that thought when the skies opened. I had taken the precaution of placing Ziploc bags over my socks, inside my boots. My attire of jeans, boots, and a red Ocean State Harley-Davidson tank top was covered by rain gear. Bob had gotten my bike in peak condition for the trip; however, it's an older bike. I used my smartphone for music and navigation, connected to the sound system by a cable. In adverse weather, I store the device in a dry place to avoid damage. The radio was an option, but I chose to leave it off until the rain had passed. And a long wait that would be. Rain adds a dynamic to the road that needs to be experienced to be fully understood. It's a different type of ride, a vigilant one, with a need to travel slowly, especially on the highway.

My first stop was a familiar rest area in Connecticut. The rain was already taking its toll on me. The precaution of plastic bags over my socks did not work. Instead, they acted as aquariums for my feet, filling up with water. A woman at the next gas pump watched as I poured the water from my boots. We shared a laugh over it. The rain accompanied me through four states. As I entered New York, it intensified. Over the Tappan Zee Bridge, traffic crawled along at twenty miles per hour. Some drivers were using their four-way hazard lights—a practice I've never understood. It reminds me of cars parked in fire lanes, in front of stores, clearly marked "No Parking." They seem to think turning on the hazards makes it OK to disobey the "No Parking" sign.

Once I was over the bridge, I opted for the Palisades Parkway, a scenic two-lane road, to guide me around New York City and the dreaded George Washington Bridge. My go-to man for all things Harley-Davidson, Bob Q., advised taking a longer, safer route, avoiding the headache of driving through New York City. The rain continued to fall relentlessly. The only thing making it tolerable was the temperature, which was in the high eighties. I pulled into another familiar rest area, one I had utilized in the past. After filling up with premium fuel, I made my way inside the convenience store. My bike was stocked with healthy snacks and ice-cold water, but I decided to treat myself to an egg-and-cheese sandwich from the store. Standing next to my bike, soaked to the bone and eating the sandwich, it occurred to me that this modest sandwich was the most delicious breakfast I'd had in recent memory. Sometimes it's the simple things in life.

What happened next almost made me want to throw in the towel. I'd used this road before to circumnavigate the city, but this time, I found myself staring at an unfamiliar sign: "George Washington Bridge All Points North to New England Ahead." Were my eyes playing tricks on me? How was this happening? I could see Bob Quattrocchi shaking his head and saying, "I said to go *around* NYC!" With precision timing, the rain came down hard. Not only was I on the bridge, I was also heading in the wrong direction—meaning I would be going back over it, in the other direction, and getting the full tour. (Perhaps this would be a good time to turn on my four-way hazard lights.) From the corner of my eye, I could see people running over the bridge in the pouring rain. It felt like I was on the set of a disaster movie. The joggers proved that people just as crazy as I were braving the weather this Saturday morning. *A shout-out to my father, Robert J. Higgins, a longtime marathon runner.*

I had to get off this fucking bridge. The rain beading up on my helmet's visor made it hard to see anything. I took the first exit. Without navigation (my phone was stored in a dry place to avoid damage in the rain), it became necessary for some old-school technology: looking at street signs. Over my shoulder, I made out the familiar red-white-and-blue Interstate 95 South sign. I doubled back and looped around, getting myself back on course. Stopping to wait out the rain had never entered my mind. My goal was to be in Richmond to meet my best friend, Jeff; spend the night; and travel to Boogie's Wrestling Camp in the morning. With my type A personality glowing, changing plans or waiting for a change in weather did not compute. I had a mission. In the words of Paul Rodgers from the song "Cut Loose," I had to "keep on rollin' down that road."

I had traveled through Southern Rhode Island, Connecticut, and New York—and after crossing the George Washington Bridge twice, I was now entering New Jersey, once again in the steady rain. My spirits were very low; the pity party was in full swing. Before leaving Rhode Island, I'd detailed my bike, spending hours shining and polishing every inch. The leather had been treated with cleaner and conditioner, the chrome was glistening, and the paint was shining. But after hours in the rain, any sign of my labor had been washed away by Mother Nature. The New Jersey Turnpike can be a long, lonely stretch of highway. At times, it feels like it will go on forever. My body remained soaked to my very core. The last time my underwear had felt this wet for this long, I was a toddler. I began to think I needed to stop and regroup. After all, I had the entire month off. With Boogie's Wrestling Camp open only on Sundays from noon to 4:00 p.m., I told myself I could visit the following week. But I knew in my heart that I wanted to make every effort to arrive on schedule.

My fortune took a sudden turn for the better when, up ahead, I could see nothing but blue skies. My mood shifted to joy. I could make it! The moment I rode from rain to sun felt like *The Wizard of Oz* shifting from black-and-white to color. I pulled into a rest area for gas and to use the bathroom. It was time to finally change into dry socks and drawers. (Everything else dries in the wind.) I reconnected my smartphone and resumed my playlist. The first song queued up: "Gasoline & Guns" by Electric Mary. Heads turned as I started the bike at the busy rest stop. The unmistakable sound of Pete Robinson's guitar blasted from my speakers. I revved the engine a few times and put her in gear. As I pulled away from the entrance to the rest area, two twenty-something girls stopped and raised their fists in approval. They let out a big "Woo!" as I rode past, pointing directly at them. This moment is not easy to do justice to. It was as macho as it gets. I resumed my adventure in the bright sunshine. Enjoying my freedom, riding in the USA, aligned with my Australian companions, Electric Mary.

I was back on course to meet "Handsome" Jimmy "The Boogie Woogie Man" Valiant. My questions still needed to be asked, and I felt hopeful that he had the answers:

*How do you determine the next right thing to do in life?
How do you know it's the right decision?*

Ready or not, here I come.

CHAPTER 2

Chasing a Childhood Dream

*There are many ways to calm
And many ways to burn
I have been to war
And never did I learn
There are many ways to learn
And many ways to hurt
I have seen the one
And never did I learn*

Electric Mary, "Long, Long Day"

ONCE THE POURING RAIN THAT PELTED MY FACE LIKE BBs had passed, I began to enjoy the ride. I reflected on my personal experience in the wrestling world. My story is not about making it big; it's the more common story of *not* making it, and life in the aftermath. From my first thought of pursuing a career in professional wrestling, the deck was stacked firmly against me. For starters, I had an average-looking physique at best, far from the superhuman look that's usually associated with a pro wrestler. In addition, I had no contacts or connections to get my foot in the door. The term *second generation* did not refer to me. Having relatives in the business is a common path into many professions, and wrestling is no exception. I was just a fan who loved wrestling so much that I had to start doing it.

During the early '90s, I worked as a courier driver for Airborne Express, a company best described as a poor man's FedEx. I liked the job itself very much. For starters, they didn't drug test, a very appealing component for me. I lived deep in addiction from my early teens until my late thirties. During that period of my life, any job including wrestling—became impossible for me to maintain without drugs and alcohol. My daily routine included rolling out of bed and smoking pot right away, a practice commonly known as "wake 'n' bake." I continued to get high throughout the day. In the evening, I added cocktails—a lifestyle I embraced for nearly thirty years. Never for one second did I ever think this behavior was a problem. I was in complete, total denial.

While working for Airborne Express, I covered the North Attleboro and Plainville areas.

That meant I serviced the Emerald Square Mall. In this gigantic mall, filled with beautiful women, I met a twenty-one-year-old Irish beauty named Shannon. I had delivered packages to almost every store in the mall at one time or another. It was, by far, the highlight of my day. The day I walked into Shannon's boutique for the first time, her beauty mesmerized me. Her dark hair, blue eyes, and dazzling ivory smile struck me like nothing before. I was determined to ask her out. In fact, the very next day, without a package to deliver, I returned to her store and informed her that I was not there on official business. Instead, I was there to ask her out on a date. She smiled, wrote her phone number down on a piece of paper, and slid it across the counter with supreme confidence.

"I get off at nine," she said, and I walked out of the store on cloud nine.

I had only taken a few steps back into the mall when I realized I'd forgotten her name. I walked back into the store and openly announced my memory lapse.

She laughed and said, "Shannon."

I returned a few minutes before 9:00 that evening and made small talk as she closed the store. She was dressed in black from head to toe, her outfit rounded out with a black leather motorcycle jacket. We went to a restaurant inside the mall and sat at the bar.

After we ordered drinks, she lit a cigarette, took a drag, blew out the smoke, and said, "Mind if I smoke?"

I hated cigarettes with a passion.

"No. Of course not," I said.

I was too taken by her charms. As the night progressed, we shifted our position to facing each other. Our legs touched as we continued to become acquainted. I was smitten beyond words. When the establishment closed, we started to walk toward the parking lot. We held hands, as we both felt something special happening. Shannon stopped in her tracks, remembering her car was in the employee parking lot down the road. She asked if I could give her a ride. That, of course, was a no-brainer. I drove her back to her car. We sat in my car, completely relaxed. She looked over at me and asked if I wanted to get baked. I didn't think it was possible to be more attracted to her, but after her offer to smoke some weed with me, my desire to be with her shot off the charts.

It was in my car that we kissed for the first time. She went back to her parents' house in Massachusetts, and I went home to my apartment. From that day forward, we were inseparable. She was a dream come true for me. She began to stay overnight at my place more and more often. She would go home for a day and return with more clothes. She took over my closet and bedroom, and I loved every minute of it. In my eyes, she could do no wrong. She loved motorcycles. She liked to have fun, and she was always upbeat. I mean *always*. She changed her hairstyle in drastic ways without warning. One time she arrived at my apartment with the entire side of her head shaved.

Noticing my surprised expression, she asked, "What?"

"Nothing, it's just that you shaved half your head," I replied in a monotone voice.

"I know! Isn't it awesome?" she said with a laugh.

I did the best I could to keep up with her. A missing piece in my life was now in place. In addition to driving for Airborne, I kept busy as a martial arts instructor, establishing karate and self-defense programs at local health clubs and gyms. My long days were made longer by substance abuse.

I lived in the Arctic section of West Warwick, Rhode Island, renting an apartment above the Hong Kong Restaurant on Washington Street. In those days, Arctic's nightlife featured a bar on every corner. At times it could be scary. The people who would frequent the local watering holes were tough as nails. They would fight at the drop of a hat, never giving a second thought to swinging a pool cue at someone's head. The women who hung out in the bars were also really tough. Some were missing teeth and seemed unable to get through a sentence without using the F-word at least three times. In reflection, it was always eventful and mostly fun. From Ronnie's Last Chance Saloon to Johnny Ray's, a new adventure awaited, seven days a week. Other establishments included the Arctic Café, Washington Street Café, Benoit's, Café Jericho, The Windsor, and just up the street, the Come Along Inn.

None of these fine establishments had money tied up in decor or furniture. They all smelled like booze, cigarettes, and—as you got closer to the bathroom doors—piss. Most had pool tables, pinball machines, and if you were lucky, a bowling machine with a puck that slid along a hardwood surface under the pins. The machine itself was about waist high. You would bend over and hold the puck in your hand, moving it back and forth a few times on the table before letting it go. When you took your turn and pushed the puck down the lane, the pins would turn up. There was always a can of sawdust nearby to help the puck glide with ease. We called it *the cheese*. Local bands played on the weekends. They were true Rhode Island honky-tonks.

The area also featured the Palace Theatre. A strip joint that eventually changed its name to the Arctic Playhouse. From my second-floor windows, the roof of the Playhouse connected to my building. I could climb out of my window and stand on the roof of the Playhouse. It felt like standing inside an empty swimming pool. At the end of the rooftop, a trap door in the side of the wall led to the dancers' dressing room. The girls would hang out and smoke cigarettes at the door. They all knew me and would call me to my kitchen window to chat on their breaks. From time to time, I'd receive requests from the dancers to crash on my couch if they found themselves fighting with their boyfriends or too drunk to drive home. When you drive through the area today, there is no trace of the vibrant setting I describe. Father Time has worn away some of it, and man has reshaped the architectural landscape of this once-notorious town.

During this time period, while I was hanging out in my apartment with my friend Clinton Perry (who would soon become known as Clint Rampage), an article I was reading in the *Warwick Beacon* jumped off the page. A new professional wrestling school had opened in Providence and was holding open tryouts. An unnamed former WWF (now WWE) wrestler was in charge. Seeing this article in the *Warwick Beacon* was one of the few times I had ever experienced a vision of my future. I knew what I wanted. I wanted to become a professional wrestler. The self-realization was powerful. From this moment of ignition in 1992—when I was twenty-nine years old—through 2003, the wrestling flame burned strong and bright in me.

Prior to reading this article, I'd gone from one crappy job to another. I always settled for less. I had no awareness that my drug and alcohol use was playing a defining role in every decision I made, including who I surrounded myself with and where I worked. In my twisted mind, I thought that becoming a professional wrestler would catapult me to a new life and surely impress Shannon. I knew nothing about breaking into the wrestling business. Social media and cell phones were a long way into the future. Clint and I decided to attend the open tryout. For years, we'd beaten the crap out of each other in karate school, and we could hardly wait for a transition to wrestling.

The school was in an old warehouse on the outskirts of Providence, located in a mostly vacant industrial area near the post office on Corliss Street. It took time to find the place. There were no signs or anything to indicate any type of business existed in this run-down area. We eventually found it, and when we stepped inside the so-called wrestling school, I noticed a boxing ring with two ropes, a top and middle, with the bottom ropes missing. (A boxing ring generally has four ropes, while a traditional wrestling ring has only three.) The sound of dripping water came from the corner of the dark room. It was cold and damp. Welcome to entry-level wannabe wrestling.

A well-conditioned man in his early twenties stood alone in the ring. It appeared my friend Clint and I were the only ones attending the open tryout. We introduced ourselves. To the best of my memory, the article did not mention a fee to try out; however, a $5 fee was required to continue. We gave him the money and went right into the ring. I had several questions.

"Who is the former WWF wrestler in charge?" I asked.

He mentioned a name I'd never heard of. My skepticism continued to grow as red flags kept popping up like daisies. I consider wrestling to be a serious, legitimate sport, with my preoccupation dating back to my earliest memories. I love all the traditional New England sports teams, but I've never felt obsessed with them the way I have with wrestling.

I subscribed to print newsletters known as "the sheets." Dave Meltzer's *Wrestling Observer Newsletter* and Wade Keller's *PWTorch* arrived weekly in my mailbox. I wrote letters to both, and some were published. Wrestling had not yet been exposed at the highest level as being entertainment. Fans who are aware that wrestling matches are predetermined are sometimes known as *smart marks*. They know that the outcome of a professional wrestling match is fixed, but could not care less. I fell into this category. My favorite explanation as to whether or not the wrestling business is fake or fixed came from a former coworker and friend known as JC.

"Wrestling is all bullshit," JC once told me. "It is most definitely fixed." Then, after a short pause, he added, "Unless the belt is on the line. Then it's real."

For me, that explanation will be hard to top in my lifetime. That is a true fan. You see, wrestling is like no other sport or form of entertainment on the planet. Fans are so passionately bonded to the sport, they become emotionally invested to the point of either loving or hating wrestlers. They become consumed by the whole thing. At times, being a wrestling fan is more real than what is going on in the ring. People start fan clubs and newsletters with thousands of subscribers. The real human emotion that takes place in the ring and in interviews is undeniable. Some wrestlers, like Dusty Rhodes, Ric Flair, Hulk Hogan, the Von Erich brothers, and Jimmy Valiant, could talk people right into arena seats. They were capable of being so believable with the delivery of the words they were saying on television that the fans just *had* to be in attendance to see what the outcome would be.

While some people have no use for wrestling and possibly consider it beneath them, wrestling fans love it and feel no need to explain *why* they love it. I personally believe that people who snicker at wrestling and turn their noses up to it miss out on some of the most incredibly dramatic moments in sports history. These moments create human emotion more powerful than anything I've witnessed in any sporting event or movie. It's not even close. One example (among countless others) of what I'm referring to took place on May 6, 1984, when Kerry Von Erich defeated Ric Flair for the NWA World Heavyweight Championship in front of over forty thousand fans in Texas Stadium. It was as emotional a moment as any I have personally witnessed in all of sports history.

Several different story lines unfolded for this match. Some were man-made, while others involved tragedy and fate. If you are not familiar with the Von Erich wrestling dynasty, let me set the stage for you. Fritz Von Erich was a wrestler-turned-promoter in Texas during the time period of this historic match. He had six sons, and all but one became professional wrestlers. The Von Erich boys were incredible athletes. David Von Erich was widely recognized as the chosen one to someday become the NWA World Heavyweight Wrestling Champion. Sadly, David passed away while on a tour of Japan at the age of twenty-five. The official cause of death was acute enteritis.

Ric Flair was scheduled to defend his World Title against David at a mega-wrestling event, appropriately renamed the David Von Erich Memorial Parade of Champions, on the home field of the Dallas Cowboys. David's brother Kerry, known as "The Modern Day Warrior" stepped in as a replacement for his deceased brother, setting the stage for the match of the century. Kerry was a perfect physical specimen. His amazing athletic ability rounded out a unique fresh look for a pro wrestler. He was young and handsome, with long hair. He gave the fans something new to watch, and more importantly, to get behind and support.

Ric Flair was a classic heel, or bad guy. Although he did have fans wherever he went, he was pretty much despised against any of the Von Erich brothers, especially in Texas. Flair traveled from city to city and town to town to face the top wrestlers around the country and the world. He was a master at making others look like they were going to beat him—but Flair would always get himself disqualified, or find another way to escape with his precious title belt. The psychology or formula he used was executed to perfection, time and time again.

On this day, it appeared Flair would be surrounded by the entire state of Texas, with nowhere to run or hide. Wrestling in the Dallas area back in those days was not a sporting event. It was not a fake wrestling show. It was very serious. It was real life to those who followed it—and especially those who lived it in the ring. Thanks to cable television, I was able to watch the weekly TV show featuring the Von Erich boys, *World Class Championship Wrestling*, on Channel 25 out of Boston. I loved the show and was really into the Von Erichs.

After several failed attempts by David, Kevin, and Kerry to defeat Ric Flair, it felt like this might be the day. Although I did not see the match in person, I did watch it on TV without knowing what the outcome would be, so it felt the same as watching it live. I remember sitting at home in the family room, excited about the buildup and the hope that Flair was finally going to lose to Kerry. As the match got underway, my father walked into the room and commented on the size of the crowd. It was like looking at a sea of people, and quite unique because the football field was covered with seats filled with fans. It was an incredible sight on television. My father made a snide comment about not understanding how so many people could be interested in a wrestling match. I was dying for him to exit the room so I could resume watching in peace.

In the end, Kerry did, in fact, pin Ric Flair. He became the new NWA World Champion. His brothers, mother, and other family members, along with other wrestlers on the show, ran out to the ring to congratulate and hug him as the fans at ringside and the entire state of Texas joined in on the celebration. In the crowd, I could see people crying tears of joy and feeling relief that Kerry had beat Flair in the name of his brother David.

Watching back home in Rhode Island on tape delay, probably a few weeks after the fact, I still felt a part of what I was witnessing on TV because I had tuned in to the show every week and was so emotionally invested. At this point, I had never witnessed the Red Sox or Patriots winning a world championship. This felt like the same thing to me.

Our new friend in the boxing ring seemed clueless. He had no idea what the sheets were. He didn't use any terminology that I'd picked up by this point. Red flags continued to surface all around us. And Clint and I were so green you couldn't even call us green. Our new trainer wanted to begin by giving us both a standing vertical suplex. Learning to fall or take a bump is a good place to start in wrestling training. This might also occur after countless hours of conditioning, depending on who is doing the training. But taking a suplex is *way down the road*. It's amazing we walked out of there that first day still in one piece. Deciding to ignore the list of red flags, I volunteered to go first. The execution of a suplex for both people should never be attempted on the first day, let alone be the first thing taught. Regardless, our host for the tryout moved in for the kill. He wrapped his left arm around the back of my head while we faced each other. Next thing you know, we were standing side by side, facing opposite directions. He then grabbed hold of my sweatpants (the most common attire for a wrestling wannabe) with his right hand, just below the pocket. Without informing me he was about to possibly paralyze me for life, he cinched me up with all his might, lifting me off the ground and powering me over his head. I was now completely upside down. My momentum carried me toward the hard canvas as he dumped me on my side. Only by the grace of God did I land without injury.

Clint clapped his hands together.

"OK, my turn," he said.

For the record, Clint was in top physical condition—a fearless competitor and a force to be reckoned with. The next thing I knew, Clint was in the air upside down with his legs flopping around. Instinctively, he clutched our not-so-professional wrestling instructor, grabbed tightly around his neck, and they fell to the floor in a heap. Clint popped up.

"Let's do it again!" he said.

The truth is, we both had a screw or two loose. Neither of us had the sense to see how dangerous this was. On the ride home, I expressed concern about the legitimacy of the no-name school, but we decided to return for a second session—the reality being, this was our only option. The next day we arrived for our second session to a ring full of aspiring wrestlers. Our first visit had been reserved for brand-new marks. We met the members of this glorified backyard group. Everyone was kind and welcoming, but I had great concerns when I noticed that no one seemed to care about learning the art of pro wrestling. Just getting in the ring and winging it seemed to be their status quo. Still, my self-serving desire to wrestle outweighed my concerns. Before we did anything, they informed us of an upcoming wrestling show. They wanted Clint and me to wrestle each other at the event. It appeared that after taking one suplex, I was qualified to perform on a live show and was deemed *ring ready*.

We both needed names. I mentioned this to my parents, and my mother seemed annoyed.

"What is wrong with the name I gave you?" she asked.

I settled on the name "Hurricane" Higgins. Clint kept his first name, adding the surname "Rampage." We invited family, friends, and coworkers to witness the big fight. Admission to the event was free. It would have been a crime to charge for this crap. The marquee should have read, "Two Untrained Men Too Old for Wrestling Trying Not to Kill Themselves in a Boxing Ring Missing the Bottom Rope." That would have been just about right.

The event drew a standing-room-only crowd of around twenty-five people. It was standing room only because there were no seats around the ring. The lighting was dim. A construction trailer left behind long ago served as the locker room. A door at each end of the trailer gave the appearance of the wrestlers coming from separate dressing rooms—at least, in *our* minds. A small cassette boom box served as the sound system for the night's festivities.

The first match of the evening: *Higgins vs. Rampage*. Being the first match always appealed to me. The crowd was fresh and curious, not yet exposed to any terrible wrestling. A near give-in at this level. Not only would I appear in the first match, I'd also be the first wrestler to emerge from the locker room. Once the music hit, I would shift gears, springing out of the locker room door and wowing the crowd that consisted of my family, friends, and other onlookers. Only one problem: the music never hit. I stood ready to coordinate my entrance with music, only to have technical difficulties arise. This was a reoccurring problem at independent wrestling shows, one that would dog me for years to come. It never failed; either the music system would suddenly malfunction, or they'd play the wrong music. My ring entrance music that evening would have been "Rock You Like a Hurricane" by the Scorpions—as generic as could be. Luckily for me, "Hurricane" Higgins had only one match. My attire, black Reebok bike shorts about two sizes smaller than necessary, with the big "R" logo on the side. My gut was pushed out so far, I could hardly see my black sneakers. The look was crafted to offend all audience members, even my family and friends. In sharp contrast, Clint "Rampage" looked the part. Ripped to shreds, he looked like a pro wrestler.

We moved forward without music. The match itself was brutal. Being untrained, we laid in every shot—meaning we beat the shit out of each other. Basic wrestling etiquette was absent simply because we didn't know it. We talked freely to each other, making no attempt to hide our conversation. At one point, we spilled out of the ring onto the floor. I picked up a heavy folding chair and waffled Clint from behind, striking him in the back of the head. The impact sent him into the metal ring post, knocking him unconscious. His legs were jelly as I tried to pick him up. Clint is one tough bastard, so upon regaining consciousness, he managed to come around and finish the match. He landed a *sunset flip* for the three count, securing a hard-fought victory that, in many ways, was like a real fight. The small crowd seemed pleased with my defeat. Clint was a heavy fan favorite.

What happened next was the first of several *in the right place at the right time* moments during my time in the wrestling world. After the show, two men approached us. One of them I recognized as Bob Evans. We knew each other through a mutual friend, Cody Boyns. Cody hosted a weekly wrestling cable access television program, along with his brother, Jody. It featured local wrestlers in a talk show environment. At some point during the show, Cody would attack his brother with some really fake-looking wrestling punches and moves. It was so bad, it was awesome. In addition to the television show, Cody hosted a weekly radio show in Providence. He had excellent guests on the show, like the manager of the professional wrestling tag team Midnight Express, Jim Cornette, and former four-time American Wrestling Association (AWA) World Champion Nick Bockwinkel. I would call in to the show every week to offer my "expert" opinion on the wrestling world. I remember telling Nick Bockwinkel how much I disliked the way the WWF presented wrestling. He promptly told me I was not speaking from a position of authority and really had no idea what I was talking about. He was right.

Bob Evans told us he'd enjoyed our match. He also thought we were crazy. At no point did he criticize any training we'd received. He said he felt we needed more *formal* training. He explained that with proper training, we could become professional wrestlers. He hoped to point us in the right direction if we so desired. I can't stress enough how polite, respectful, and sincere Bob came across. He was, and still is, a genuine person. Although he was just a young kid then, he had been trained and was working matches around the New England area. Today, "Brutal" Bob Evans is a highly respected wrestler, manager, trainer, and promoter. His career spans four decades. Sharing his extensive knowledge with countless men and women, Bob improves their craft and personal character, both in and out of the ring. I'm proud to be the first of many wrestlers trained by this consummate professional. More importantly, I'm honored to call him my friend. Clint and I jumped at the chance and took him up on his offer.

The new school was about an hour from Rhode Island, located in Freetown, Massachusetts. On Clint's and my first visit, our eyes were opened wide. From outside the door I could see a clean, well-lit space with wrestling photos on the walls. In the center of the room stood a beautiful, brand-new wrestling ring. We had arrived at our new home: Coastal Pro Wrestling (CPW). Inside the ring were men who looked like wrestlers, wearing professional gear and boots. The first memorable sound I heard was like a cannon blast: the unmistakable sound of someone taking a bump. Bob greeted us at the door. He introduced us to our new wrestling family. First up was promoter Frank Castanhinha, a nice, quiet man with a mild resemblance to Captain Lou Albano. Next, we met trainer Brian Brieger. I recognized Brian from television. During a WWF televised match, Papa Shango had brought down the house lights with his voodoo powers, and once order had been restored and the lights had come back on, his opponent lay motionless in the ring, flat on his back, his boots on fire. That was Brian.

Several wrestlers practiced that day inside the ring at the Coastal Pro Wrestling school, including Johnny Royal, Rip Morrison, and a sixteen-year-old kid named Nick Steel, the son of promoter Frank. As I walked across the magical threshold, crossing into the wrestling school for my very first time, Nick was literally coming off the ropes. He catapulted himself through the air without taking one step. His momentum carried him to the center of the ring, above his opponent who was motionless and flat on his back. He landed on his opponent's prone neck with his right leg fully extended in a seated position. It looked like he had decapitated the man. He popped up to his feet immediately after the impressive move and walked toward me. The guy he executed the move on also got right up and appeared to be fine. Nick rested his arms on the top rope.

"How was that?" he asked.

I stood there totally in awe of what I had just witnessed.

"That was fucking awesome!" I said.

He nodded.

"That's called a stealth leg drop," he replied.

After our brief exchange, he returned to his work in the ring. Nick seemed as if he'd been born to enter the squared circle. He possessed a powerhouse physique and long curly hair. He already knew the ropes of pro wrestling at a very young age, and to top it off, he could bench-press in excess of four hundred pounds.

After we'd survived our experience at the wrestling venue in Providence, the time had come for Clint and me to learn the art of pro wrestling.

Brian Brieger is an excellent teacher. I respect him immensely. His method of teaching includes never asking anyone to execute anything he can't do himself. Years later, when I opened a wrestling school, I carried on his philosophy. Brian had WWF experience. The others also had experience working for independent groups, like the New Bedford-based Yankee Pro Wrestling, who have a long, storied history. Before becoming involved in wrestling, and without social media, I was unaware that an independent wrestling promotion was running shows on a regular basis just over the state line in Massachusetts. The key people responsible for training most of the wrestlers in YPW were Silvano Sousa, Gino Caruso, Phil Apollo, and the late, great "Gorgeous" Chris Duffy. From time to time, additional help came from "Dr. D" David Schultz and the "Boston Bad Boy," Tony Rumble, among others. Coastal Pro Wrestling had gotten off the ground with several people making an exit from Yankee Pro Wrestling to embark on this new promotion—a bold move, to say the least. It was much easier to wrestle for an established promotion than try to start something new in the same area. At the time, I had no knowledge of these wrestlers branching out on their own, not that it would have made any difference. I was excited to be at CPW. The new school provided safe, quality training. We learned to take bumps for weeks. The emphasis was always on safety. We drove from West Warwick to Freetown as often as possible. The hour-long drive gave me time to smoke pot on the way to practice. On the ride home, I added a twelve-pack of beer and more weed. I continued this behavior my entire time in wrestling.

The same core group attended training sessions regularly: Clint, Bob, Nick, Brian, Rip, Johnny, and Sky King. From time to time, others would drop in, with Frank outside the ring, overseeing the operation. Frank was kind, but a bit unpredictable. On one occasion, he entered the school with a shotgun in hand. He began pointing it in all directions. Wrestlers dove from the ring for cover. Brian was clearly terrified. I liked Frank very much.

After a few weeks of training, a new student joined the school, a four-hundred-pound African American powerhouse named "Mo Pain." The now-deceased Kevin McCone. We became fast friends. Mo moved with the agility of a man half his size and weight. His laid-back nature and his great sense of humor made him a welcome addition to the CPW family. CPW announced a live event that would be taking place on December 12, 1992, in Seekonk, Massachusetts. I looked forward to observing the show from the crowd, but to my complete surprise, Clint and I were booked to wrestle on the show. This would be my first legitimate pro wrestling match. My opponent, also making his debut: "Mo Pain."

The name "Hurricane" Higgins did not set the wrestling world on fire. I held no attachment to it and welcomed suggestions for a new ring name. During practice one evening, potential names were bandied about. The group offered suggestions, none of which I remember.

Brian looked at me and said, "I've got it: Tully McShane, the Irish Prince."

Tully Blanchard is a world-famous wrestler. While I have a similar-looking face, my in-ring ability did not come close to his. With no other ideas, I settled on the name. I couldn't have known it at the time, but years later, I would team with Erich Sbraccia to win the NWA World Tag Team titles in a match featuring Tully Blanchard as one of my opponents. The big win came on October 24, 1998, in Cherry Hill, New Jersey, at the NWA 50th Anniversary Show.

The Coastal Pro Wrestling match with Mo marked both our debuts and took place in a VFW hall with a capacity crowd. The ring was too big for the room. The low ceiling made it difficult to execute moves from the top rope. A manager named Felix "The Mind" Edison was assigned to me for the evening. He had a slight build and a big mouth, and wore a cheap suit and glasses. His job was to lead me to the ring as a member of his stable of wrestlers. He fit the part very well. Once again, I was happy to be positioned in the first match of the evening and the first wrestler out of the dressing room. The crowd was full of energy. In attendance were my parents, my brothers Kevin and Jeff, my buddy Dave O'Rourke and his son, Justin, and some of my coworkers from Airborne Express. Also in attendance was my new girlfriend, Shannon. She had no reference point for wrestling. She hadn't attended the glorified backyard match in Providence, thank God. This would be her first exposure to her boyfriend in the ring. It took a very understanding girl to date a wrestler in the first place. The idea of watching your boyfriend don spandex shorts and fifteen-inch-high patent leather boots is not for everyone. Shannon was a good sport and offered support and encouragement every step of the way.

I remember having doubts about attempting certain high-risk moves—like a top-rope sunset flip, a move that had me diving off the top rope as if the ring were a swimming pool. I would be diving over my opponent who was standing in the center of the ring, facing me, and bent over at the waist. I would need to clear his back, grab his hips, and flip myself over to my back, through his legs, and then up into a seated position, rolling him up on his back. What could go wrong?

In these times of doubt, Shannon would look me in the eyes and say, "You know you can do this, and I know you can do this, so go fucking do it." She would tell me that if I started thinking about getting hurt, I probably would. She provided me with great confidence in my athletic ability. Her belief in me helped me to overcome fear and take necessary risks in the ring. She would say, "If you can't beat fear, do it scared."

A nice group had turned out to cheer me on, and they quickly learned that I was not a fan favorite. "Mo Pain" had enlisted half the city of Taunton, Massachusetts, to support his effort and debut. The match went well. This time, I had proper wrestling gear: a black singlet to conceal my gut and some black knee pads. A pair of black-and-white patent leather boots rounded out the outfit. The boots were on loan from the locker room. Immediately following the match, I needed to remove the boots quickly for the next wrestler who needed them. This time, I had ring music. I used the song "Rock Warriors" by the Rods. Not very original, considering a music video featuring Randy "Macho Man" Savage used the same song. My role in the match was to take a beating from pillar to post, a scenario I became quite familiar with in the years that followed.

My favorite memory from the match had me in the corner of the ring. Mo pulled me from the corner while using my momentum to push me toward the other corner, directly across the ring in front of me. This enabled me to somersault over the top rope, landing on my feet on the ring apron. As I made my way along the apron, Mo charged, decking me with a clothesline and knocking me to the floor. I found myself at the feet of his cheering section. Trying to regain my senses, while also getting away from his fans, I made a retreat to my manager for advice and a breather.

The flip over the top rope is a move made famous by "Nature Boy" Ric Flair during his incredible career. My attempt at his trademark move has a memorable story to go with it. The low ceiling had several ceiling fans around the VFW Hall. They rotated a few feet above the top rope. As I flipped over the rope, the back of my heel came down on top of one of the fan blades, breaking the blade with incredible, unplanned timing. It made a loud snapping sound, and the crowd loved it. I was unaware it had happened until after the match. I had little chance of defeating my younger, larger, and more powerful opponent. He was full of energy and quite fast, beating me in every phase of the match. It was only a matter of time before he would put me away. He punished me for a solid ten minutes. I once again bailed out of the ring to consult with my manager. I hoped he'd have an idea for how to turn the tide in my favor. As we plotted strategy together, Mo reached over the top rope, grabbed me by my hair, and with sheer power, pulled me up to the ring apron. He set me up for an untimely return to the ring, known as *coming in the ring the hard way*. This meant I would be coming over the top rope—not of my own choosing—with a standing vertical suplex. Because I had nothing left, little effort would be needed to execute this move and pin me. But as my opponent hoisted me up, my manager grabbed his ankle, causing Mo to lose balance. He fell onto his back, with me landing squarely across his chest. My manager continued to hold his ankle down, helping me secure an unlikely pin-fall victory over "Mo Pain."

This turn of events outraged the crowd. I loved the feeling of pissing off so many people at the same time. My manager and I made a quick exit from the small venue, back to the safety of the locker room. My payoff for the evening? A measly $10. But to me, it felt like a million; someone had actually *paid* me to wrestle. After the match, my family and friends gathered in the VFW bar. I joined them, feeling elated and accomplished. Everyone seemed to be enjoying themselves, offering high fives and pats on the back. Everyone except for one person: my mother. She seemed far from impressed. After watching her son get the tar beaten out of him, she had the privilege of watching the rest of this independent wrestling show. This is where it all begins for most people—entry-level wrestling. After my match, she witnessed another contest, one featuring journeyman wrestler John Callahan, a veteran of the ring. The match could only be described as a bloodbath. Up close and personal, there was no denying that bloodshed in wrestling is real. To make matters worse, in this case, it was self-inflicted with a razor blade.

Right in front of her eyes, my mother watched John spill a gallon of his own blood, to the delight and complete entertainment of the rabid crowd. My mother was a veteran of community theater, but this did not resemble any type of entertainment to her. I was told later that her observation of the crowd cheering on this spectacle had disturbed her deeply. This turned her off to the sport completely and permanently. After the show, everyone gathered in the VFW hall bar. I was on cloud nine, feeling good about my performance. At one point, my mother pulled me aside, away from the post-match celebration. She placed her hands on both my shoulders. She wanted my complete and undivided attention.

Once she had it, she asked, "Have I ever asked you not to do something?"

I was not sure what she was getting at.

"No, not really," I replied.

"Well, I'm asking you not to do this. You are better than this. It's dangerous, and I don't like it. Please do not do this anymore," she pleaded.

Without hesitating, I said, "Mom, I'm definitely going to be doing this again."

Disappointment filled her face. I could not only see it; I could feel it. My mother had made her dislike of wrestling crystal clear, but I could not grant her wish. I was hooked. My father was equally unimpressed with wrestling. My love for wrestling, along with my new attire, left him with questions of his own. He chose to address his inquiry to Shannon, assuming she would know best. He asked her if I was gay.

Shannon laughed and said, "No, he's just a little flashy these days."

In later years, when I began to make a name for myself, my mother had opportunities to see my wrestling accomplishments in a positive light. When I became one half of the NWA World Tag Team Champions, she told me how proud her father would have been. I have very vague memories of my grandfather and asked her why. She revealed that he'd loved wrestling. Shocked, I asked her why she'd never told me this. She explained when she'd seen me glued to the TV screen as a child watching wrestling, it had reminded her of him. She hadn't wanted to encourage it. Still, it felt good to hear about this since my grandfather had died when I was a young boy.

Another time my mother saw my wrestling accomplishments in a positive light was when my cousin Lauren asked me if I would visit a sick child at Hasbro Children's Hospital. I was more than happy to do so. On Christmas morning, my parents accompanied me to visit a young boy named Billy. I brought the championship belt with me. When we entered the hospital room, Billy was in the middle of a blood transfusion. It was a difficult sight for any day, let alone Christmas.

When I took out the belt, Billy sat right up in bed and exclaimed, "WOW!"

The nurse instructed him to stay still.

He looked at her and in a commanding voice said, "But he's got the belt!"

The nurse laughed.

"You've got a point," she said, "but please lie down and stay still."

My mother liked the situation very much and instructed me to visit every room on the floor. Each time we left a room, she said, "Let's go to another." It was not a request; it was an order, and she led the way. This was back when we used a Polaroid camera for photos, and we took a bunch of photos of the children with the title belt for them to have as keepsakes. My mother and I left the hospital arm in arm. She loved the experience. It was almost like she was saying, "At least something good is coming out of this nonsense." It felt wonderful to receive a positive reaction from her. She never did warm up to the wrestling world, but that was one of the best Christmas mornings ever. I would often remind my parents that my father was an athlete (a marathon runner) and my mother performed in community theater, singing, dancing, and acting. When you put the two together, you get a professional wrestler. I'm sure a baseball player or a movie star would have been easier to accept. What can I say—they got me instead.

Coastal Pro Wrestling gave me the opportunity to break in to the local wrestling scene and gain experience. Top-notch talent filled the locker rooms: Bill Wilcox, "Freight Train" Fulton, John Callahan, along with future WWE stars like Scott Taylor—who went on to become "Scotty 2 Hotty"—and PJ Walker Polaco a.k.a. "Aldo Montoya" and "Justin Credible." The experience I gained at CPW allowed me to move up the ladder and branch out to other wrestling promotions on the independent circuit. I remember watching Bill Wilcox wrestle "Freight Train" Fulton and quickly coming to the realization that I had a lot to learn. Luckily for me, I was in the right situation to do just that. While at CPW, I received an introduction to tag-team wrestling. Nick Steel pulled me aside one day and informed me that the two of us would be forming a tag team. His level of intensity was intimidating at times. I mean, the kid was barely old enough to drive, but he understood the dynamics of tag-team wrestling inside and out. At the time, I was twenty-nine. He told me my new name was "Terror" Tully McShane, and he was "Nightmare" Nick Steel. It wasn't a question, like, "How do you feel about this?" He was bringing me up to speed on what was going to happen next. He told me our tag-team name would be *The Dark Side,* and our ring music would be "A Touch of Evil" by Judas Priest. Our catchphrase would be "God forgives. The Dark Side doesn't." He tossed a denim vest at me.

"Here, start wearing this out to the ring," he said.

He also had thick towing chains to wrap around our necks as we walked to the ring.

I stood there thinking, *Woo, I'm happy I'm on his team and not his opponent!*

He instructed me to call him every single day.

When I asked why, he said, "We are a team now. We need to get to know each other much better."

If I missed a daily call, my phone would ring at 11:00 p.m., and on the other end of the line a voice would say, "Why didn't you call me today?" He reminded me that we needed to know what each other was thinking.

I didn't think it was possible for anyone to be more serious about wrestling than I was, but Nick made me look like a slacker. I never questioned any of his ideas. Not that it would have mattered. He was not looking for my opinion. Luckily, all his ideas were really good—from ring attire, to in-ring moves, to music. Years later, I found myself in tag-team matches against the likes of the Public Enemy, the Headbangers, the Dudley Boyz, PG-13, and the Eliminators. All of the tag-team knowledge Nick infused in me was carried along and utilized throughout my entire career.

Like many independent promotions, CPW disbanded. In time, I broke out on my own, which led to my experiencing the petty side of wrestling. Frank and Nick, the father-son promoter-wrestler duo, had protected me. They'd never once stood in the way of my furthering my career. In fact, they encouraged me to wrestle wherever I could, as often as possible. Sadly, not all promoters operate in good faith. Anytime I made a new connection with a wrestling group, the person in charge would issue an ultimatum: if I wanted to work for them, I would need to be with them *exclusively*. This seemed ridiculous, considering the payoff would be $20 to $25. Not to mention they might run shows once a month or so, if we were lucky. The idea is to wrestle as often as possible. Wrestling in front of a live audience is the best way to gain the valuable experience necessary to move up through the ranks. I always agreed to the silly terms of promoters at first; then I did whatever I wanted. I was fortunate to work often during the early years.

Tragically, while I was writing this book, Nick Steel passed away unexpectedly, leaving behind his wife, Jennifer, and three children. He was just forty-four years old. I was heartbroken and grief stricken upon hearing the news. Nick was a warrior. A physical warrior as well as a spiritual warrior. From a young age, he offered practical advice and opinions. I remember having serious conversations with him when he was a teenager. Then I would walk into his bedroom to find wrestling posters on the wall. I would say to myself, "Holy shit, he's just a kid." We stayed in touch over the years. His conservative values were in place almost from birth. His love of family, friends, and God were unparalleled. He was a natural-born teacher. The list of successful professional wrestlers that were influenced by Nick Steel is long. On a side note, I never had to worry about jumping or timing when Nick suplexed me. It was always over before I knew it. I would have wanted Nick to read this book to be reminded of how I held him in such high regard. In my heart, I believe he knew. I love you, brother. See you on the other side.

CHASING A CHILDHOOD DREAM

Nick Castanhinha a.k.a. "Nightmare" Nick Steel
March 25, 1975– February 15, 2020
(Photo courtesy of Jason Schneider)

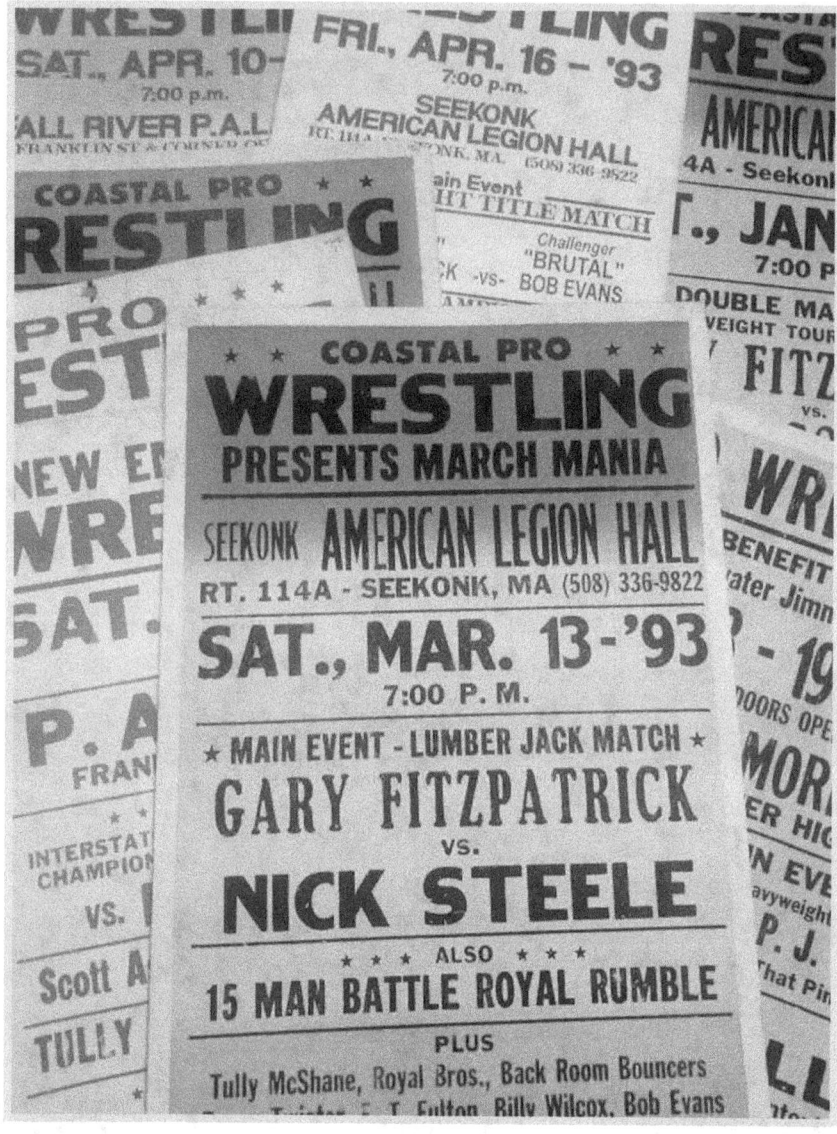

Things began to change quickly in my personal life. My time with Airborne Express ended abruptly. One day, on my regular route in North Attleboro, a snowstorm broke out. The ground was already covered from a previous snowfall. I was in a rush, as usual—a trait that goes hand in hand with addiction. To save time, I took a shortcut through a snow-covered parking lot. Turns out, the parking lot was a small pond. Suddenly, the van was floating in the water. The first indication: water was pouring in the doors as the van bobbed up and down. I rolled down the window and climbed onto the roof, bringing the remaining packages with me. Lying down, I reached into the window that I had just climbed from, and grabbed the corded microphone to call for help. I then managed to jump to shore. Standing there, looking at the silver delivery van, I was mainly annoyed that this would make me late for wrestling practice. Shortly thereafter, management wished me well with my wrestling career and showed me the door. I tell this story in a lighthearted way, but it was embarrassing and sad. For the rest of my twenties and thirties, I worked in nightclubs, trying to make wrestling my full-time profession. I was a full-blown alcoholic and drug addict, living from day to day.

Around this time, an unexpected turn of events unfolded. The store Shannon worked for closed its doors for good, and she informed me that she had been offered a new job with a much-deserved promotion at another mall. I was happy for her until I found out it was in Worcester. That meant she would be staying at her parents' house more and staying with me less. I was obsessed with becoming the best pro wrestler I could be, and Shannon took on her new job as she did everything—like a badass. We saw each other less and less. We were on two different lifeboats, holding hands until we simply let go. Our boats drifted off in different directions. We never officially broke up; our time together had just run its course. Shannon had more style, personality, and charisma than any of the wrestlers I was around. Her wardrobe was unique, filled with sexy outfits that she wore perfectly. She was the most incredible dancer I had ever seen. I would take her to nightclubs, and she would walk out alone onto a dance floor full of people and begin to feel the music as I watched her from the crowd. In no time, the floor would be cleared of everyone except Shannon because she needed space to move. She always made me feel like I was the only man in the room—even when the room was full of other men and women watching her dance. I loved her deeply, but neither of us could prevent life from moving forward. Almost six months after we parted ways, I received a message from Shannon on my answering machine on my thirtieth birthday. She sang the lines of "Happy Birthday," adding "from Shannon" at the end. Then she hung up. I sat looking at the machine, feeling sad and missing her. I wanted to call her back but decided not to. In my heart, I knew that would be the last time I'd ever hear her voice.

More change came when Clint informed me of his decision to hang up his wrestling boots for good. As a husband, father, and new homeowner, his priority was his family now. He couldn't risk the possibility of injury, and I understood completely. To this day, I hold Clint in the highest regard. A superior martial artist, he's always thinking outside the box. His philosophy for self-defense: it should be practiced under any and all conditions. He stands ready in all situations.

One night back then, Clint suggested we practice self-defense while drunk. After all, an attack could happen after a few drinks. The idea made perfect sense to me. To prepare for our training, we consumed several Captain Morgan and Cokes. Sometime after midnight, we drove to a cemetery in the Crompton section of West Warwick. Dressed in winter jackets, hats, and gloves—all the added accessories being Clint's idea—we got right into it. Before long, a police cruiser approached, flashing a bright light in our direction. A female officer emerged from the car.

With genuine curiosity, she asked, "What's going on here?"

We both stood there in silence.

She pointed her flashlight toward Clint's car. A single Budweiser can sat on the hood.

"Who does that belong to?" she inquired.

In unison, we both said, "Me."

Clint then sprang into action: "Officer, we are here tonight practicing self-defense techniques. You, of all people, should understand how important that is. What if—"

"Stop," she interrupted, laughing. "As long as there are no warrants out for either of you, I'm going to leave you to it."

She was pretty *and* confident. Considering our size and appearance, it was impressive that she never called for backup. Once she'd received the result of the routine background check, she told us to be safe and to have a good night. We'd dodged a major bullet. As she began to walk back to her cruiser, relief set in . . . though mine was short-lived.

Clint decided to blurt out, "Officer, he's single!" Of course he was referring to me. Then he offered this: "Officer, maybe you should give him your phone number, and the two of you can go out on a date."

I stood, once again silent, in complete disbelief. She took Clint's suggestion in stride, but decided to pass on his offer.

Once we were alone, I screamed at Clint, "What the hell is wrong with you?!"

He remained calm and asked if I thought she was hot.

"Yes, of course she is," I said, "but we could be in jail right now!"

He held his ground, pointing out that it was an opportunity to meet a nice girl with a good job. Clint is one of those people with good looks and charm, even when he's not trying. We resumed our self-defense moves, entertaining the dead—just another night hanging out with Clint Rampage.

I had no intention of hanging up my wrestling boots; I hadn't even broken a bootlace yet. The time had arrived for me to take some drastic measures and jump-start my nonexistent career. I needed to get my foot in the door, so I went to the Providence Civic Center when the WWF was in town. My goal was to make myself known to the right people. With hardly any experience under my belt, I was completely clueless as to just how unprepared I was for this level of wrestling. I walked to the back door of the arena and was promptly stopped by security. I explained that although they may not know me, I was one of the new wrestlers. They stepped aside and held the door for me. *Wow*, I thought, *that was easy*. This was the first of several lies I told that day.

The only option for me to get in the ring for the WWF would be in the role of a jobber, (also known as an *extra* or *enhancement talent*). A jobber is best described as someone who loses a one-sided match. Pitting a polished, more established wrestler against a far lesser talent (that would be me). The man in charge of these jobbers was another legend from my youth, Tony Garea, the same man who had wrestled "Handsome" Jimmy Valiant at Mount St. Charles Academy many years earlier. At the time, WWE was still called WWF, and they used local talent from whichever part of the country they happened to be touring for the purpose of losing to one of their established wrestlers. These matches, taped for television, were known as *squash matches*. If I wanted to wrestle for the WWF, Tony Garea was the man to see. Always a gentleman, Tony greeted me with a handshake. He knew what I wanted before I opened my mouth. He asked who trained me.

"Paul Roma," I said. A lie. I knew some of Paul's students and felt that giving a known wrestler's name as my trainer might help my chances.

He asked how long I had been wrestling. I said five years. Another lie. He seemed amused by my ring name, Tully McShane.

"OK, Tully," he said, "be at the next television taping in White Plains, New York, next week." Then he asked if I needed tickets for the show that evening.

That was it. Just like that, I was in. The only problem: everything I had told him was a lie.

As instructed, I arrived at the Westchester County Center in White Plains, New York, on the morning of August 17, 1993. Once again, security stopped me. Only this time, I *was* one of the wrestlers. Once inside, I located Tony Garea. He claimed we had never met and he had never told me to come today. I stood silent in disbelief. Without another word, he turned and walked away.

I raised my voice: "Yes, you did!"

The New Zealand native stopped and turned back toward me.

"I did?" he asked.

"Yes," I affirmed.

He smiled.

"I must be losing my mind," he said. He asked my name again. He told me to hang out and said he would talk to me later. He said to relax and enjoy the day.

I never did relax that day. With each passing moment, reality set in. One by one, a who's who of the wrestling world arrived at the building: the Steiner Brothers, "Mr. Perfect" Curt Hennig, Razor Ramon, "Macho Man" Randy Savage, and

Vince McMahon—all coming to work. It hit me that I would be facing a member of the WWF roster, in a WWF ring, in a matter of hours. Tony returned, asking if I knew Razor Ramon.

"Yes, of course I do," I said.

He wanted to know if I had any reservations about taking his finishing move, the Razor's Edge. This move would have Razor facing me, putting my head between his legs, and flipping me over his shoulders. He'd hold me by my armpits and press me over his head. He'd then fall forward and drive me into the canvas on my back.

"No problem," I told Tony, and he instructed me to introduce myself to Razor and listen to his instructions for the match.

Razor's real name is Scott Hall—a well-seasoned pro and future WWE Hall of Famer. He had paid his dues years before I had ever even thought of becoming a wrestler. When I introduced myself to Razor, he was very polite and friendly—a nice warm-up before he beat the shit out of me. Razor had recently captured the WWF Intercontinental Championship title. This would be a non-title match.

As I walked to the ring, the air felt warm. In fact, everything felt warm—the air, the lights, my body, everything. Before I entered the ring, I was completely blown up. This is a wrestling term, meaning I was already tired. In fact, I felt exhausted. The fans in the front row jumped on me quickly.

"Who in the fuck are you?" they yelled. "We have no idea who you are! You fuckin' bum!" You know, just your average words of encouragement from fans. The reality: I was being led to slaughter. Once in the ring, I was supposed to stay in my corner, showing no emotion or enthusiasm. The sound of screeching tires filled the arena. Miami-style music began to play. The crowd erupted. Razor had an endearing trademark move of throwing a toothpick into the face of his opponent after the referee had finished his instructions. He threw his toothpick into my face like one would throw a dart. Once he completed this insulting gesture, the match got underway.

Vince McMahon called the match, with Randy Savage doing color commentary. The wrestling match was short. Razor immediately unleashed his arsenal of moves at my expense. He outclassed me in every way—a journeyman pro against a guy who was high and had sixteen matches under his belt. He executed a belly-to-back suplex from the top rope, driving me to the mat. That move inspired Randy Savage to say, "Welcome to the World Wrestling Federation!" A fall-away slam from the middle rope almost sent me out of the ring. Then Razor set me up for the Razor's Edge. Pushing my head between his legs, he extended his arms to the side to signal the end was near. Hurling my body over his shoulder first, then military pressing me over his head. I could see myself on the giant video monitor known as the Titantron. A surreal moment. During the match, I'd failed to throw a single punch. Razor thanked me while he covered me for the pin, and he thanked me again in the backstage area. My payoff this time around? $150!

Unless you've experienced trying to enter the pro wrestling fraternity, you might not understand the concept of being happy about getting beaten up. On the ride home, battered and bruised, I was thrilled. Some kids want to grow up and play for the Boston Red Sox or the New England Patriots. Not me—I wanted to be a professional wrestler, and I had just wrestled the Intercontinental Champion on national television in a WWF ring.

It would be another six years before I would get another chance in the WWF.

The "Boston Bad Boy"

I'm Boston born
And Boston bred
And I'll be Boston bad
Till I'm Boston dead

Tony Rumble

MY OBSESSION WITH WRESTLING GREW WITH EACH passing day. The idea of working a nine-to-five job was no longer on my radar screen. The desire to make my dream a reality was so strong that I became willing to do anything to achieve it. Fresh off my WWF pounding, I traveled to Hanover, Massachusetts, for a show promoted by the infamous "Boston Bad Boy," Tony Rumble. Born Anthony David Magliaro, Tony Rumble would become my manager, mentor, and close friend in the months and years ahead. A cult figure in the wrestling world, Tony was extremely well known despite never having a run with a major wrestling company. He is best known for his time in International Championship Wrestling (ICW). During the '90s, Tony branched out on his own with a brand-new company, the Century Wrestling Alliance (CWA).

On January 22, 1994, I drove my 1985 Buick LeSabre, equipped with a Pioneer Supertuner, to Hanover High School. In the past, Clint Rampage would have been my copilot, but with him hanging up the boots for good, I was on my own. Even though I knew a slew of hungry young wrestlers, I decided to fly solo this time. I felt my chances of getting booked on the show would be greater if I was alone. I arrived early in the day. So early, the wrestling ring had not yet arrived at the building. I now considered myself experienced. In reality, I was still completely green. I was just a notch above clueless. But after all, I'd wrestled Razor Ramon on television. That had to count for something. Surely Tony would know Tully McShane.

I sat in the bleachers, watching the ring crew set up the ring. Workers from the school set up folding chairs on the basketball court. I decided to walk into the locker room. The first person I encountered was "Hacksaw" Jim Duggan; he was sitting alone playing solitaire. A two-by-four rested against the lockers. In the next aisle was a true wrestling legend, King Kong Bundy.

"Hey, kid," Bundy said, looking up at me from a bench.

Deeper in the locker room sat Tony Atlas and Tito Santana. I said hello as I walked by. Once out of their sight, I heard Tito ask Atlas, "Who the hell is that?"

"Some young whippersnapper, I reckon," Atlas replied.

Then the door behind me flew open. In walked Tony Rumble and Patrick J. Doyle. I didn't know who Pat was then, but I quickly surmised he was Tony's right-hand man. He managed all the television activity for the CWA. I came to learn that Tony and Pat shared a very close bond, like father and son. Pat looked up to Tony, as we all did. It was my move to introduce myself, just like when I'd met Tony Garea.

I walked up to Rumble, extended my hand, and said, "Hi, I'm Tully McShane. I have my gear with me, if you can use me today."

Looking back, I can see that "if you can use me" is exactly what promoters do; they use wrestlers, and when it's over, the wrestler says, "Thank you." Every time a wrestler steps into the ring, it involves taking a risk. Injuries happen. A new, inexperienced worker, like I was in my early days, is more than likely going to be on the receiving end of a solid beating. With full knowledge of this, we still offer sincere gratitude.

To my delight, Tony agreed.

"OK, you can work with me," he said. And just like that, I was in.

I was about to learn that one-sided squash matches also take place on independent shows. Any input on the match from me would not be necessary. I learned in wrestling school to always put my opponent at ease—to never tell them what I want to do, but rather remind them that anything they want to accomplish in the match is fine with me. Making a veteran professional wrestler aware that I know my place is a good way to minimize the physical pain coming my way.

Tony worked a very basic match. I would attack him before the bell. After the sneak attack, I'd put him in the corner. I'd then attempt to pull him from the corner by his arm. He'd reverse it, catching me with a short elbow across my chest. Tony would then apply the Boston Crab, a wrestling hold which would find me flat on my back with him standing over me, looking down on my prone body. He would proceed to reach his arms under my knees, pulling my legs off the ground. Then he'd turn around on his pivot foot, facing the other direction, maneuver me onto my stomach, pull up on my legs, and increase pressure on my lower back while he settled into a deep squat, forcing me to submit or give up. What could go wrong?

Before the match, Tony sat me down to set me straight. He hated the name Tully McShane. For a moment, I felt crushed. But then he explained that his idea was to put me under a mask for this match, and if things went well, bring me back for future shows.

"Of course," I told him. "Whatever you want."

Tony was a pleasure to be around. I'd watched him on television for years. The ICW aired Saturday afternoons on

WPRI-TV12 in Providence. This was a big step in the right direction for me. As a wrestler, promoter, and all-around television personality, Tony brought a wealth of knowledge to his new wrestling company. His connections ran deep in the wrestling world. He made a living on the independent circuit, not an easy thing to do.

Left to right: Vic Steamboat; the "Boston Bad Boy," Tony Rumble; and me (Knuckles Nelson)

The show in Hanover had an early-afternoon start time of 2:00 p.m. The high school gym was full of wrestling fans. Tony promoted shows with famous wrestlers and he also utilized up-and-coming wrestlers to create a perfect mix of talent. The shows were sold to organizations as fundraisers. Groups could raise large amounts of money in one night. This allowed wrestlers to work in front of big crowds. Everybody was happy. Aside from my WWF adventure, I was used to around fifty people in the audience. On this sunny, cold winter day in Hanover, thousands filled the gym. It was awesome.

I had finally purchased my own black-and-red patent leather wrestling boots. And black kneepads with big red stars in the center, just like Jimmy Valiant. I had also come across some long, black skate laces at a local flea market that created a better look for my boots than basic white laces. I wore a generic black singlet—basically, a one-piece pair of shorts with shoulder straps. A new dynamic came about for this match: I would be wearing a mask. Another first for me.

Tony supplied the mask. As he handed it to me, I asked him, "What is my name going to be?"

He looked at Pat and asked, "What should we call him?"

Slightly amused, Pat said, "Oh, I don't know. What about the 'New Hampshire Nightmare'?"

Tony asked if that was OK with me.

"Yes, of course, whatever you want," I replied.

"Perfect," Tony said. And the "New Hampshire Nightmare" was born . . . or so I'd thought. A short time later, as I wandered around the school lobby, killing time before the show began, I noticed *Tony Rumble vs. The New Hampshire Nightmare* had already been printed in the program. I guess anyone could have put on that mask. The match went well, with only one hiccup. Instead of delivering the elbow to my chest, Tony hit me square in the mouth. If I had turned my head to the side, the consequences would have been less severe. Under the mask, my mouth filled with blood.

Back in the locker room, I removed the mask; my face and mouth were covered in blood.

Tony Atlas walked over, looked at my face and said, "Kid, that's good for the business."

Receiving feedback like that from "Mr. USA" gave me a feeling of accomplishment.

Atlas went on to say, "Now go clean up your face, find Rumble, and thank him for the opportunity to be in the ring with him."

I did exactly as I was told. My payoff: $100. Much more than I'd expected. Tony told me he didn't have change for a one-hundred-dollar bill. He called me the next day and asked about my mouth. I told him it was my fault for not turning my head to the side and assured him I was fine. He thanked me again. He told me he had an idea for a wrestling character that he wanted to run by me. A rough-and-tumble brawler from Reno, Nevada, named Knuckles Nelson. Tony felt I could go far with the idea. I loved the name. I thanked him for calling, and we hung up. This was the first of countless phone conversations between me and the "Boston Bad Boy." My new wrestling name was Knuckles Nelson.

Over the years, I've received many compliments on the name. One night in World Championship Wrestling (WCW), legendary wrestler Arn Anderson told me it was an "outstanding moniker." In fact, everyone loved the name. I always give Tony Rumble credit for coming up with the idea.

Tony booked me on all his shows from that day forward. He also introduced me to Jeff Katz, my best friend and longtime conservative radio personality. Back then, Jeff lived in Revere, Massachusetts, across the street from Erich Sbraccia, who would eventually become my tag-team partner. And Tony Rumble lived around the corner. Now that's what I call a cool neighborhood! During the mid '90s, Jeff worked at AM talk-radio station WRKO in Boston. Tony recruited Jeff as an on-air personality for CWA's weekly television program *Mass Madness*—a show featuring wrestling matches, music videos, and in-studio interviews and vignettes designed to build up feuds and promote upcoming live events. Jeff broke into the wrestling business with "Pretty Boy" Larry Sharpe, bringing his knowledge and experience to the CWA. Doing interviews, promos, and hosting the show, Jeff elevated the entire presentation. I worked with Jeff at live events, and occasionally on television, but that was the extent of our involvement back then. Jeff was single—but then he met the love of his life, Heidi Jaillet. It was a pleasure to watch and, at times, listen to Jeff and Heidi's relationship blossom. Jeff liked to call Heidi while he was on the air. They spoke while the city of Boston eavesdropped on their conversation.

The era was filled with growth and opportunity. Thanks to Tony Rumble, I continued to land in excellent situations that furthered my career. I can sum up my experience working for Tony with a story from February 3, 1996: Tony called to inform me of a high-level independent show taking place in Cherry Hill, New Jersey, *The Eddie Gilbert Memorial Show*, that he'd managed to book me on. On my own, I would have had zero chance of getting on that show. Scott Dickinson, Tony, and I made the drive from Boston. Upon arriving in the parking lot, Tony was quickly surrounded by fans seeking photos and autographs. Inside the building, dozens of wrestlers were attempting to get on the show—the scene was pure chaos. Among those scheduled to wrestle were Dory Funk Jr., Jerry "The King" Lawler, Doug Gilbert, and Tom Brandi, to name a few. Emerging from this herd of people was Jim Cornette.

"Tony Rumble, you old dog! How are you?" Cornette asked. "Hey, can you do us a favor and book this clusterfuck?"

Tony just smiled. At that moment, I knew I was with the right person. He then proceeded to put me in a tag-team match. My partner, opponents, and the referee were all from the New Jersey area, making me a total outsider. They planned the match as I stood by silently.

At one point, Tom Brandi, one of my opponents, turned to me and said, "We work together all the time, so we will take most of the match. At some point, we will get you in there, brother." They all called me brother, even the referee. They had no interest in calling me by my name.

Although it felt condescending, the entire situation was fine with me. I was aware of how lucky I was to be there in the first place.

Tony Rumble approached us, inquiring about the match. The three of them ran through the details with great enthusiasm. I stood quietly, watching the animated description continue.

Finally, they revealed the finish of the match: "We will tag in brother [that's me], hit a big move, and pin him, 1–2–3." We all stood there, waiting for Tony's feedback.

The "Boston Bad Boy" responded, "I like it, except for the finish. Here's what I want you to do. Just before Knuckles is tagged in, I will already be at ringside, slipping him a pair of brass knuckles. After he's tagged in, he will knock out both his opponents and the referee. Then he will turn on his partner, knocking *him* out as well. The four of you will sell like you're dead, and me and Knuckles will stand tall in the ring." Keeping a straight face, Tony looked at me. "Is that OK with you?" he asked.

"Yes, brother," I said. I couldn't resist.

The four of them stood there in shock. Tony walked away. They all hated the scenario Rumble presented. In the end, the entire match was scrapped, and I wrestled "The Inferno Kid," using the brass knuckles finish and scoring a victory in the first match of the night. That, ladies and gentlemen, is the way Tony Rumble always treated me.

During the fall of 1999, I had a short break from wrestling with no shows booked until after Christmas. My cousin Jimmy enlisted me for a cross-country road trip. He was moving to California from Rhode Island. We had worked together in various Rhode Island nightclubs, including JR's Fastlane, Mustang Sally's, and Club Fantasies. My cousin was not a wrestler but easily could have been. Along with his good looks and friendly personality, he was blessed with massive arms, earning him the nickname "Jimmy Fat Arms." Always up for an adventure, I gladly accepted.

We drove a beautiful white Mustang convertible from Rhode Island to Los Angeles. We made many stops along the way. Jimmy was in a serious relationship, and I was single. On the trip, I drank and smoked pot in earnest. He was setting up a new life for himself, and I was along for the ride, still living day to day. We had a blast driving across the country on what would be our last adventure together. With our vastly different lifestyles, we lost track of each other after that trip. Jimmy offered to show me all the tourist attractions, but I wanted to go directly to Hollywood and hang out. I was attracted to the street life, so we went to Hollywood and Vine, cruising with the top down. I found LA to be so different from Boston. A quick summary: Boston is Aerosmith, and LA is Mötley Crüe. It was a great experience. I had so much fun that I neglected to check in back home. Before social media and cell phones, a landline hooked up to an answering machine kept me in touch with the world. After a few days of partying in Los Angeles, Jimmy dropped me off at the John Wayne Airport, and we said our goodbyes.

Inside the airport, I located a pay phone to check my voicemail for the first time in a week. I had several messages, including one from Jeff Katz. He sounded weak and serious. He called me Brendan. Everyone in the wrestling community called me Knuckles or Knux. It was rare to hear my real name in wrestling circles, especially from Jeff. As I stood in the busy airport, Jeff delivered the shocking news.

"Brendan, something terrible happened. Tony died. Please call me."

The words did not register at first. The next message, also from Jeff, repeated the sad news. Jeff must not have been aware that I was on vacation. He called again, clearly confused about why I hadn't returned his call. I turned my back to the wall in disbelief. My knees gave way as I slid down the wall until my rear end touched the floor. The receiver was still in my hand, up to my ear, its thick silver cord fully extended from the pay phone. My vision, now at knee level, took in countless pairs of legs passing by in both directions. Among all these people, I sat, unable to move, as alone as I had ever felt. The phone line went from a busy signal to silence. I hoped someone, anyone, might stop to ask me what was wrong. Finally, I gathered myself together as best I could. I still needed to catch my flight to Logan Airport in Boston.

As I walked along, a voice behind me asked, "Are you all right?"

It was Steve Blackman, a WWF wrestler. This might sound pretty random, but wrestlers live in airports, and Steve had recognized me from past shows. After I told him the awful news, he walked with me for as long as he could, and then told me to hang in there as he continued to his destination. Death had come calling in the past, but this was the first time a close friend of mine had died so young and so suddenly. Tony had taken me under his wing. We'd spoken for hours on the phone. He'd never asked me for anything in return for all the incredible opportunities he'd presented me with. He is a man I still love, respect, and miss very much. I later learned that many others had had similar relationships with Tony: Rich Palladino, Sheldon Goldberg, Bull Montana, Jeff Katz, Patrick J. Doyle, and Erich Sbraccia, to name a few. Tony's death marked the beginning of the end of my time in the wrestling world.

My flight began boarding, and I was running late. This was before 9/11, when traveling was much more relaxed. I approached the metal detectors and placed my lone bag on the baggage belt. The next thing I knew, I was surrounded by members of the LAPD. As my bag passed through the x-ray machine, several pairs of brass knuckles became visible—props for my wrestling character. One of the countless lessons passed on by Tony Rumble is to always have your wrestling gear with you, as you never know when you may need it.

You'll recall that the entire brass knuckles idea came from Tony. I was fortunate to have wrestled well-known stars, and, thanks to Tony, the idea was to have them outperform me in every way until Tony would slip me the brass knuckles and distract the referee, giving me time to knock out my opponent—my last resort as certain defeat loomed. The emotional outrage from fans was always amplified when they felt emotionally invested in the wrestler who I assaulted. The list of wrestlers feeling the brunt of my cheating ways included Tito Santana, Tony Atlas, Jimmy "Superfly" Snuka, Tom Brandi, Perry Saturn, and Devon Storm, to name a few.

The police did not see it the same way. But my story did make sense. My look was spot-on for a '90s wrestler: long, flowing dark hair, a deep tan from daily tanning sessions, weightlifting pants covered in skulls, a No Limits string tank top, black Magnum boots, laces untied with pants inside boots, the ensemble rounded out with a black leather fanny pack. Luckily, I'd smoked the last of my weed on the ride to the airport, avoiding complicating matters further. The officer in charge explained that he didn't know the laws in Massachusetts, but in California, possessing brass knuckles is a felony—and in my case, times three. I maintained my status as a pro wrestler. I opened my bag, which emitted a foul locker room odor. I offered my gear and boots as further proof. The stench seemed to be adding credibility to my story. I pulled out my eight-by-ten-inch headshots, and for some reason, that won them over.

"Hey, can you sign one for my son?" one of the officers asked.

"Sure," I said. I was happy to oblige.

The mood quickly changed. The deal they offered was they would keep the brass knuckles and photos, and I would get to catch my flight. I couldn't wait to tell Tony Rumble the story. Then I remembered he was gone. How symbolic to have my namesake, brass knuckles, an idea thought up by Tony, confiscated moments after I'd learned of his death.

With Tony gone, never again would I hear ring announcer Rich Palladino say, "Being led to the ring by his manager, the 'Boston Bad Boy' Tony Rumble from the Combat Zone, representing the Brotherhood—Knuckles Nelson." The New England wrestling landscape changed forever when Tony passed away. A big happy family, with Tony leading the way, turned into a broken home. Under Tony, we each knew our position. Everyone enjoyed being part of the CWA and NWANE family. Without a strong leader, we splintered off, with several people, including myself, promoting wrestling cards around

New England. Left behind was a trail of harsh words and bad feelings that took years to repair. At times, it felt like the bad blood and deep wounds could never be healed. I remember the president of the NWA, Howard Brody, calling me and asking what the hell was going on up there in New England. He told me, "Tony Rumble would not be happy with all the bullshit going on." Howard was right. The date November 13 will always hold three distinct memories for me: First, it's my brother Kevin's birthday. Second, it's the date Felix Unger was asked to remove himself from his place of residence. That request came from his wife. If you are too young to remember, that is a reference to Neil Simon's *The Odd Couple*. Third, it's the date that Tony Rumble passed away.

During the '90s, Tony Rumble promoted the premier wrestling events in the Northeast. Thousands of fans flocked to unique shows featuring young up-and-coming talent alongside established wrestling stars. The locker rooms featured Kevin Sullivan from WCW and Jim Cornette from WWF scouting talent and promoting wrestlers to the next level on the spot. I'm unaware of any other independent group able to make that claim during that time period. The roster, a who's who of wrestling, included: Jerry "The King" Lawler, "Hacksaw" Jim Duggan, King Kong Bundy, Tony Atlas, Tito Santana, Jimmy "Superfly" Snuka, Lou Albano, Tommy Dreamer, Tazz, Vic Steamboat, Sgt. Slaughter, The Public Enemy, Demolition Ax, Erich Sbraccia, Matt Bloom, Ric Fuller, Perry Saturn, John Kronus, Bob Evans, Abdullah the Butcher, Scott Dickinson, Dan Severn, Damien Demento, Rick Martel, Matt Borne, Steve Keirn, Steve Bradley, Ron Zombie, Tre, Mike Hollow, Naoya Ogawa, Billy Silverman, Rich Palladino, Jeff Katz, Curtis Slamdawg, the Mercenary, "Slyck" Wagner Brown, the Power Twins, Kevin Landry, and many others.

As a wrestler, Tony's first match found him looking across the ring at Bruiser Brody. His second opponent was "Superstar" Billy Graham. Tony Rumble left an indelible mark on the wrestling world. In a universe with no coincidences, I wrote this chapter on November 13, 2018, without realizing it was nineteen years to the day after my dear friend's passing.

Tony felt at home with a microphone in his hand. He coined some amazing phrases:

"What's cookin', rubberneck?"

"We ain't having fun till they gotta call 911."

"Cream rises to the top. So does scum. How do you think I got here?"

And his trademark, which proved to be a sobering truth:

"I'm Boston born and Boston bred, and I'll be Boston bad till I'm Boston dead."

See you on the other side, brother.

Tony Rumble and me

CHAPTER 4

Japan

Overanalyze myself
Overestimate my worth
Overcompensate my time
Overutilize my mind
Organize to change my ways
Organize to waste my days
Organize to work things out
Organize my own self-doubt
. . .
No one does it better than me

Rusty, "No One Does It Better Than Me"

IN JANUARY OF 1999, PRIOR TO TONY RUMBLE'S PASSING, I started wrestling in Japan. Touring the Land of the Rising Sun was another amazing opportunity made possible by the "Boston Bad Boy." Tony had introduced me to several people in the wrestling world, including Shunsuke Yamaguchi. Shun worked for *Weekly Gong* wrestling magazine as a photographer. When I was wrestling for the WWF, I would run into Shun at television tapings and also at National Wrestling Alliance (NWA) shows. We became friends. He could always be found at ringside taking photos of the biggest moments in wrestling history. Shun always made me feel welcome with his easygoing personality. He would later go on to make up one half of the WWE Japanese television announcer team, along with the commentator Funaki. One night, Shun called me asking if I was interested in going to Japan. His brother, Wally, was involved with a new promotion, and several American wrestlers were invited to join the tour. Yusuke "Wally" Yamaguchi (a.k.a. Yamaguchi-san) was a well-known wrestling personality in Japan, as well as a manager in the WWF, leading a stable of Japanese wrestlers known as Kai En Tai. Shun arranged our travel and itinerary. All I needed to know was the time of my flight and which airport. We left Logan Airport in Boston and arrived in Portland, Oregon, for a layover. At the airport in Portland, we met other members of the tour. Wrestlers from Minnesota welcomed us with open arms, building our camaraderie and group momentum. This was my introduction to wrestlers Derrick Dukes and "Wild" Bill Irwin. They were easy to recognize, since I'd watched them both on television for years. Wrestlers have a way of looking out for one another on the road. We all seemed to bond right there on the spot, creating a safe environment for everyone. It's like safety in numbers—or strength in numbers, in our case.

"Wild" Bill was the most accomplished in our group of travelers. A journeyman wrestler who'd competed in the World Wrestling Federation, National Wrestling Alliance, World Championship Wrestling, American Wrestling Association, World Class Championship Wrestling, and on many tours of Japan. He quickly set the tone, passing along his experience of dos and don'ts as we prepared for a long journey across the planet. He easily could have kept to himself, but he did the complete opposite. He got to know us and formed friendships with my tag-team partner, Erich Sbraccia, and me. We were the new guys in the group. Derrick Dukes also went out of his way to make friends with the guys from Boston. After a long—and I do mean *long* flight—we touched down in Tokyo. A line of taxis took us directly from the airport to the first show. This was news to me; I only realized it when we arrived at an arena instead of a hotel.

Inside the locker room, we met Wally, who pointed across the room to our opponents and asked if we spoke Japanese. This was the first of many pranks Wally played on us. We approached our opponents and introduced ourselves. They used a strange gimmick known as the "Cola Powers." "Pepsi Boy" and the "Cola Kid" both wrestled under masks with full-body outfits. Apparently, the idea was for them to resemble a can of Pepsi and a can of Coke. Through an interpreter, we discussed a very basic match. Our opponents seemed unwilling to cooperate with our ideas, but eager to execute their own offensive moves, quickly setting a tone that they wanted to look as good as possible against the American wrestlers.

Program guide with my name in Japanese

Once we hit the ring, the experience was very positive. The NWA name had taken a downward turn during the '90s in America. The oldest governing body in wrestling watched its biggest member, WCW, leave the organization and begin recognizing its own champions. The NWA was left with a small collection of independent promotions to carry on with. In Japan, the name still elicited great respect. Our status as NWA World Tag Team Champions felt much more prestigious in Tokyo. Japanese wrestling fans are very knowledgeable. They respect history.

Our first match of the tour ended with a double countout and no clear winner, setting the stage for a series of matches all over the country. The following morning, the manager of our hotel held up the morning newspaper and a pen as I passed by. At first, it didn't register that he wanted me to sign it. He stepped out from behind the desk to inform me that my picture had made the front page. The hotel manager raved about Ric

Flair, Kerry Von Erich, and Bruiser Brody as I autographed the paper for him. From there, we boarded a bus for the rest of the tour. We made daylong bus trips from town to town. We really got to know one another on that bus. Wally handpicked his guys. Some were from Japan, and the others were from Korea, Mexico, Australia, Great Britain, and the USA.

The bus rides allowed us to see the majestic country, unlike tourists traveling to typical locations. We traveled to big cities, small cities, villages, and towns—seeing the land in a whole different way. I kept a video camera handy and did my best to record the trip. We traveled by day, wrestled at night, and partied until the sun came up. We slept on the bus and never went to a gym. We ate like crap the entire time.

Wally Yamaguchi and his son with me and Erich

I never understood who ran the show or who was going to pay us; I kept good faith and enjoyed myself. Wally ran the locker room with complete privacy, or "kayfabe"—a term related to not exposing the wrestling business to outsiders. As part of that, he also requested that I turn off my video camera during booking meetings. During the tour, we all wrestled one another at some point. The real payoff was the wealth of international wrestling experience. Being in the ring with an opponent who has difficulty speaking English or doesn't speak English at all will quickly reveal how good of a worker you are. Having a flow or succession of moves in a match without speaking to your opponent or planning it out beforehand is part of being a good worker. It's very real.

The travel itself was grueling. The options for food were limited. Sometimes we'd shop at 7-Eleven or a convenience store for breakfast and snacks before hitting the road for a long day of travel. The opportunity to maintain a normal workout schedule was a challenge. During the tour of Japan, major camaraderie was built among everyone associated with the promotion. By the end of the tour, we'd become brothers and sisters. Strangers two weeks prior, we were now close friends for life. We wrestled every night in a different location. Some shows were in small towns or villages, and others were in cities. I almost never knew where exactly I was. I would call home and be asked the question, "Where are you?" My answer would always be the same: "Somewhere in Japan." After we'd traveled from Tokyo to Fukuoka, making many stops along the way, it was time to come home. I kept it in the back of my mind to be grateful for the experience, but no one had been paid yet. At the airport, I met the moneyman for the first time. One by one, each wrestler met with him.

Through Wally, he thanked me and paid me a thousand dollars in American money. I did not have a big enough name to negotiate a better payoff. I'd simply showed up at the airport and hoped for the best. A thousand dollars is not considered a good payoff for an established wrestler, but considering the free trip to Japan, along with the experience I'd gained and the incredible time I'd had, it felt like a million dollars to me. Before they left, they provided me with the dates for the next tour.

The NWA World Tag Team Championship belt

Back on American soil, I stayed busy working for the NWA and WWF. I enjoyed a new level of respect from other wrestlers and promoters, having competed in Japan. About six months later, in June of 1999, I returned to Japan. This time, the unknown was no longer a part of the experience. I took the initiative to incorporate ways to make money on the road in Japan. I went to local department stores at home and bought all the WWF T-shirts on clearance racks. I paid as little as $3 per shirt, packed them in my travel bag, and sold them in Japan for five thousand yen—about fifty American dollars. I sold out at the first show of the tour. During the second tour,

I felt at ease and grateful. The same basic group had returned from around the world. Erich and I continued to defend the NWA tag-team titles. We were improving as a tag team with every match. However, outside the ring, we drove each other crazy. Erich's a responsible guy. At the time, I was not. He had a family. I was single. He was careful. I was reckless. By the end of this tour, we had become a bit sick of each other—not completely, but at times, noticeably so. I remember returning from Japan and getting off the plane in Boston. We walked away from each other without saying goodbye. I didn't know it at the time, but the last night of the second tour of Japan would be our last match as tag-team partners. When we returned to Boston, we had a title defense the next night in Dallas, Texas. Erich dropped a bomb on Tony Rumble, informing him that, for personal reasons, he was quitting wrestling and would not be going to Texas. Erich hadn't shared this information with me while we were in Japan. To this day, I don't know if he had made the decision prior to our trip to Japan, or if he'd decided to quit once we'd returned home. For me, this had been what we were working toward. We had become a solid tag team. We were at the doorstep of the WWF and WCW. The unstable and uncertain life of an unsigned, independent wrestler had forced Erich to hang up his boots and resume a more traditional nine-to-five life. Today, Erich is a successful businessman. At the time, I didn't understand how he could have left us high and dry during a title reign. It left Tony Rumble and the NWA in a very difficult situation. I didn't have a family or a regular job to worry about. Today, I have a better understanding of his decision.

Tony Rumble and me, Dallas, Texas, 1999
(Photocourtesy of Rob Moore)

The next year would be eventful, both in and out of the ring. My longtime friend and manager Tony Rumble would pass away, Erich Sbraccia would retire for good, and Jeff Katz would move away from Boston. I briefly teamed with Ric Fuller as a replacement for Erich Sbraccia, and we quickly lost the NWA World Tag Team titles on June 17, 1999, to the Public Enemy in Bolton, Massachusetts. The reason for the title-change loss was to put me with a more permanent tag-team partner. Ric Fuller was on his way to WCW. This was easily explained to the wrestling public as Tony Rumble using different combinations of his stable of wrestlers, known as the Brotherhood. A third team was formed with Dukes Dalton. On June 19, 1999, we won and regained the NWA titles, defeating the Public Enemy in Dorchester, Massachusetts. On September 25, 1999, we defended the NWA World Tag

Team Championship for the last time in Charlotte, North Carolina—dropping the belts to Team Extreme at the NWA 51st Anniversary Show. After losing the belts for good, and with all the loss in my personal life, my wrestling batteries finally began to run down.

One night, after midnight, my phone rang. On the other end of the line was my old friend Shun Yamaguchi.

He said, "Hey, Knuckles, you want to go back to Japan? Things are getting busy over there."

I sat up in bed, suddenly feeling elated.

"Of course, I do," I told him.

After the previous tour, the promoter had failed to give me a return date, leaving me with the impression I might not be going back. Just another bit of bad news in a year filled with bad news. Shun explained that the wrestler known as "Pepsi Boy" had moved to New Japan Pro-Wrestling, and they needed someone to replace him on the upcoming tour. Shun also wanted several other wrestlers for the upcoming tour. I thought Dylan Kage could fill the role of "Pepsi Boy." I also enlisted Brian Day and Luis Ortiz to join the tour. The news got even better when I found out Shun Yamaguchi would also be coming on the tour to serve as a referee. It all lined up perfectly. Returning for the tour was "Wild" Bill Irwin, and new additions were hardcore wrestler Vic Grimes and the well-traveled superstar Barry Darsow. This tour became one for the ages. I made sure my bag was once again full of WWF T-shirts to sell to fans on my third tour of Japan. With my traveling flea market, I would have plenty of cash on the road. Wrestling in Japan is vastly different from wrestling here in North America. In Japan, they take care of wrestlers, at times paying for meals and drinks. They transported us on a state-of-the-art tour bus. They also paid for hotel rooms. In the States, it's get yourself to the show, and that's it. At least back then, anyway.

Being on the road with this group was a blast. Barry Darsow and Bill Irwin together provided hours of entertaining stories. They both had accomplished so much in the wrestling world and were willing to pass along their wealth of experience to the younger guys. They made sure we had fun, but also kept us safe at every turn.

Wally Yamaguchi ran a very professional locker room. Throughout this tour, attendance at shows was low. I didn't make much of it at the time. I was earning so much extra money selling the T-shirts, I never took an advance on my pay (like the others did). I wanted all the money that I earned to come home with me. On the second-to-last night, Wally called me down to the hotel lobby. He handed me a booking sheet with multiple dates that took me into the next year. This meant we would be going back and forth to Japan regularly for the foreseeable future. He told me I should give the promoter/moneyman a T-shirt out of respect for allowing me to make money on the side during his shows. I agreed with Wally and approached our employer to present him with one of my American shirts featuring the Rock. His face lit up. He immediately removed his shirt, exposing a large potbelly, put on his new shirt, and shook my hand with both of his hands. Wally stood off to the side, giving me a nod of approval.

During this tour, Barry Darsow was a busy man. During his incredible career, Barry developed several famous wrestling personas: Krusher Khrushchev, Demolition Smash, Repo Man, and the Blacktop Bully, to name a few. He was called upon to use multiple gimmicks in Japan. He also wrestled as one of the Super Destroyers during this Japanese tour. The original Super Ds were a masked duo consisting of Bill and Scott Irwin. One night at dinner, I told Bill Irwin, Barry Darsow, and Wally Yamaguchi how much I had loved the Super Destroyers in my youth. It didn't appear at the time that the three of them cared much about my admiration; my comments seemed to fall on deaf ears. But the following night, I realized they must have been listening when they allowed me to wrestle as a Super Destroyer on some of the shows. I was Super Destroyer #21. The number was kind of a light-hearted joke referring to the number of people who'd wrestled as a Super Destroyer over the years. It was a personal honor for me.

Left to right: Barry Darsow, me (Knuckles Nelson as a Super Destroyer), and "Wild" Bill Irwin

Two weeks later, on the last night of the tour, we drank in the hotel lobby all night. One wrestler decided to streak naked down a busy street on a dare. Our bus driver drank us all under the table every night. He started hitting on a young male wrestler who was not at all interested in his advances. Barry Darsow and Bill Irwin debated who the greatest tag team was: the Super Destroyers or Demolition. The next morning, everyone paid the price for the previous night of drinking. We staggered onto the bus. Our driver appeared to be fine and in tip-top condition, but the rest of us were in rough shape. As we pulled away from the hotel, I noticed Wally was not on the bus. Even his brother, Shun, seemed puzzled by his absence. We didn't get far before the driver pulled over to the side of the road. Most of the group was fast asleep. I could see something was not right. Shun and other Japanese members of the group appeared to be pleading with the driver. I began to video the exchange. After we'd sat there for a good half hour, Barry Darsow and Bill Irwin finally asked what was going on.

Front cover of Japanese wrestling program (I'm in the upper right corner)

The promoter, known to us as *the moneyman*, had skipped town without paying anyone, leaving us high and dry. Wally had *also* decided to leave the group without a word to any of us. It was bad enough for the wrestlers, but the bus driver would not move until he got his money. A complete nightmare unfolded before my eyes. We had round-trip plane tickets, but no idea of our location or how to get to the airport. The days of whipping out my phone to use GPS navigation had not yet arrived. One of the road crew members went to an ATM and took out his own money to pay the bus driver. This satisfied the driver enough to start driving again, but after traveling a short distance, he pulled over again. Apparently, the payment the driver had received would only get us a short distance. He was definitely sending us a message. He wanted the rest of his money, or we'd all have to get out and walk. Two wrestlers from Australia, Mark Mercedes and Billy Cole, made the ill-advised decision to get off the bus and fend for themselves. They gathered their belongings and exited the bus with one member of the road crew. The decision held some merit since they needed to go to a different airport to catch a return flight to Australia.

"Do not get off the bus!" Barry Darsow said in a serious tone. "This is a bad idea."

They ignored Barry and said goodbye to us all. I had my camera rolling the entire time. Shun ordered me to stop filming, but I ignored his request. This was happening, and I needed to record it. After we pleaded with the driver to take us to the airport, he finally did. Not sure why he'd changed his mind, but we were happy he had. I filmed the Aussies standing on the street as we pulled away. They got smaller and smaller until they finally disappeared in the distance. We finally made it to the airport in Osaka and returned to America.

I never had hard feelings about not getting paid. After all, I was traveling back and forth to Japan on someone else's dime. I was wrestling every night against quality opponents and gaining an unparalleled international experience. Up until that point, we had been treated like royalty. I still wanted to return to Japan. I always felt grateful I'd been given the chance to go in the first place.

The decision to leave us on our own, hours away from the airport after a night of heavy drinking, fell squarely on the shoulders of Wally Yamaguchi. I never received an explanation as to why we hadn't gotten paid or why Wally had left us without a word. His unwillingness to face us and explain what was happening had left everyone on the bus feeling a variety of emotions. Some were upset, while others were happy to be going home. It's a shame to have that as my final memory of touring Japan as a professional wrestler. The truth is, I never got involved in wrestling for money. It was simply for the love of it.

Front cover of another Japanese wrestling program

Salisbury Beach

*Lost in a world of pain
And I walk away
With the radio on
Oh, better ride the storm
Let it take me home
When the love is all gone
I'm a big bear with a mind insane
I'm a hair, hair, hair's breadth away
If you know what I mean*

Rusty, "Hey Now"

DURING MY TIME IN THE WRESTLING WORLD, I TRAVELED extensively—locally, regionally, and around the world. In July of 1995, prior to my adventures in Japan, I discovered Salisbury Beach, Massachusetts.

This small town and long-time tourist attraction with a carny atmosphere would become my home. At the time, Salisbury Beach was home to video game arcades, batting cages, bumper cars, Willey's Candy Shop, souvenir shops, and two pizza stands side by side: Tripoli's and Cristy's. Anyone who frequents the beach surely has a favorite of the two. At night, the action picked up in the bars and nightclubs. Drinking establishments blanketed the beach: Bevie B's, the Sands, the 5 O'Clock Club, the Normandy Lounge, the Sidewalk Café, the Dugout, the Beach Club, Uncle Eddie's, and Ten's Show Club. Something for everyone, day and night.

Smack-dab in the middle of the madness was Champs Arena, a small wrestling venue in a prime location. A row of buildings similar to a strip mall lined the street, just a few feet from the ocean. One of the storefronts was slightly different than the others: the glass picture windows were filled with wrestling posters and headshots of local and nationally known professional wrestlers. Once you'd stepped inside the lobby, you'd find wrestling merchandise and memorabilia for sale alongside a concession stand. Deeper inside the venue, as you passed through a curtain, you could feast your eyes on a former WWF wrestling ring, long retired from the big time and now making its home in the minor leagues of wrestling. The ring was way too big for the space, with the top rope about five feet from the ceiling. It was not possible to properly execute moves from the top rope, at least for me. I was unable to stand up straight without hitting my head on the rafters in the ceiling. Champs Arena had the capacity of holding a few hundred people, with an upper deck around the perimeter of the building adding a nice touch when the room was full. The walls were painted bright yellow. It was not a good look for television taping, but this place was not about TV; it was about live wrestling shows. The locker room was small and usually cramped during a show. It did have a shower stall with hot water—a welcome perk at the end of the night. My first visit to the beach felt like I'd gone back in time to the 1970s. Everything seemed old and a bit run down. Still, people flocked to visit this place on a regular basis, spending money and having a great time. I would put the beauty of this stretch of beach and coastline up against anywhere in the world. Especially during the summer. The crystal-clear blue water and enormous waves still occupy my memories. Prior to my first visit, I had never heard of Salisbury Beach. Over the next decade, it would become my home. Here I met some of the nicest and most unique people I've ever known.

Champs Arena had the potential to do extremely well. Unfortunately, the people in charge did not have good heads for business. Big City Mike, a four-hundred-pound man, opened Champs with the best of intentions. His lack of business experience quickly reared its head. For starters, he felt the need to tell everyone he was "Typhoon" from the WWF. He bore a facial resemblance to the real "Typhoon," Fred Ottman, but the story was a complete fabrication. Another guy used to suggest to people that he was "the Mountie" from the WWF. Again, his face did maybe look a little bit like the real "Mountie," Jacques Rougeau. I've never understood the need to impersonate or claim the identity of another person. To each his own, I guess. I have a difficult enough time being myself.

Big City Mike was a kind man. But kindness is not necessarily in the top qualifications needed for building a successful wrestling business, or any business, for that matter. After obtaining a small-business loan, the first thing he did was take his family and friends out for Chinese food. Topping that, he proceeded to rent a beachfront condo he couldn't possibly afford. Champs Arena was doomed from the start. In the beginning, Champs kept a busy schedule, running weekly shows on Fridays, Saturdays, and Sundays. Attendance was good at first, with plenty of beachgoers to fill the seats. The building had air-conditioning, making it even more appealing on hot summer days.

I quickly became a regular performer at Champs Arena. After commuting for the first couple of weeks from Rhode Island, I moved to the beach and spent the next nine years of my life there. Unlike Big City Mike, I rented a small cabin, a mile from the beach. Wrestling on weekends would not pay the bills, so, like a good alcoholic, I secured a day job at a liquor store a few doors down from Champs. I quickly found work at the bars. I set myself up in a great situation in my new community. Back in Rhode Island, the state athletic commission still regulated wrestling as a real sport. They made it nearly impossible for a small wrestling company to run a show unless they paid a premium to the commission. In other words, independent wrestling was dead in the Ocean State. Moving to the beach afforded me a great opportunity to stay busy and continue to pursue my dream of having full-time employment in wrestling. Anything resembling a normal life evaporated, and I never looked back. Getting married, settling down, and starting a family never entered my thoughts. A decision I came to deeply regret years later. I moved from one woman to the next. Never getting too close to anyone in order to keep my options open. My antennae for the next female conquest always stayed up. A lonely, fearful, and disconnected life. In many ways, I was no longer a member of society.

Once I invaded Salisbury Beach, I focused on wrestling, weight training, cycling, working my multiple jobs, and partying all night long. I burned the candle at both ends, living a healthy lifestyle and a destructive lifestyle at the very same time. I had one goal: to become a full-time professional wrestler. Already in my thirties, I was too old for serious consideration. A glaring fact I chose to ignore. My body needed serious work. Due to my heavy drinking, I always had a gut. Not a look usually associated with a WWF Superstar. Tony Rumble had told me that he felt the reason I'd remained unsigned to a contract was my average appearance among the giants of the WWF and WCW. He'd told me I would never be taken seriously unless I got into much better shape. I made that a priority.

My typical day started at 5:00 a.m., when I'd wake 'n' bake and down a cup of coffee; then I'd jump on my bicycle and peddle to the local gym below Brothers Pizza. I made the two-mile ride every day, rain or shine. The gym was empty at 5:30 a.m., and I took full advantage of it. Then, I'd pedal home, eat, and head to Tiger's Liquor Store, waiting for it to open at 8:00 a.m. Tiger was a charming guy. I loved him. He liked me, but made it clear that I was *not* to sit outside the store with my shirt off on beautiful summer beach days. He told me I would scare off his customers. He golfed all day, so as soon as he would leave the store, I'd take off my shirt and sit out front.

From time to time, he'd drive by, yelling from his car, "Put your shirt on!"

He would also call the store, and when I'd answer, he'd say, "Put your shirt on, Knux."

"How do you know I have my shirt off?" I'd ask.

"Just put a shirt on," he'd say and hang up.

I loved the guy, so after a while, I kept my shirt on.

After work, I went to Champs to hone my craft. They needed a trainer for a growing wrestling school, so I took the job, adding to my already full life. After practice, the nightlife heated up on the beach. My drinking and drug use were completely out of control. Every night, I'd barhop until closing time. This led to reckless sexual behavior, playing Russian roulette by having unprotected sex with women I'd met only hours earlier, a pattern I continued for years.

I worked hard at getting into shape. I grew my hair out. I became a local cult figure around Salisbury Beach, especially after making an appearance on *The Jerry Springer Show*, playing a deranged ex-boyfriend. I wrestled in the WWF and WCW, but all people wanted to talk about was Jerry Springer after they'd seen me on the show. While I enjoyed a nice life of wrestling, training, and working multiple jobs on the beach, my old friend *Big City Mike* watched his business go down the drain. One bad decision after another, and not taking advantage of all the additional ways to make money on the beach during the summer, led to Champs Arena closing its doors for good before it ever really got off the ground. Big City Mike died shortly after that.

My favorite match at Champs took place on December 17, 1995, right before they closed permanently. Billed as "The Nightmare Before Christmas," the main event featured *Knuckles Nelson vs. Cactus Jack* in a "Falls Count Anywhere" match. This means, the action can *and will* spill out of the ring—especially with Cactus involved. A wrestler can attempt a pinfall in any location, in or out of the ring. The entire card was filled with excellent talent, including the Eliminators (Saturn and Kronus), Tony Atlas, and referee Scott Dickinson. This was just prior to Cactus Jack (Mick Foley) making his debut in the WWF. Cactus had already achieved legend status for his work in WCW, ECW, and most notably, his hardcore matches in Japan. This was a big match for me.

Cactus arrived right off a plane from Japan. I introduced

myself and let him know I was up for whatever he wanted to do. I wanted it to be crystal clear that I was only interested in listening to his interpretation of the match ahead of us. We were strangers at this point, and I hoped to put his mind at ease and tell him I would never take any cheap shots or try to outshine him during the match. Similar to when Rocky Balboa told the boxing promoter how he would perform as a sparring partner with Apollo Creed in the movie *Rocky*.

A major snowstorm in the dead of winter almost killed the show. There were fewer than one hundred people in attendance. In the middle of summer, they would have been lined up around the block to see Cactus Jack in a (at the time) rare New England appearance on a small independent show. But this didn't stop us from having a great match. The crowd was really into it and followed along with emotional outbursts. I think multiple dynamics were in play: First, Cactus was in town. A novelty at the time. Second, I was a well-known wrestler on the local scene with a reputation of being a bit crazy; everyone wanted to see how I was going to match up with an already established lunatic in the sport. In reality, Cactus Jack is a kind, sweet man and extremely easy to like. In the locker room, he sat quietly reading a book. I only remember this because my brother Kevin was also in the locker room and had asked Cactus if he had taken his name from a Robert Ludlum novel featuring a character by the name of Cactus Jack. He revealed to us the name did not originate from the Ludlum book.

Cactus gave me the green light to attack him from behind. We brawled all over Champs Arena. The action spilled not only outside the ring, but also outside the building and into the street. The wind howled off the Atlantic Ocean. Cactus suplexed me onto a snowbank. He rolled me up in a small package on the freezing pavement. That alone motivated me to kick out of his pin attempt. We made our way back inside the warm arena. Eventually, Cactus hit a swinging neckbreaker outside the ring on his way to victory. He treated me with respect and had been open to anything I had suggested for the match. Later, whenever I ran into him at WWF television tapings, he always went out of his way to make me feel at home. A mild-mannered man, but indestructible in the wrestling ring.

Four years into my living at the beach, Tony Rumble passed away, but I continued to work for the World Wrestling Federation when they came to the Northeast. Drinking and drugging were no longer fun. It became work to feed my addictions, and it took its toll on me in different forms. My memory began to fail. I frequently forgot things. Someone could tell me something, and I would forget what they said seconds later. This was, of course, a major problem when creating a wrestling match with opponents. From my experience, wrestling is not choreographed. At least, back then it wasn't.

I discussed the match with the people I wrestled just prior to going to the ring. At times, I would be meeting my in-ring foe for the first time in the discussion of the match. If a wrestler is properly trained, the match comes off fine. If something doesn't happen as discussed beforehand, the only people who know are the ones who planned it. Once in the ring, everything is much more real than is generally assumed. As a jobber (or an *extra*—or to really dress it up, *enhancement talent*) in the WWF, my role was to help make other wrestlers look good. I hardly ever had input in the match.

After my early-1990s experience of getting annihilated by Razor Ramon, I hoped to return to the WWF with more experience and a meaningful role. It was not meant to be. At my age, and considering my lack of ability and problems with addiction, they did not consider me someone worth investing time and money into. I was lucky to have been there at all. Thousands of wrestlers fall short without ever stepping into a WWF ring. It's a major accomplishment to do so at any level on the card. Several top wrestlers always made me feel welcome, regardless of my position in the show. Matt Bloom, Chris Jericho, Mark Henry, Big Show, Edge and Christian, and the Hardy Boyz, among others, treated me like one of the boys. I managed to hide my substance abuse enough to wrestle Hardcore Holly, the Headbangers, Big Boss Man, and Ken Shamrock.

My issues with addiction took center stage one night at the Fleet Center in Boston. On August 30, 1999, The Dudley Boyz—Bubba Ray and D-Von—were making their debut in the WWF, and their opponents would be me and WWF veteran Tim McNeany.

The match we discussed was much more competitive than

the usual squash match. So much so that Tim spoke up, feeling they were giving us too much offense. Bubba explained that where they came from, Extreme Championship Wrestling (ECW), everything was fifty-fifty in the matches. The brother duo, already established stars, treated us with respect. Tony Garea joined our pre-match conversation. He agreed with Tim, and our offense became limited. To my disappointment, the match had been altered, but still wouldn't be a squash match. We came to the ring first, both of us known in our hometown of Boston. The crowd was red hot as the Dudley Boyz came out to a huge ovation. Standing in the ring, I felt the heat all around me. I started the match for my team—D-Von Dudley, for his. Prior to the match, I'd found a secluded spot in the back to smoke pot—a routine thing for me to do before a match. As we locked up, I forgot the opening spot even though we had gone over it a dozen times. I sent D-Von into the ropes, and as he came off the ropes, we collided in the center of the ring. All my fault. I'd failed to execute a simple hip toss. The crowd booed. I couldn't recall anything like this having happened before in the ring, and I'd picked a hell of a time for a major fuck-up. Bubba became enraged on the ring apron.

"Kill him! Kill him!" he screamed.

I felt horrible. This was their debut in the WWF, and I had just ruined it. We managed to get back on track and finish the match. They executed their signature finishing move on me, the 3D. It was a long walk back to the locker room.

Backstage, I approached the brothers to apologize. They were not upset and let me off the hook right away. To this day, that moment still makes me sick to my stomach. The Dudley Boyz went on to become WWE Hall of Famers, and I went on to work in public transportation. I'm sure they got over it much faster than I did.

I put the final dagger in my time with the WWF at a television taping in New Haven, Connecticut. Tony Garea asked me to bring along another local wrestler of my choosing for back-to-back TV tapings in New Haven and Providence. I enlisted my friend Curtis Slamdawg to have the privilege of being seen by the WWF. The first night, Tony Garea told me to put together a short, five-minute match between the two of us. He said he didn't care who went over—who would win. We had a short debate as to who should go over. Of course, we both presented good reasons why we deserved a victory. In the end, I shamed Slamdawg into putting me over—letting me win—by reminding him that I'd gotten him booked in the first place. Just before our match, they scratched it. I told Slamdawg we should leave early because I wanted to start drinking. He took my word for it, and we left early. The next night in Providence, Tony Garea expressed his disappointment in my decision to leave early. He asked that I never do that again. Then he shook my hand. Over the course of the evening, several other office people who had never spoken to me before shook my hand. They were saying goodbye. The reality set in. Even my denial couldn't stop it. I would not be signed to a WWF contract. The door remained open a crack because I seemed to have nine lives in wrestling.

A few days later, I called Jim Cornette, inquiring about future TV tapings. He informed me the office wanted to look at new talent—and just like that, it was over. I hung up the phone with no plan B. I was still very much addicted to wrestling. I found myself unemployed with no medical insurance—a drug addict and alcoholic, creeping up on forty years old.

If I found myself face-to-face with Vince McMahon

today, I would thank him for having given me the incredible opportunity to step inside his ring. To me, that is a bigger honor than playing at Fenway Park, Gillette Stadium, and the Boston Garden combined. I would also apologize for not having been at my best while in his ring. Addiction leapfrogged over my respect for the business, my opponents, and myself. I will never know what it's like to be at my best in the ring.

Wrestling Star Wars logo

It didn't take long for me to follow a path taken by other wrestlers in my situation. My background was filled with teaching experience (karate and wrestling), so I decided to open a wrestling school. It seemed like a logical move, but in reality, it was a way of holding on to my life's passion, which was also beginning to take shape as another addiction. During my time in the wrestling world, I lived from day to day without health insurance. At times, I didn't even have a bank account of any kind. I spent money while never saving. My idea for a wrestling school started with a budget of zero. In order to get my not-so-original idea off the ground, I needed a quality wrestling ring. The cost would be roughly $5,000. A location for the school and the expenses were still unknown. The events that unfolded prove that if there's a will, there truly is a way. Salisbury Beach introduced me to people who would be instrumental in getting my idea off the ground. The person playing the most integral role was a four-hundred-pound man known to most as Buddy. His more formal name was Elwood K. Apt Jr. We became fast friends, and soon his wrestling persona, "Big Woody," was born. His impressive knowledge of sports, including wrestling, provided countless hours of conversation. Woody was a very likeable man. I met Woody when I took a job as a truck driver for a seafood company in Seabrook, New Hampshire. One day, the door to the clam house flew open and in stepped Woody.

"Hey, Knuckles, what's happening," he said. He went on to tell me he was pleased to learn we would be working together.

I liked him immediately. He was sincere, plain and simple. Woody knew who I was from attending wrestling matches at Champs Arena. That boosted my ego greatly. He was a tremendous chef, always cooking something wonderful and inviting me to dinner. He also had a wonder dog named Duncan. They became my family throughout the entire time I lived on the seacoast. Woody and Duncan were not the only family I had in the area. My godfather, Joe Gliottone, and his wife, Carol, live on Plum Island. Joe is from Providence, and during his journey in life, he landed just a few miles from Salisbury Beach, providing family connection and comfort for both of us. Joe is also a master chef, inviting me to breakfast, lunch, and dinner while I was living in Salisbury.

While I scouted a location for my new school, Woody introduced me to a man named Gilbert Bonk. Gil wanted to promote a wrestling show to raise money for Pop Warner football. A former amateur boxer, Gil stood tall at six foot three. His fundraising and promotional skills could only be described as relentless. Gil would take me around to local businesses and make introductions. He wanted the community to get to know me and vice versa. Everyone liked and respected Gil. Some of the business owners would see Gil coming in the door and immediately empty their pockets in a joking gesture. They knew Gil was always fundraising for some worthy cause.

Champs Arena had closed years earlier, the potential of the venture never reaching fruition. Here was my chance to bring pro wrestling back to the beach, this time, presenting a quality product. Not that quality wrestlers hadn't competed at Champs; that was not the case at all. It was the overall presentation that would be vastly improved with me at the helm. Gil worked long and hard to make the Pop Warner benefit show a success. It lit the fuse for a new era of wrestling in Salisbury Beach. Our venue would be the Beach Club Pavilion. A massive two-level structure literally right on the ocean. The building sat on huge poles sunk deep into the ground. At high tide, the building was no longer on the water—it was *in* the water. The pavilion section of the building being considered for the show was once a video arcade. Now it sat vacant. Plenty of space for a ring and crowd.

The show drew over one thousand people and featured wrestlers from NWANE under the NWA banner. It fell on the eve of Jeff Katz's leaving Boston for a new position in

Las Vegas. Held on April 22, 2000, the main event was a dog collar match for the NWA New England Championship. *Champion Curtis Slamdawg vs. Challenger Knuckles Nelson* was a match in which the combatants wore dog collars around their necks, connected by a twelve-foot chain. Slamdawg had competed in dozens of this style of match. It would be my first. Slamdawg and his brother, the Mercenary, were long-time favorites of Tony Rumble. The crowd filled the Pavilion with optimistic curiosity. Most of the wrestlers were making their first appearance in Salisbury, but others, like Tony Atlas, were no strangers to the beach. Tony had wrestled in Champs Arena. He had also wrestled decades earlier at the Frolics. A much bigger venue and a location for WWF wrestling during an earlier era. The quality of wrestling on this card kept the crowd engaged from beginning to end.

During the main event title match, I brawled with Slamdawg for a solid ten minutes before referee Scott Dickinson was inadvertently knocked to the canvas after Slamdawg shoved me into him. My opponent capitalized on this opportunity by bringing three folding chairs into the ring while Dickinson was semiconscious down on the mat. Slamdawg opened two chairs and put the third one flat on top. He picked me up and powerbombed me through the chairs. A devastating wrestling move normally ending on the mat—but in this case, I was the lucky recipient to instead land violently on a metal folding chair. Slamdawg pulled the referee back into position, shaking him as he returned to his senses. He then pinned me to retain his title.

Slamdawg left his mark on the town, grabbing the house microphone and expressing his dislike for Boston and his love for New York. This infuriated the Massachusetts residents who dominated the audience. Slamdawg made comments about Boston sports legends Raymond Bourque and Nomar Garciaparra. New England sports fans take sports *very* seriously. Having a wrestler from the Big Apple defeat a wrestler from Beantown—on Massachusetts soil—made it personal. He left the ring victorious and quite pleased with himself. Many in attendance expected me to win, considering I was a resident of the town and also the promoter. But I was transitioning from wrestling to an office position, so I felt having Slamdawg win was the right business thing to do.

In the wake of a successful show, I continued to search for a location for my wrestling school. I decided to continue trying my hand at promotion. After Tony Rumble died, I briefly helped run NWANE. They decided to go in another direction and no longer wanted my help. I opened my own office, called Wrestling Star Wars, a tribute to World Class Championship Wrestling (WCCW). The following year, I promoted shows at the Pavilion. Just getting by, I learned, by trial and error, how to effectively promote wrestling. My approach was to provide quality wrestling above all else. Making sure everyone got paid, even if it meant I didn't. At first, I rented a ring and chairs for every show. A costly expense. During this time, I watched the Pavilion's management change hands twice. On the morning of September 11, 2001, during the catastrophe and chaos around the country, I asked Mr. Harold Nabhan, the owner of the Pavilion, to open my wrestling school in his building. Harold is a man I respect immensely. He gave me the green light to open my school, and we agreed that I would live in a small office apartment overlooking the Atlantic Ocean. I could now promote shows, run my school, and live all in one location with an extraordinary ocean view. Giving me the space to run an alternative business is something I remain grateful to Mr. Nabhan for to this day. I've never called him by his first name out of complete, sincere respect.

My new school needed a name. Tony Rumble was a well-known figure in the section of Boston known as the Combat Zone, which was also the fictional hometown for his stable of wrestlers, the Brotherhood. I can still hear the music playing now. "Dirty Water" by the Standells filled the air as ring announcer Rich Palladino eloquently announced, "Being led to the ring by the founder and leader of the Brotherhood, the 'Boston Bad Boy,' Tony Rumble, from the Combat Zone in Boston." The school name was a no-brainer: the Combat Zone. It was a tribute to Tony, a man who'd helped me and so many others and had never asked for anything in return.

The next order of business was a wrestling ring. This was a major obstacle when operating on a budget of zero. A conversation with a friend about what I was trying to accomplish led me to someone willing to put up the money for a brand-new ring. Everything fell into place. Frustrated by the failure of Champs Arena, I was determined to bring quality professional wrestling back to the area. Working with money out of pocket, I went to Home Depot. Droplights above the ring and gallons of black paint on the walls and ceiling transformed a warehouse space into a television studio, small arena, wrestling school, and my residence, all under one roof—and all a few feet from the Atlantic Ocean. It was pretty cool to get up in the morning, open my bedroom door, and watch my idea and vision come to life. I had one hell of a living room.

The black paint gave the illusion of a much bigger space. When a match was being filmed properly, the droplights over the ring allowed only the first few rows of fans to be visible on television. Through trial and error, I perfected the space. Silver duct tape on the ropes and a beautiful set of stairs for the wrestlers to enter the ring. The stairs were built by Elwood Apt Sr., Big Woody's father. In a relatively short time, I created a TV studio to go along with the brand-new wrestling ring. I went to the local marina in Newburyport and purchased a small hammer and a bell shaped like a mini version of the Liberty Bell to add the final touch to my venture.

Renting chairs is an expense I couldn't afford, and purchasing them was not an option. That's when the law of attraction kicked in and blessed me with a major break. Another person I met while living in Salisbury Beach was Matt Bloom. He was just starting his journey in the wrestling world at the time. Matt is a very generous man. He introduced me to a nightclub owner, Mark Filtranti. That led to a job working nights for Mark at his gentleman's establishment, Ten's Show Club, while I spent my days getting the school opened. One night, I arrived at work to find all new tables and chairs in the club. I quickly located Mark and asked about his plans for the old chairs.

He smiled and said, "I'm going to give them to you. They are out back. Come pick them up anytime."

The so-called "old" chairs were in great condition. Unlike uncomfortable folding chairs, these stacked, and had cushions on the seats and backs. The chrome-finished frames looked great on television. Mark gave me the chairs, refusing to accept any type of payment. A good thing since I didn't have any budget for chairs . . . or anything else, for that matter.

As Boston Celtics great Kevin Garnett once said, "Anything is possible." I'd learned the formula for promoting wrestling from Tony Rumble, which included not depending on tourists to fill new seats, but instead, building a fan base from the surrounding towns. To do that, I needed television exposure. I approached the local cable station with an idea for a thirty-minute program called *This Week in Wrestling*. The guys at Channel 12, right over the border in Amesbury, Massachusetts, came on board, but challenges mounted quickly. The program director and crew at the station had no experience in filming wrestling. And they had even less interest in letting me educate them on the subject. From beginning to end, the relationship was rocky. I attempted to pass along what I'd picked up at WWF TV tapings, in addition to sharing what I had learned from Patrick J. Doyle and Tony Rumble in my CWA-NWA days. They ignored me and did whatever they wanted, frequently making the show look like crap. My hands were tied, and I had no choice but to go along with their thickheadedness and, at times, incompetence. The reality was, they were all I had.

Between promoting shows, teaching at the school, and producing a weekly television program, I had found my niche and a way to stay involved in wrestling. As a wrestler, I had lived a self-serving, selfish life. In my new role, I was helping people try to pursue their dreams. It felt good to offer young men and women a place to take a shot at wrestling—and in some more serious cases, advance their careers. My good fortune continued. I became aware that a well-traveled professional announcer named Brian Webster lived in my area. I figured if I could land Brian to host my TV program, that would dramatically elevate its credibility.

To everyone's delight, Brian joined the team. He never brought up money. He trusted that I would address the subject when things got up and running. With Brian's classic clean-cut image, my long-haired-degenerate demeanor, and the happy-go-lucky Big Woody in the mix, we created excellent chemistry on and off the air. Famed wrestler Terry Funk once said that the number one reason to be in wrestling was to have fun—and we were doing just that.

This Week in Wrestling taped 102 episodes. The show took place in the Adelphia television studio and showed matches from the Combat Zone. This allowed us to promote upcoming shows mixed with interviews, music videos, and vignettes showcasing the Wrestling Star Wars talent.

We aired in twenty-seven towns on the North Shore. Each week, I drove to Newburyport, Haverhill, and Lawrence, delivering the weekly show on VHS tape to the cable companies. The roster was handpicked by me: the commissioner Gil Bonk, senior official Shun Yamaguchi, and the wrestlers: Fred "The Rocket" Curry, Ron Zombie, Dylan Kage, Kidd USA, Astroman, Brian A. Day, Curtis Slamdawg, Donnie Rotten, Big Woody, the Mercenary, Arch Kincaid, Tony Gangsta, Nikki Roxx, and D. C. Dillinger, along with future stars, like Eddie Edwards and Velvet Sky. I decided to use top-notch independent wrestlers and stayed away from expensive wrestlers who were known from television. Tony Rumble once explained that well-known wrestlers made absolutely no difference when it came to attendance but cost a bundle to bring in—usually requiring a plane ticket and a hotel room. The idea was to keep the doors open and stay in business.

My uneasy working relationship with the crew from Adelphia didn't last. On extremely short notice, they decided to stop producing our TV show. This left me in a quandary. Thinking the show could end without notice, a sixteen-year-old kid named Derrick Mitchell took over. Derrick worked at another cable company in Haverhill. When I stopped in to deliver weekly tapes, he would offer feedback on the show. At times, he would laugh at how bad it was. He was interested in helping me make the show better, but as long as Adelphia was involved, they would have considered this kid a threat.

I liked everything Derrick had to say; we were always on the same page. He had a handle on how things should be done. When I told Derrick that Adelphia had dropped us, he gladly took the reins and breathed new life into *This Week in Wrestling*. I would pick him up at his house and drive him to the TV studio to edit the show each week. He improved everything he touched, and I mean *every single* aspect of it. So I let him do whatever he wanted. The kid was—and still is—brilliant.

My personal favorite story from Wrestling Star Wars took place one night prior to a live event at the Combat Zone. Big Woody came into the back room to let me know WWE Superstar John Cena was in the building. He had bought two tickets and was sitting in the crowd. Since he was dressed in sweats and a ball cap, no one realized who he was. His father was making his debut as a manager on the show.

A few weeks prior, John Cena Sr., a.k.a. John Fabulous, showed up at the Combat Zone to ask if he could be a part of the promotion in some capacity. He threw himself on the ground to demonstrate his willingness to take bumps if needed. He had a lot of enthusiasm, and I welcomed him into the fold. Bad Company had just released a new song called "Joe Fabulous," and I suggested he use the name John Fabulous for a ring name and use the song.

For his debut, he'd painted glitter dollar signs on a briefcase, put on a suit and tie, and John Fabulous was born. He went on to manage several wrestlers, including me, when I would make an occasional in-ring appearance.

The night John Cena Jr. came to the Combat Zone, I instructed Woody to give him his money back and tell him to enjoy the show. Woody returned a short time later to let me know that Cena had refused to take the refund; he wanted to support wrestling and pay for his seats. Time and time again, people will appear at the door of a wrestling show, expecting to get in for free because of who they are. They also want whoever they bring along with them to receive complimentary tickets. It was such a pain in the ass. But John Cena, a major star in wrestling, insisted on paying for his tickets, proving what a class act he is. That, boys and girls, is how it's done. From that day forward, I've always paid for tickets, even when I'm invited to attend for free.

One of the perks I offered my wrestlers at the Combat Zone was a high-quality VHS tape of their matches that they could use to help them to get booked with other promotions. John Fabulous asked for a copy of his first match for Wrestling Star Wars, and I was happy to oblige. A few days later, he called, letting me know that I had given him a tape filled with pornographic material by mistake. He was *not* amused by the honest mistake I had made. In addition to his wrestling personality, Mr. Cena was also a justice of the peace, marrying couples for years. To say I was embarrassed is a huge understatement. I drove to his office to bring him his actual wrestling tape and attempted to explain my blunder. He was a good sport about the whole thing and continued to manage wrestlers for Wrestling Star Wars.

During the summer of 2002, the door began to slowly close on my wrestling promotion. The core group of wrestlers no longer wanted to work for me. My drunken behavior after one of the shows forced longtime friends to break ties with me. I tried to make amends with everyone, but the damage could not be repaired. I began using wrestling school students on the shows, some of whom were not ring ready. Our transition from featuring the top independent wrestler in New England to students filling out the wrestling cards was not going to draw fans to the arena.

I stopped paying everyone, insisting that the opportunity to appear on my TV show and work in front of a crowd was compensation enough. I stooped even lower, suggesting a bottle of alcohol or a bag of weed would ensure a spot on the card.

In the past, my office would hold after-parties for out-of-town wrestlers who would be staying overnight. The following morning, excellent wrestling practice sessions would unfold, featuring a mix of students and experienced wrestlers. Our having well-trained men and women from all over New England in the same place at the same time allowed different philosophies to blend into a single practice. You might think conflict would arise, but it never did. We introduced students to conditioning that was conducive to wrestling. We ran drills. We taught them how to put together spots (a series of moves in succession). Then we would have matches. It was awesome. Dylan Kage, Ron Zombie, and Freight Train Dan all helped train my students. We had so much fun in those days. But I replaced those valuable sessions with locked doors and canceled practice. Instead of attending lively gatherings after a show, I sat alone in my office, hating myself. The heart and soul that I used to create the Combat Zone and Wrestling Star Wars was gone. Like a blanket had been thrown over my entire body. Drinking and drugging had stopped being fun a long time ago. I lived on a beautiful beach, yet I spent most of the time indoors.

On September 28, 2002, two days after my birthday, Wrestling Star Wars closed its doors for good. The crowd that night was made up of fewer than fifty people. I sat alone in my office. In front of me, on a large round table, bottles of liquor, two ounces of pot, and a variety of pills. A stack of thirty-packs of beer sat on the floor next to me. I decided I would consume all of it in one sitting. Feeding my addictions until everything was gone. Over the next two days, I isolated myself in my office, drinking and drugging in earnest. Knocks at the door and telephone calls went unanswered. I couldn't get drunk or high. For some reason, I felt little effect. Instead, I felt completely empty. I felt the same way two nights earlier standing in the middle of a bar filled with people. Everyone had been drinking and having a good time while I'd stood in the middle of the crowd, feeling so alone that my chest hurt. Three days later, I attended my first meeting of Alcoholics Anonymous.

Design courtesy of John Rodeo

Courage to Change the Things I Can

Get on your knees
And beg for this
Don't say please
And then resist
You don't wanna talk about it
It's over and done
Gasoline and guns
Your time will come
And here's the deal
You start messin' with another man's home
And the burnin' steel

Electric Mary, "Gasoline & Guns"

JUST ONE DAY AFTER THE LAST WRESTLING STAR WARS show, I sold my wrestling ring to journeyman wrestler Astroman. He came to the Pavilion to pick it up with a helper, Benny the Bronx. The three of us loaded the ring into a truck. The moment felt surreal. Astroman placed his hand on my shoulder.

"Don't worry, Knuckles," he said. "I'm in charge now."

I watched with a heavy heart as they drove away. I walked back to my office, trying not to notice the empty space where the ring once stood, surrounded by empty seats, but the image is etched in my memory forever. Tony Rumble had said he would be involved in wrestling until the day he died. That turned out to be true. And I'd believed the same for myself. Shun Yamaguchi had suggested I take a nice vacation. He'd felt that closing the doors might be a decision I would live to regret, that taking a break and returning fresh was a viable option. Like most people, Shun was not aware of my real problem. I didn't need a spa weekend; I needed a lifestyle change. The time was upon me for some serious soul-searching.

Even back then, I'd longed for the same answers to the questions I later hoped to ask Jimmy Valiant during my trip to Virginia: *How do you determine the next right thing to do in life? How do you know it's the right decision?* Without realizing it, I became willing to open my heart and soul to a new way of living. I can pinpoint the moment, as I stood on the beach, looking out at the horizon. I was abusing my mind and body, and that needed to change. In need of answers, I did what any thirty-eight-year-old would do: I called my mother. She seemed prepared for the call. I told her something was seriously wrong with me, but I didn't know what exactly. Without mentioning a topic, she guided me in the right direction. She revealed how difficult it had been to watch her son getting beaten up for years. She had no love for wrestling. From day one, she'd asked me to do something else. She'd once told me that even if I were to become the world champion, she would never endorse my decision to become a professional wrestler. She told me she'd worried about my safety and well-being the entire time I wrestled. She feared that she would someday receive a phone call informing her I was dead. Back then, it seemed like a wrestler was found dead in a hotel room every other week. The combination of worrying about the self-destructive lifestyle I was living, along with the physical punishment of wrestling that I'd sustained, caused her sleepless nights.

Fortunately, she was now receiving a phone call from me, still very much alive. I knew I needed help. I wasn't sure what was wrong with me or what type of help I needed, but the phone call was a step in the right direction. She asked if I'd be open to receiving a phone call from Brian W., a longtime family friend. I'd always liked Brian but hadn't seen him in years. His parents and mine had been friends since the 1960s, and I had known him my entire life. I welcomed the call.

The next morning, Brian called. I was still starting my day by smoking pot, and shortly after that, planning my first drink of the day. I stood looking out the window at my million-dollar view of the ocean, smoking from a pipe as the phone rang. When I answered, Brian sounded upbeat and happy, a warmth in his voice.

After the pleasantries, he said, "Your mom tells me you think you might have a problem with drugs and alcohol."

I quickly fired back, "No, not really."

He was smooth with his approach. He backed off and changed the subject to wrestling. We had a nice conversation. Like most drunks, I enjoyed talking about myself. Brian asked if I'd be open to meeting him in Providence. I agreed, unaware of the reason we would be getting together.

"How about tomorrow?" he asked.

I hadn't realized he'd meant right away; I'd been thinking in a few weeks.

I paused before replying, "Sure, ok."

On October 2, 2002, I drove to Rhode Island to meet my longtime family friend. We met at Dunkin' Donuts on Admiral Street, near Providence College, where I jumped into his black pickup truck. A few years my junior, Brian seemed calm and mature. He left the parking lot, and we were on the road to destination unknown to me. We drove to a building on Pitman Street with lots of people outside. I had no idea we were at the Salvation Army. In the parking lot, everyone said hello to Brian. In front of the building, more of the same. Once inside, I discovered the hall was full of men and women ranging in age from very young to senior citizen. I noticed a podium off to the left in the distance. Rows and rows of metal folding chairs in front of the podium. More chairs along the walls and around the entire room. Blue banners were strung up on the walls with unfamiliar slogans written in yellow, like "First Things First," "Easy Does It," and "One Day at a Time." Straight ahead, there was a table with coffee and snacks. Brian asked if I wanted coffee. I quickly declined.

People continued to greet Brian with handshakes and hugs. Brian introduced me to a dozen or so people in a short period of time. He suggested we grab a seat. We sat all the way in the front, just across from the podium. An attractive woman stepped up to the podium to welcome everyone.

I leaned over to Brian and asked, "Where are we?"

The woman and Brian said, "Alcoholics Anonymous" almost simultaneously.

I wasn't sure what that meant. I knew Andy Sipowicz, a character on the television show *NYPD Blue,* was in AA, but that was the extent of my knowledge of the program.

The woman at the podium told her story of drinking and blacking out. Even though the terminology she used was foreign to me, I somehow knew exactly what she was talking about. My focus was not on her message, however, but rather on her good looks and her hardcore stories of drunken behavior. Getting her phone number was my priority. I didn't know at the time that women in AA couldn't be less interested in some idiot like me who might be contemplating the idea of getting sober.

My biggest takeaway from my first AA meeting was the friendly way everyone treated one another, displaying genuine kindness and sincerity. A scenario I had not been a part of in some time. On the ride back to my car, Brian handed me a small pamphlet. A meeting list book for the entire seacoast back home in Salisbury. How he'd gotten his hands on it, I'll never know. I lived over one hundred miles away. Brian suggested I go to meetings. He said to show up and everything would take care of itself. I had no idea what he was talking about. I wanted to believe him. I needed something to hold on to. I needed hope.

Brian became my first AA sponsor. I called him every single day. Due to the distance, we maintained our relationship over the phone. He made himself available during the painful process known as early sobriety. I talked and he listened. He consistently offered the same advice. Always in the form of a suggestion. "Don't drink—go to meetings." That may sound like a command, but it's comparable to telling someone who's getting ready to jump from an airplane to pull the cord if they want the parachute to open. Brian is a family man with a wife and, at the time, two small children. He always made time for me, even with his already full schedule.

I bet it was an absolute pleasure to sponsor me in those early days. I was defiant and a know-it-all. Questioning everything he suggested. I did what I wanted. I learned things the hard way before settling into a new lifestyle, one that no longer included smoking pot and drinking alcohol on a daily basis. Everything in my life changed. My wrestling operation closed for good, which left me unemployed. Attending AA meetings became my job. Twice a day, I went to meetings. A noontime meeting in Newburyport and one at night in a variety of locations. What a relief it was to broach the subject of addiction in rooms full of people who knew exactly what I was going through! They offered me solid advice, reminding me that I could have my misery refunded anytime I wanted by simply leaving and returning to my old ways.

Friday nights I traveled to Harvard University in Cambridge, Massachusetts, to another program, Marijuana Anonymous. This program is similar to AA, except it's for potheads. I loved that meeting. I connected with people in MA, just like in AA, because I belonged there. I identified with everyone and the common struggle of trying to give up smoking pot after years of daily use. The next six months, I made great strides on the path to recovery. From drinking and smoking pot daily to stopping completely. An accomplishment I would never have thought possible. Unfortunately, at the time, I was the last person to see the progress I was making. Attempting to hold down a job during the roller-coaster ride known as early sobriety was not possible for me. A common term that best described my condition during the first six months: *unemployable*. I was unable to work for multiple reasons. My new routine looked like this: Sleep until late morning. Eat breakfast, followed by a noontime AA meeting. Return home and sleep until dinnertime. Get up, eat dinner, then attend another AA meeting at night. Return home, watch television, and attempt meditation before turning in for the evening. I'd sleep like a baby until 11:00 a.m. the next morning. Then I'd get up and repeat the process. This went on for a solid month. I was physically and emotionally drained. The only remedy was rest.

Slowly I incorporated other activities into my routine. Some familiar, some new. I returned to the gym. I slept less during the day. I became friends with group members. I began to socialize. I started going to church. I started to drink lots of coffee in early sobriety. It started to affect my sleeping pattern, so after a while, I cut back on my coffee consumption. The only way I was able to keep a roof over my head and food on the table was by receiving financial support from my parents. They could see my dedication to getting sober. They helped me keep food on the table and gas in my car during a time I simply couldn't work. Without their help, I would have ended up on the street. It is possible to get sober while unemployed *and* homeless. Luckily, I never had to test that theory myself.

My godfather, Joe, and his wife, Carol, also supported my quest for a new lifestyle, inviting me to their home as a frequent dinner guest. My life got better. My health returned as I discovered working out at the gym sober for the first time. This is my tip of the day: if you want to have the best possible workout, don't smoke weed before you go to the gym. Here I was, in my late thirties, experiencing life through a sober lens for the first time as an adult.

A definite problem started to unfold. I exhausted my savings. Asking my parents for more financial help just didn't feel right. I was running out of money. Anyone who has ever experienced living off a savings account knows that you watch it dwindle day by day until it's gone. They say getting sober is like walking out of the woods. You have to spend as much time walking out as you spent walking in. My thought process was clearly still in the woods somewhere. My situation led me to believe that AA must not be working. How could it be, if I were broke? I began to think that quitting AA made sense. The idea of getting a job never entered my mind. What happened next was another example of my being in the right place at the right time.

One day, I went to my daily noontime meeting in Newburyport with every intention of quitting AA. I sat down in the meeting with exactly three dollars in my pocket—and to my name. My sick thinking took over. Quitting the program was all I could think about. The group's secretary approached me—a long-haired Grateful Dead fan named Sam, complete with a tie-dyed shirt. A sweet, gentle man, he asked if I would speak at the meeting.

I folded my arms, looked straight ahead, and firmly said, "No."

Sam told me he thought I had a good message and hoped I would reconsider his offer to share my experience, strength, and hope with the group.

I looked at him and asked, "What part of no don't you understand?"

He politely excused himself to go find another speaker.

Apparently, being an asshole still came easily to me. My plan was to leave the meeting, drive to the beach, use my last three dollars on two slices of beach pizza, and reevaluate my life.

When the meeting ended, I rose from my seat and walked outside without a word to anyone. This meeting had an average attendance of about fifty or so people, many of whom stood and socialized in the parking lot after the meeting.

In the lot, a voice behind me called out, "Hey, Brendan!"

I turned around to see a man I did not recognize. He asked if I was working. My first reaction was to be offended. Why would this guy think I'm *not* working? Luckily, I got over myself quickly.

"No, I'm not," I said.

He introduced himself as John H., extending his hand for a shake. He informed me that he owned a landscaping company. It was April, and he desperately needed help with spring cleanups. He said I could start right away if I wanted. He offered me fifteen dollars per hour in under-the-table cash at the end of each day. Considering my current situation—an ex-wrestler in early recovery with a total of three bucks in my pocket—I gladly accepted.

Next thing I knew, we were driving off in his truck,

straight from the meeting. We drove to West Newbury, a beautiful town filled with expensive homes and manicured lawns. My new employer explained that I would start on my own while he went to work on another account at a different location. A perfect situation unfolded. John needed help, and I needed a job. Plus, I've always loved landscaping. After a few hours, John returned and scanned the yard I had just finished cleaning.

"I'll pay you twenty dollars per hour," he said, pleased with my effort. He shared his plan for the summer: work ten hours a day, six days a week, stopping for lunch and the noontime meeting. This, of course, ended any plan I'd had of leaving AA. I can't make this shit up. This really happened. John paid me for five hours of work, and instead of taking me for beach pizza, he took me out to dinner. We got along great. I spent the next two summers working for John.

One suggestion in AA is to take a low-stress job in early sobriety. Pushing a fifty-two-inch Gravely lawnmower while dressed in cutoff jeans and work boots with no shirt definitely qualified. Over the summer, John and I became close friends. Thanks to him, I was also making a good living. Landscaping is seasonal work. I needed to find a job for the fall.

Across the seacoast, word spread of a new World Gym opening in Seabrook, New Hampshire. With perfect timing, I transitioned from landscaping to working the desk at World Gym. I had a plan of returning to one of my loves, teaching karate. The gym's owner, Tim Johnson, had realized his vision of running a brand-new, multilevel, state-of-the-art fitness center. Tim treated everyone with respect and kindness. I admired the way he always paused before responding to questions. We became training partners, which gave me a chance to pitch my idea of a karate program. He gave me the green light, and I resumed my longtime role as a karate instructor, sober for the first time.

World Gym allowed me to return to the workforce. I received medical insurance for the first time in over a decade. Eventually, Tim promoted me to night manager. We trained in the morning, and I closed the gym at night. I found myself in the best condition of my life. Everything continued to improve. Working at the gym opened the door to a social life, and I even began dating. Little by little, AA started to take a back seat to my having a good time. I called Brian, my sponsor, less and less. In time, I stopped calling altogether. I attended fewer meetings until I stopped completely. I no longer associated with people in the program, including some coworkers at the gym who I knew from recovery meetings. My new life at the gym was now fueled by arrogance. I believed I no longer needed AA.

Brian took AA seriously (and still does). Once he finally got me on the phone, he asked direct questions: "Are you going to meetings?" "Are you drinking?" I answered no to both. He told me that if I was no longer attending AA meetings, there was no reason to continue our sponsor/sponsee relationship. I agreed, moving closer to the edge of the cliff. The reality was, I'd never stepped foot on the path to recovery. I'd fallen into the misconception that going to AA meetings and the fellowship that accompanies that, in addition to the sober time, would be all I needed for a healthy life in recovery. The real recovery process would not enter my life until many years later. It's quite possible that the real message of recovery was being transmitted to me back then. The problem was, I wanted to take the message and mold it into something I could make work for me. I was far from ready to hear the truth. My self-will was working overtime.

The gym had roughly five thousand members. Yet I decided to get involved with someone who drank and drugged in earnest. She was sixteen years younger than me. Just prior to my achieving two years of very shaky sobriety, I was angry most of the time. I was dishonest. My sexual conduct was despicable. I lashed out at people, having no control over my rage. I blamed AA for all of it. I concluded that the program did not work for me. My new girlfriend made a strong case, suggesting that sex would be much better if we got drunk first. I agreed and popped open a bottle of champagne. I want to be crystal clear about this next part. When I was a drinker, having champagne was not considered drinking. After a few glasses of bubbly, I moved on to one hundred-proof vodka. In my book, that's real drinking. After twenty-two months without drinking or drugging, I relapsed. Unlike my previous decades of drinking, during my relapse, I couldn't get drunk. I seemed unaffected by putting alcohol in my system. Smoking pot always went hand in hand with drinking, and it didn't take long to pick that up again. I found marijuana equally ineffective. During my youth, drinking and smoking weed was fun, with my incredible stories of romance and traveling the globe, enjoying exciting times. My relapse was a complete nightmare. Then I sank to a new low. With the help of my demented female companion, I entered the world of prescription drugs. Percocet and Vicodin, when combined with alcohol, brought me as close as possible to the effect I wanted. My much younger girlfriend educated me on faking injuries to get my hands on the dreadful medications we desired.

I have one nightmarish memory of lying on a bed in a hotel

room, fully conscious yet unable to lift my head or move any of my limbs. I was paralyzed. My girlfriend, motionless next to me and in a similar condition, asked, "Isn't this great?" My soul had not yet been fully extinguished because all I could think was NO. *This is not great.* It was the single most horrible feeling I have ever experienced.

It didn't take long for my employer and coworkers to notice a change in my behavior. I went from being a dependable person to someone no one wanted to work with—just like it was toward the end of my wrestling days. As night manager, I worked unsupervised. I walked around the facility with a red plastic Solo cup, normally used for protein shakes. Mine was filled with one hundred-proof vodka on the rocks. I made frequent trips outside to smoke pot. I told my training partner, Tim, that I had an "injury" and stopped working out and teaching karate classes. I was barely existing, living from day to day again. My karate students would see me at the gym and express how much they missed class. I would lie, telling them that when I recovered from my injury, we would be back at it. The idea of getting sober again seemed impossible. I needed help, and this time I knew it—unlike the previous decades of drug and alcohol abuse, when I lived in denial of my problems. From July 22, 2004, until late November of the same year, my life was a living hell. As Thanksgiving passed and Christmas approached, I gave up hope of returning to a sober life.

World Gym in Seabrook had the appearance of a fitness club in Los Angeles or Miami. State-of-the-art in every way. At night, I worked at the juice bar—a common place for members to congregate and socialize—chatting with members and making post-workout protein shakes. Just before I relapsed, I had made so much progress in recovery that I decided to go back to school. I applied for a loan and suddenly had the funds to pursue an education. Instead of following through with the original idea, however, I spent the money on a four-month binge. One night, I sat at the juice bar, feeling complete despair. An acquaintance of mine from the gym, Maria, sat down to chat after her workout.

She looked at me and said, "What's wrong with you? You look like shit."

Without hesitation, I spilled my guts. I told Maria that I had totally fucked up my life. I had almost two years of sobriety, and I had decided to drink and drug again. I explained that everything was out of control. Then I caught myself and stopped talking. I stood there looking at her mouth, which was shut in silence. Maria was friends with Tim, my workout partner and employer. She was also a respected business owner in the area. I had just exposed personal information about myself that could result in my losing the only thing I had left, my job.

She sat quietly for a few seconds.

"It's OK, Brendan. I've been sober for fourteen years," she disclosed. Her revealing her sobriety meant there was a good chance that she would keep my living hell to herself. "What would you like to do about this?" she asked.

I stood there with a blank look on my face.

"I don't know," came out of my mouth. I felt relief in telling her the truth, but I still needed direction.

She reframed the question: "If you could do anything right now, what would that look like?"

"I would like to go home to Rhode Island," I responded. I felt my time on the seacoast had run its course—from the first time I stepped out of a car and looked around Salisbury

Beach until this moment. I felt the circle becoming complete. My gut was telling me it was time to go home, even before Maria asked what I wanted to do. I had a girlfriend who was deep into her own addiction with no intention of stopping. Everyone, including me, knew that dating her was a bad idea.

Maria went so far as to ask me, "What do you see in her?"

If I had answered the question honestly, I would've said I saw a person just as sick as I was and just as self-destructive as I was, needing help, like I did. If I moved back to Rhode Island, I could reconnect with my AA sponsor, Brian. Our previous relationship had taken place over the phone due to our distance from each other. He'd helped me in the past, and my hope was that he would help me get sober again. Being around him in person and attending meetings together sounded like a great idea.

Maria took out her cell phone and made a call.

She spoke to someone on the other end: "Hey, Anthony. Are you still looking for a driver?"

She put the call on speakerphone, and a voice said, "Yes, I am."

She told him, "I have your man sitting right in front of me."

He replied, "No, no, no. I need someone familiar with Rhode Island."

She laughed and said, "He is from Rhode Island, and he's moving back. Can he get an interview?"

"Sure," he said. "Bring him in tomorrow when you come down."

"Will do," Maria said as she hung up.

Let's review. I'm sitting in a gym in Seabrook, New Hampshire. A woman I know by first name only appears in front of me. I can't find my ass with both hands. I'm deep in addiction. The next thing I know, I have a job interview in Rhode Island the very next morning. Just like the day I decided to resign from AA and met John the landscaper, another angel has come into my life, allowing fate to take over.

Maria worked for a large company based in Rhode Island. This opened the door to new possibilities. She told me she would vouch for me on two conditions: First, I needed to stay away from my demented girlfriend. Second, I had to return to AA.

I paused before asking, "Can I think about it?"

Maria laughed and said, "Sure, you can think about it, but don't be an asshole. There's not much to think about."

That's the power of addiction. I had a golden opportunity to point my life in a good direction, a chance to return to my home state of Rhode Island, a chance to start over, an opportunity to be around my family again and reconnect with my AA sponsor, but I needed to think about it.

Luckily for me, I accepted her terms. The next day, on a cold late-November morning, Maria and I drove to Lincoln, Rhode Island. The man on the phone was a stranger to me, as I'd been away from the Ocean State for a decade, but he was a well-known public figure to most people in Rhode Island. He owned a hugely successful company. Turns out, I had gotten the job over the phone. The interview was a mere formality. During the informal meeting, Anthony told me the job entailed delivering tools and materials in a small box truck to job sites around New England. The starting pay and benefits were more than I expected. I thanked him as we shook hands, sealing the deal. He told me the only thing left was a drug test. My heart dropped into the pit of my stomach.

When Anthony needed to leave the room momentarily,

Maria came back in. I told her this might not end well since I couldn't pass a drug test. Before she could respond, Anthony returned. He repeated that I needed to go for a drug test.

Maria suggested, "Let me take him for the test in New Hampshire. I need to get back."

"Great," Anthony responded. "Welcome aboard, Brendan."

That was the last time a drug test was ever mentioned. Maria had faith in me that I would get my act together once and for all. Another easy sober job had appeared for me without my having to put in much effort. My fears and doubts intensified as we left the parking lot in Lincoln, Rhode Island. My ability to make good decisions was clouded by four months of hard drinking and drugging. I expressed my gratitude to Maria before confessing that a big problem loomed: I had no idea where I would live once I was back in Rhode Island. The new job expected me to report the following week for my first day of work. Getting the job was only a portion of my pulling off this improbable move.

We stopped at a convenience store, and Maria stepped inside. She returned with a copy of the *Providence Journal*. She opened the paper, and immediately located an apartment five minutes away, in Smithfield. She called the number associated with the ad, engaged in a brief conversation with someone on the other end of the line, and drove directly to the apartment. The smell of fresh paint wafted through the air as we walked inside. A man holding a paint roller greeted us. He informed us that he was the property owner and told us to take a look around.

Maria scanned the place, looked at me, and said, "It has potential."

The owner agreed. He asked her when she was looking to move in.

"It's not for me," she responded. "It's for him." She pointed at me.

He seemed disappointed. I told him I was hoping to move in soon, next week, if possible.

The man said, "I'll need a deposit to hold it for you. This place will go quick."

Maria took out her checkbook and secured my new digs. Landing the job and finding a place to live had taken less than an hour. I promised her I would pay her back.

She laughed and said, "You bet your ass you will."

Maria is one of the angels who was placed in my life. In time, I did pay her back.

I returned to Rhode Island on December 1, 2004. I left the seacoast with little fanfare. I packed my car with my belongings, got on the road, and Maria followed me in a pickup truck containing the rest of my stuff. Filled with emotion and hope, I merged onto Route 95 South in Salisbury for the long trek to my new, old home. I passed a gigantic American flag suspended from a crane, dancing in the wind. With perfect timing, the song "Don't You (Forget About Me)" by Simple Minds came on the radio. I turned it up to maximum volume, and tears streamed down my face as I sang along. The song fit like a brand-new sock. A new beginning was waiting for me at the end of the ride.

Each summer, I return to the seacoast to visit my family members there, Joe and Carol. When I first arrived in Salisbury Beach back in 1995, and throughout the time that I lived there, not much changed over the years. Now, each time I visit, a little more of the area I once knew disappears. A new business here. A new condo development there. Someone who has moved away or died. A feeling of change in all directions. My memories of Salisbury Beach will live in my heart forever.

COURAGE TO CHANGE THE THINGS I CAN

Left to right: Big Woody, Joe Moakley, me, Tony G., Bull Montana

CHAPTER 7

Welcome to My Nightmare

When your head gets its fill of emotions
And your eyes let the world know what it is
You better hold on tight
And get ready for the slide
Cause it's all
Coming down on you

Rusty, "All Comin' Down"

I SETTLED INTO MY NEW LIFE IN RHODE ISLAND. I FUMBLED along in my new job and began my second go-around in recovery. I spent the next four years of my life making progress and regaining financial stability, but my life was devoid of passion. I missed the wrestling world. Doing what you love is light-years away from doing what is necessary to pay the bills. I focused on sobriety and attended AA meetings regularly. I was picking up the pieces from my relapse. I reconnected with my AA sponsor, Brian. I returned to the treadmill of: Don't drink—go to meetings. For me, that meant following a formula for abstaining from drugs and alcohol, and not much else. I was angry most of the time. I had no idea how to be in a relationship of any kind. I kept everyone at a safe distance. I was sober, but it was not a pretty sight. I knew how to abstain and fell into a trap, believing that time away from alcohol and drugs could treat what was wrong with me. I ignored the many possible avenues within the program that could have unlocked a happy life for me. This led me to believe that AA was not what it was cracked up to be. I was on a treadmill, practicing phony recovery. My mind never stopped racing. And I was about to embark on the most emotionally painful period of my life.

Working in a field I had no interest in felt like wearing shoes on the wrong feet. I could do it, but it was uncomfortable. In

2010, six years after I had moved back to Rhode Island, I applied for a job with the Rhode Island Public Transit Authority. In true Rhode Island fashion, I secured the position with help from a family friend. It's not uncommon in Rhode Island to land a sought-after position based on who you know—as opposed to being the most qualified person. Sadly, I felt little passion for my new career. However, I quickly recognized and embraced the idea of long-term security, and I remained optimistic about my new path in life. A public bus operator gains experience through trial and error. The techniques needed for dealing with people who ride the bus are not taught in the five-week training period. It's *on-the-job* training, and at times, warfare. From behind the wheel, I found myself frequently saying, "I can't believe that just happened."

    I had an easy life growing up, with the help of successful parents. We lived in a big, beautiful home in Scituate, Rhode Island, with a loyal dog, Brownie, a fluffy cat, Heidi, and a massive backyard with goats to take care of. I had a wonderful childhood, never once worrying about where my next meal would come from or where I would sleep for the night. Both of my parents were always present, providing my two brothers and me with every opportunity to have a comfortable life. In my new position at RIPTA, I encountered people who were unable to make the same claim. I observed people living in constant overwhelm. Desperate to stay off the streets, they appeared to be in a daily struggle just to feed themselves and their children. This new environment shocked me. Like any new job, I dealt with a variety of firsts. First day, first time behind the wheel, first time driving a new route, first time being spit on, first time being threatened, first time being assaulted, first time having a lit cigarette flicked in my face. I also became aware of the lines drawn between bus operators and management. Drivers take a lot of abuse on the road and rarely hear any positive or complimentary feedback. But the slightest mistake or complaint directed at a driver is swiftly addressed. A battle taking place long before I arrived and one that's sure to continue after I'm gone. One never knows when the next incident will occur; they're not from day to day, but from bus stop to bus stop. One needs to personally experience the dynamics to truly understand what I'm talking about.

All drivers have stories of adventures on the road. They happen every day. Some drivers despise passengers while maintaining a pleasant demeanor on the surface. Others prefer not to hide it at all. The same holds true for some passengers. I promised myself I'd never adopt this line of thinking. After my first year on the road, I learned firsthand the reason all sides feel conflict. A new driver enters into a sink-or-swim environment. When a veteran bus passenger becomes aware of a new driver, either by his uniform number or his face, they will, usually out of boredom, test the driver's patience. Having utilized public transportation for years—and in some cases, a lifetime—a veteran rider of public transportation can treat a new driver like fresh meat to toy with. After having been bullied throughout most of my youth, I went to great lengths as an adult to ensure those days were behind me for good. Between karate, wrestling, weight training, and a genuine dislike of bullies, I know how to fight fire with fire in confrontational situations. You might think, *Hey, good for you,* but management does not endorse fighting fire with fire as an employee of the Public Transit Authority. This created an immediate dilemma for me. As a bus driver, I found myself facing seriously twisted behavior from passengers. I approached each day with a positive outlook and tried my best to avoid conflict. Try as I did, it found me anyway. This is one example:

It was a beautiful Saturday morning in Bristol, Rhode Island, a quiet town with a picturesque shoreline, a friendly bike path, and a world-famous Fourth of July parade. I stopped at a bus stop to pick up a man who was waiting alone. What could go wrong? As soon as I opened the door, he fell into my lap. He was highly intoxicated. He pushed his way off me and back to a standing position. He told me he loved me several times. I attempted to make a deal with him.

I said, "Look, here's the deal. Two things. First: stop breathing on me. Second: you can ride if you behave."

He agreed. The bus had a few other people scattered throughout. The man took a seat, and as soon as I resumed driving, he started yelling at a woman across the aisle from him. She sat in silence. I reminded him of our agreement. He ignored me. He continued to scream at the woman.

He told her, and I quote, "If you don't stop looking at me, I'm going to punch you in your motherfucking face." He then stood up and started moving in her direction.

I stopped the bus and opened the door. Then I got out of the seat and cut him off. This put me between the two of them. The woman remained seated and silent the entire time. Next, he turned his attention directly to me. He began to taunt me. His breath was brutal. His body gave off an odor best described as a combination of booze, cigarettes, baby powder, and body odor. He was more revolting than anyone I'd ever encountered in my life.

Next, he whispered, "Go ahead, motherfucker, put your hands on me." He repeated himself as he stood so close to my face you couldn't slide a piece of paper between us.

Without hesitation, I grabbed him by the back of his jacket and the seat of his pants. I walked him to the front of the bus to the open door and threw him off the bus in the same manner I would throw someone over the top rope in a wrestling match. I quickly turned to close the door, but like lightning, he jumped back onto the bus and punched me in the back of the head. Man, he was quick. Especially for a guy drunk off his ass. I turned around, and with all my might, pushed him in the chest, sending him, once again, hurtling to the ground, landing directly on his back. I should mention that he was landing on grass each time. But he got up again! He lunged toward the open door, only this time, I managed to close it before he succeeded in his attempt to resume our dance.

I called the dispatcher to request police assistance. The situation was not looking good for him or me. As a new driver, I didn't know the correct protocol; a situation like this had never come up in training. My intuition told me that I hadn't handled the situation in a way that would get my employer's seal of approval. My coworkers, on the other hand, would probably offer me a high five.

The zombie-like man paced outside the bus until a single police officer arrived. He was white, in his early twenties (if that), well over six feet tall, and thickly muscled. He told the man to stand on the curb and be quiet—a request the man was unwilling to comply with. That put the officer immediately on my side. The officer ordered the man to sit on the ground. The officer, looking more like a wrestler than a cop, got on the bus and asked me what had happened. Before I could answer, the woman finally spoke. In fact, she *yelled,* "This is all because he is black!" I looked at her, thinking to myself, *I just tried to prevent this guy from punching you in the face.* Now that the police were on the scene, she was crying racial foul. The officer walked off the bus and asked the man if he had any needles or anything else on him that he could be cut with. The man said no. Then the officer pulled a needle out of his jacket pocket, and the incident swayed heavily in my favor. I left the man on the sidewalk with the officer. After the bus had gotten back on the road, the woman continued to remind everyone that the entire incident revolved around the guy being black. That was the last time I came to the defense of a passenger.

My first five years were filled with crazy stories from the road. I've been physically assaulted multiple times. I've had a lit cigarette flicked in my face by a person standing on the sidewalk outside the bus because I didn't know the answer to his question. I've been spit on by passengers and have received threats against me and my family. In most cases, the person in question, male or female, had made a mistake and boarded the wrong bus. Once I bring that to their attention, I become the bearer of bad news, and the entire situation becomes my fault. After living through challenging situations, I became unapproachable, giving the cold shoulder to management, coworkers, and passengers. I began comparing my line of work to someone in an office or a factory, wondering if they, too, were being subjected to such sick behavior. My employer had no interest in investigating any of the incidents I brought to their attention. I drove home from work each day wanting to quit my job. I became the bitter bus operator I'd promised myself I'd never be. Days turned into weeks. Weeks turned into months. Months turned into years. Years turned into a decade. I stayed in a job I hated, never leaving and, instead, finding reasons to justify staying. Anyone dealing with the public has a story to tell. The following happened right in front of my eyes:

The Fourth of July is traditionally a time for family, friends, cookouts, and fun in the sun—unless one chooses to work overtime and drive a public transit bus for the day instead. One perk in this profession is the opportunity to work overtime, including all weekends and holidays. There is no such thing as a slow day in public transportation. People who ride the bus depend on our service 365 days a year. On this day, the temperature soared into the high nineties. My assigned bus for the day had a broken air conditioner. I sat in Kennedy Plaza, watching hot, sweaty people board the bus. Before long, the bus filled to capacity, with standing room only. People packed themselves into the aisle like sardines. Once the bus was loaded, I slowly moved it past City Hall and out of the plaza. I started up Washington Street, and the bus swayed from side to side like a boat in the water. As I turned left on Empire Street, a loud argument erupted. Before long, it had escalated into a full-blown fiasco. Dozens of sweaty bodies, packed in the aisle, were moving in an unsettling manner. A fistfight was in full swing.

All buses have an emergency button for situations just like this. I pushed the button. A female voice responded to my distress call on the two-way radio, inquiring about my situation. Simultaneously, a man with revolting breath, who was standing directly over my shoulder, began screaming, "Do something! Do something!" just inches from my face. In near one-hundred-degree heat, I told the dispatcher a fight had broken out on the bus. I asked for police assistance at the corner of Broad and Empire Streets.

The dispatcher calmly said, "In order to send the police, I need your location."

I responded, "A brawl has broken out, and I just told you my location!"

She decided this would be a good time to explain to me that she would not be spoken to in the tone I'd used. She directed me to change it, or our conversation would be terminated. This was, of course, the perfect storm: extreme heat, broken air conditioner, complete chaos on the bus, and a supervisor—sitting in an air-conditioned space—unaware of the dangerous events unfolding on my end. The bus was now stopped against the curb, with both its front and back doors open. The two involved in the melee spilled off the bus through the back door and onto the sidewalk. To my complete shock, the participants were two women, and both had small children with them. One with a toddler, and the other with an infant wrapped in a blanket. Police and fire personnel encounter far worse than I do in day-to-day life, but this ranked first as the most disturbing scene I'd ever witnessed. The woman with the toddler ran off, dragging her son by his fully extended arm. I will never forget the look on his face as he tried to keep up with his mother. He was in complete shock. The second girl paced the sidewalk, holding her baby in a blanket that was now covered in blood from the fight. The sounds of sirens grew closer, and she made her escape. Once notified, police and RIPTA street supervisors respond quickly to all situations. A special thank-you to the men and women coming to our aid in dramatic and dangerous situations. Driving home after work that day, I couldn't get the image of the small children out of my head. It disturbed me deeply. I wanted to quit my job.

Another time, I drove through West Warwick, heading toward Providence. I like driving in this area, having lived in the Arctic section of West Warwick for ten years during the '80s and early '90s. The bus was empty except for three teenage boys in the back seat, keeping to themselves. Their appearance led me to believe they were tough, streetwise kids. They played music softly as we moved through town. Device speakers of any kind need to be silent while riding on a RIPTA bus. Headphones are fine, offering courtesy to everyone on board. Since they were my only passengers, I let the infraction slide, electing to stay off their radar. Up ahead on the road, I observed a twenty-something man waiting at a bus stop. He boarded the bus, said hello, and took a seat up front. Apparently, the new rider was well-versed in RIPTA policy. Rising from his seat to address the teenagers, he told them their music was offensive and not allowed on RIPTA buses. (Technically, this was not true. As I mentioned, devices can be used with headphones.) I hoped that would be the end of it, but he was just warming up.

He turned to me and said, "Sir, the boys in the back seat are playing offensive music."

Before I could reply, he turned back to the teens, pleading with them to turn off the music. He hammered his point home. He again turned to me, except this time I cut him off, I asked them to turn off the speaker on the device. They complied without a word. I told the self-appointed bus monitor to relax, as we would be in Kennedy Plaza shortly, the end of the line.

Staying off the radar of other passengers is a good, solid strategy. But the not-so-bright self-appointed bus monitor could not let it go. He put himself directly on their radar screen. I pulled into the plaza and watched all four of them get off the bus—the three teens, out the back door, and the man, out the front. I closed both doors immediately. I made my way down the aisle of the bus to get a closer look at what might transpire outside. I watched as the complainant confronted the others. He made one final attempt to explain RIPTA guidelines. I was literally two feet away, separated only by tinted glass. One of the teens punched the contemporary-music hater square in the face. Blood spewed from his mouth as teeth fell to the pavement. Unlike the two mothers who fled the scene after they threw down, these kids stood their ground, cold as ice. This poor bastard was now on his hands and knees, picking up his teeth. It was a painful lesson indeed. Mind your own business. The bloody and badly beaten toothless bigmouth stood at the front door of the bus, screaming to be let back on. That would not be happening. He began repeating over and over, "All this over music!" From where I stood, it was all over his having run his mouth instead of minding his own business. I called for medical assistance. The damage had been done. I never encountered any of them again.

A RIPTA bus ready for action

The next story took place on the 20 Line in the Elmwood section of Providence. I can't imagine being confined to a wheelchair. The physical and emotional experience is a challenge I've never been able to comprehend. I noticed a man in a wheelchair at an upcoming bus stop. I curbed the bus and opened the door to welcome him aboard. Before I said or did anything, he addressed me.

"The day may come when you become a good bus driver, but today is not the day," he said.

I smiled at him, thinking to myself, *OK, asshole, just get on the bus.*

All RIPTA buses are equipped with a powered ramp for wheelchairs to be loaded and transported. Once he rolled onto the bus, I strapped his chair to prevent it from moving and returned to my seat. A young woman in her late teens or early twenties came aboard at the next stop. She was slightly attractive, in a crackhead, street hooker kind of way. She and the man in the wheelchair immediately began to argue. They exchanged colorful insults back and forth. The girl began to fall behind on points. The man in the chair was a master at putting people down. She told him if he said one more word, she would punch him in the face. Yes, she was going to hit a man in a wheelchair.

He fired back, "If you lay one hand on me, I'll have you brought up on charges." While making his announcement, he leaned forward, as if to stand up.

Other passengers began to chime in, encouraging the girl to hit him.

"Do it; hit him!" cried someone.

"Yeah, do it!" another prompted.

The crowd got behind her in a bizarre moment, leaving me speechless. It occurred to me that nothing I might see on television later that night could top this.

She rose to her feet and said, "Fuck it, I'll take the charges."

As promised, she unloaded on him, punching the

defenseless man silly as the other riders cheered her on. This, of course, qualifies for the emergency button. Once she'd finished administering the proper amount of punishment, she turned her attention to me.

"Open the door, or I'll have *you* brought up on charges of kidnapping," she said. Man, she was quick on her feet!

I complied with her request.

She was arrested shortly afterward. When the police arrived on the scene, the man in the chair ordered me to give a detailed account of the horrible event. I reminded him that the day might come when I'd become a good driver, but . . . "today is not the day." I told the police I hadn't seen what had happened.

Another time, in the Olneyville section of Providence, a teenage girl and her little sister got on the bus. The older girl's outfit could best be described as a porn star starter kit. She looked to be between fourteen and sixteen years old.

The younger girl looked up and said, "Mama, I don't want to go to Junior's house tonight for a sleepover. He is going to try to touch my private parts again."

I attempted to process a couple of disturbing realizations. First, they were mother and daughter. Second, the daughter was asking for help in advance.

The mother looked down at her and, as cold as ice, said, "So what? It's not the last time someone is going to touch you there."

The little girl remained calm, looked up at her mother, and said, "Fuck you."

"No, fuck you," Mama said, looking down at her daughter.

The little girl jumped up, stomping her feet at the same time, and screamed, *"No, fuck you!"*

As the entire bus awaited the next *fuck you*, they both broke out into laughter and returned to being a loving mother-daughter team. Shortly after that, they got off the bus, both telling me to have a good day. As they departed, I sat there in shock.

And the hits just kept coming. One day I was on Post Road in North Kingstown. The bus was empty, but I could see a woman up ahead with a large gym bag overflowing with clothes. She came on board and said hello as she paid the two-dollar fare. When a person is on the bus alone, they usually engage me in conversation.

She said, "What's up, bus driver? How are you doing today?"

"Great," I replied.

After a moment or two she said, "I fucking hate myself, and I know God hates me too."

Her statement was powerful. I sat in silence, thinking to myself, *I know how that feels.*

She continued, "I have been fucked since birth. I was born this way. I'm the girl who goes to the gym, has a great workout, then comes outside and lights up a cigarette. I have been arrested so many times, I've lost count." Then she started running down the charges. Mostly revolving around prostitution. "I've sucked enough dick to fill up Fenway Park," she said. "They send me to rehab, and those places are a fucking joke. They don't want anyone to get better; they want everyone to come back, over and over again. I can run those places better than any of the idiots working there."

I believed her. As she shared her thoughts with me, other passengers began to board the bus. Two other women, both appearing to be in their early twenties, sat in different spots away from each other.

My new friend then addressed the bus. "I have bottled water, granola bars, and Reese's Cups." She gave the other passengers snacks, and then she began pulling clothes from her bag. "I just came from the Mission," she said, "and they gave me all these clothes. They are like new." She held up a pair of yoga pants and said to one of the girls, "You want them?"

The girl's eyes lit up, and she said, "Yes, please."

Then the woman held up a sundress and said to the other passenger, "This would look adorable on you." She handed her the dress. Then she removed her jacket and handed it to the girl she had just given the dress to. "Here," she said. "Take this too. I don't need it. Summer is coming." She was beaten down from the streets yet simultaneously generous. She turned her attention back to me. "Look at this," she said as she held up her phone. It was a photo of a beautiful woman that I instantly assumed was her daughter. She corrected me, explaining it was *her* twenty-five years ago. She told me she did have a daughter, twins in fact, but they had been taken away from her long ago.

As we arrived at the end of the line, the three of them began to make their departure.

I asked, "What's your name?"

"Candy," she replied.

I told her that she was still young, and nothing was over.

Now on the sidewalk, she looked back at me and said, "I love you for saying that, but I have to go buy some crack now."

Then she was gone. The power of addiction trumps everything.

In fairness, not all my bus-driving stories are negative, although they do weigh heavily toward the negative side. From time to time, something inspirational or even magical occurs. This is my favorite story from the bus: It was a Saturday morning on Academy Avenue in Providence. There were roughly twenty people on the bus. Two couples sitting parallel to each other began to argue. They appeared to be non-law-abiding citizens with an evil energy about all four of them. Recognizing evil is not difficult. As my hand moved toward the emergency button, I knew I needed to address them. Then, like an angel, a young female voice began to sing:

> *You are my sunshine, my only sunshine*
> *You make me happy when skies are gray*
> *You'll never know, dear, how much I love you*
> *Please don't take my sunshine away*

The argument ended. The entire bus fell silent. This must have been what Whitney Houston sounded like at that age. The girl kept singing the song, introducing me to lyrics I'd never heard before. Her voice was effortlessly perfect. She completed the impromptu healing session just as I pulled into Kennedy Plaza. When she finished singing, everyone erupted into cheers and applause. The passengers departed in good spirits. As the passengers left, the young prodigy passed me, stopping for a high five. Without speaking a word, she looked at me, saying with her eyes, *Did you see what I just did?* She stepped off the bus and disappeared into the crowd at the plaza. The bus quickly filled with a new group of passengers. During the brief time that she'd captured our attention with her incredible voice, everything had felt perfect in the universe.

Back in 2010, my life's journey led me to the Rhode Island Public Transit Authority. Those who know me best are surprised I made a career of it. So am I. Dealing with the public is an art form learned over time. Lots of trial and error, a portion of which I just attempted to explain. The rest we live and learn. As the years pressed on, I attended fewer and fewer AA meetings. The group's message of fellowship, AA slogans, and catchphrases no longer held meaning for me. I had put down drugs and alcohol years ago, but something still was not right with me. I began to search outside the program for answers to my questions. The desire to drink and drug was lifted from me long ago and with little effort. I can't explain why; it just was. I was done. But the bulk of the work normally done by a person in recovery felt unnecessary to me. The Twelve Steps, getting honest with a sponsor, sponsoring others—I never participated in any of it. With this misconception firmly in place, I pressed on in life. I lived a painful existence filled with anger, rage, and untreated alcoholism. I knew something was wrong with me, but whatever it was remained a mystery. The absence of a solution to the problem had plagued me for years prior, and would for years to come. Slowly but surely, I made my way down this lonely path.

CHAPTER 8

Goodbye, Mom; Hello, Yoga

Everyone in peace I know
Show you round the ancient souls

. . .

List the truth before you go
And it's all gonna crash on your head
Lay you down on sheets of gold
Stand you up in dainty rows

. . .

Pull you out and let you grow
And it's all gonna crash on your head

Rusty, "Crashdown"

2

014 MARKED THE YEAR EVERYTHING CHANGED forever. Tragedy was looming as a new relationship was beginning. My new girlfriend, Dawn, and I decided to live together. My desire to move too fast was in full swing. We only had a few dates under our belt when I moved her into my apartment. She was living in a roommate situation she wanted out of, and I stepped in and gave her a key to my place. In my experience, consequences accompany moving too fast, and this would be no exception. Dawn came with a pug named Bailey. She was a nurse, and Bailey, a therapy dog. After just a month of living together, we decided to leave my longtime apartment and find a house together. We moved to the beautiful beach community of Potowomut, Rhode Island. A secluded area near Goddard Park and the Potowomut Golf Club. A neighborhood with kind, loving neighbors, private beaches, peace, quiet, and lots of sea glass. We found a lovely bungalow, and made it our home. We loved our humble slice of paradise, our dog, and our cat, Friday. Life felt close to perfect with coffee on the beach to start each day.

I'd had a thirty-year run in the weight room, but the gym no longer held the same appeal for me. Jogging was also taking a toll on my legs and body. My inner voice told me to find a new activity. Dawn mentioned a new yoga studio that was opening in our area and asked if I wanted to join her for a class. An experienced yogi, she kept herself in good physical condition. I accepted her offer to attend my first yoga class. Rhode Island Power Yoga (RIPY) opened its doors inside Stop and Shop Plaza in North Kingstown, right next to Starbucks, a prime location with built-in advertising. The busy Starbucks drive-through took customers right by the yoga studio. We drove to that first class together, and I filled out the necessary paperwork. A wall of windows from ceiling to floor separated the lobby from the studio. The class appeared to be full. Holding my mat, Yogitoes towel, and bottle of water, I entered the studio for the very first time. As a longtime martial artist and former three-time world champion professional wrestler, along with a near five-hundred-pound bench press, I felt confident upon entering the class that I would be able to keep up. The class was 95 percent female. A few men were scattered around the room. As light conversation filled the air, I noticed that everyone appeared to be well-conditioned. Walking through the door from the lobby to the studio, I felt the climate change dramatically. The air became thick and warm. The white walls were bare, and the hardwood floor, slippery. Did I mention the class was *heated power yoga?* The temperature increased rapidly. My mind began to race, attempting to process everything going on around me. Sweat poured down my face and body. With my mat and other items still in my hands, I set up camp next to Dawn. I unrolled my mat and placed my Yogitoes towel over the mat.

Dawn glanced over at me and asked, "Are you all right?"

I scanned the room, preparing for the unknown, and answered, "yes."

Dawn was unfazed by the conditions and had yet to break a sweat. This was not her first yoga class. I felt anxiety from head to toe.

The class was taught by Terry Munnelly, a longtime yoga teacher with a laid-back style and calm voice. His delivery was gentle and nonthreatening. As he walked around the room, he stopped, asking Dawn if I was with her. *Was it that obvious I was a rookie?*

"Yes," she said.

Terry then told me to watch what she did, and I would be fine. I liked that he took a moment to welcome me and offer advice. The next thing I knew, I was in Downward-Facing Dog for the first time in my life. My head was pounding. It felt like a thousand degrees in the room. Terry slowly walked around, cracking jokes and keeping the mood light.

"It's fucking hot in here," he said.

The room laughed.

Sweat poured off my forehead like a faucet on low—not dripping, but a steady flow.

While standing directly behind me, Terry said, "If your fucking yoga teacher doesn't swear, don't trust them."

The class laughed louder.

He walked in front of me, turning his hand palm up into the sweat pouring from my head.

"Wow," he said, as the sweat danced on his palm. Then he walked away from me.

Still in Downward-Facing Dog, I dropped to my knees and thought to myself, *What have I done?* I began to plan my escape.

I looked at Dawn, who was still not sweating at all, and said, "I'm going to leave." The weight room suddenly appealed to me again.

"It's OK, Bren," Dawn smiled. She said, "I'll see you after class."

I stayed on my hands and knees, in Table Top Pose. The class moved on, and I watched everyone moving together. I became aware of the room breathing together. On my hands and knees, I started to breathe along. My mind slowed down slightly. I picked up the movement of the class and joined in. On the day of my first class, I did not experience yoga. I chose the mindset of survival, holding on to the gym mentality that was engrained in my being.

Terry kept it light, cracking jokes that helped guide me through the class. He reminded us to breathe often. He mentioned that he was a New Yorker. He spoke about his dogs. He shared that he had left Wall Street to teach yoga. I stuck it out, finishing my first class.

On the ride home, I had many questions for Dawn. She confided that she felt yoga could help my long-standing issues of holding a grudge, worrying about everything, having a bad temper, and being unable to forgive. I had given up any hope of change. I felt defeated emotionally. With a decade of sobriety under my belt, I watched newly sober people achieve freedom from the bondage of self, right before my eyes. I watched countless others make positive life changes while I remained stuck in my old way of thinking. Yoga felt like it could be the solution. I read every self-help book known to man, resulting in zero change, and I was still eager to find the answers to my personal struggles. Looking back now, I see that I wasn't aware of the nature of my core issue.

In the car, driving home from yoga, I felt my confidence soar to new heights. I'd found a replacement activity for the gym. Only twice before had I ever felt this way, like a light switch had turned on. The first time was when I was twelve years old, after my first karate class at New England Tae Kwon Do Center in Airport Plaza in Warwick. I knew before entering my teenage years that I wanted to be a martial artist. There was no doubt in my mind at all. The second time was after I had read the advertisement in the Warwick Beacon for a new wrestling school opening in the area. Again, there was no doubt in my mind about what I would be pursuing next in life. The self-realization that I'd felt back then resurfaced after my first yoga class at RIPY. I knew in my soul that I would return to the yoga studio, probably the next day. Over time, Dawn and I parted ways, but I will always be grateful to her for guiding me to my first yoga experience.

My second class was taught by Philip J. Urso. Dawn was working that night, so this time, I went to class by myself. I felt ready to experience my next class. I felt more prepared. I was ready for the heat and the athletic super-yoga girls who dominated the room. It was time to continue my journey. I liked Philip right away. He mentioned being a former hockey player. He quoted from a book I love, *A Course in Miracles*, written by—or depending on what you believe, channeled from God through—Helen Schucman and William Thetford. I have never felt the need to defend the statement as to how the book came to be. Every word, from cover to cover, opens new possibilities for me to question my entire belief system since birth. The book offers alternative ideas to every core issue I hold dear to my heart. Pretty powerful stuff, indeed.

Beginning in the 1990s, I attended A Course in Miracles (ACIM) study groups, referred to simply as "the Course" by those who study and practice it. I was drawn in like a magnet. I studied the book for years. Now I was in a physical practice with a yoga teacher who was incorporating ACIM. I needed no further signs that power yoga was for me. Philip hit home with every word he spoke. On the ride home from my second yoga class, I called my mother. I shared the exciting news of my new discovery. As she was a long-time spiritual seeker herself, I knew she would appreciate this new activity in my life. My mother told me she looked forward to hearing all about it, but she had a business call coming in on the other line.

"I have to go," she said. We hung up.

The following night, my parents attended a dinner party with longtime family friends. My mother was in excellent health. She began to choke on a piece of food stuck in her throat. My father watched in horror as her face began to turn blue. Someone at the table had medical training and performed the proper medical procedure. It was unsuccessful. I was not in the room that night, so I will never know the terror felt by all. I will not attempt to tell the story. I will only say I love you all. My mother was rushed to Kent Hospital, the same place she gave birth to me. She was placed on life support. They successfully removed the piece of food stuck in her throat. Unfortunately, she had gone far too long without oxygen to her brain. The doctors feared brain damage. We were told to wait and see if she would wake up.

The next forty-eight hours found my family and friends in prayer mode. When news finally came in, it was not good. The doctors confirmed the amount of time without oxygen to her brain had, in fact, caused damage. The doctor told us that if she were to wake up, it would be unlikely she would be able to speak or recognize any of us. We would be strangers to her. The surreal decision to take my mother off life support was now a reality. One minute, Barbara J. Higgins was enjoying herself with close friends, and the next minute, I, along with my father, Bob, and my brothers, Kevin and Jeff, were making funeral arrangements at Iannotti Funeral Home.

We found ourselves with the unwanted privilege of calling our family members and lifelong friends and inviting them to come to the hospital to say goodbye. I watched people I'd known my entire life enter the hospital room one by one. I have no idea where we found the strength to endure the process of watching family and friends enter the room and break down, grief-stricken, trying to understand why this was happening. We just got through it. The doctors explained to us that we could make the necessary arrangements before making the final decision to end her life. While my father, brothers, and I sat with the funeral director, Dawn called from the hospital. My mother had taken a turn for the worse. She was failing. Dawn encouraged us to return to the hospital right away. The four of us took off in separate cars. I raced through the streets of West Warwick and Warwick with no regard for red lights, and sped into the hospital parking lot. I ran from the car up the long concourse to the building. Dawn stopped me at the top of the runway. She placed her hands on my shoulders. She told me to calm down. I was too late. She was gone. My mother had died.

Dawn is a health-care professional. A nurse who works with the elderly. Far too often, she's forced to say goodbye to residents who pass away. She also understands the experience of losing a parent, having watched her own mother die far too young. My mother did not die alone. Dawn held her hand the entire time. She told my mother she no longer needed to fight, that it was OK to let go. My entire family will always be grateful to Dawn for comforting my mother up to, and including, the moment she passed away.

In the hospital, they gave us time to gather in the room and say our goodbyes. I hugged my mother for the last time. Her skin felt icy cold. We stood as a family in a circle above her. My father was devastated and asked us to join him in saying the Lord's Prayer. A few moments after I'd left the room, I watched my mother being wheeled out, headed to another location in the hospital. The entire experience drained every bit of strength from my body. Still standing in the hallway of the hospital, my family members drifted in different directions.

I looked at Dawn and said, "I'm going to yoga tonight."

She smiled and said, "I think that's a really good idea."

That crystal-clear thought can only be described as pure instinct. I knew, without hesitation, what to do. Later, in class, I kept the tragic events of the day to myself. I set up my mat and assumed Child's Pose. I cried during the seventy-five-minute class, keeping up the best I could. I spent a great deal of the class returning to Child's Pose, concealing my grief. I left without saying a word to anyone. I felt better after having attended class. No matter what circumstances are presented (and this one was a doozy), I can walk into yoga class feeling a range of different emotions—from sad to angry, anxious to hyper, or in this case, devastated—and feel better after completing the class. A feeling that repeats itself to this day. It's an unwritten promise to myself that I believe in deeply.

Later that evening, the phone rang. On the other end was Philip from RIPY. He told me someone had accidentally taken home the wrong shoes after yoga class. He asked if I could double-check to see if I'd taken them. Although I was a prime candidate to do such a thing on this evening, it hadn't been me. Before we hung up, I told him that he had no way of knowing, but my mother had died earlier in the day. Philip offered his condolences. I told him I couldn't explain it, but I'd felt the need to go to yoga class.

"That's awesome," Philip said.

I started to cry, telling him I looked forward to getting to know him and everyone else at RIPY. He told me the feeling was mutual.

Three weeks after my mother passed away, Dawn moved out of our lovely home. She took our dog Bailey with her. So much loss to process at one time. She felt she needed to pursue her journey on her own. She moved out on a cold, snowy weekend. It continued to snow heavily that winter. Snow piles mounted everywhere—a reflection of my grief. I never imagined losing so much in such a short span of time. It was just me and my kitty, Friday, alone again.

During this time, I reconnected with a therapist from my past, Irene Tomkinson. One of the wisest human beings I have ever known. She is older than me and always provided a parental effect within our sessions. After my mother passed away, that feeling grew much stronger for me. I traveled from Rhode Island to New Hampshire to meet with her. A decade earlier, she had helped me so much, it was a no-brainer for me to reconnect with her. Irene introduced me to Unity Church. She encouraged me to go back to school. She helped me navigate through a brutal alcohol and drugs relapse. She was a second mother to me. When I had no money to pay for therapy sessions, she told me to come in to see her anyway and trusted I'd pay her back at a future date. She left it open-ended and up to me. She told me I possessed a writer's soul. In fact, she put the idea in my head that I was very capable of writing a book. That single observation she made never left me.

My chance meeting with her daughter, Shawn, led to a friendship I sorely needed at that time. Our compatibility was undeniable, at least for me. We became close, and she helped me with her ability to listen and offer gentle feedback. The support Shawn offered allowed me to release what was going on around me. I held true to form, attempting to get involved with someone new before I had even begun to process what had just transpired with my former girlfriend. This led to my ruining a beautiful friendship with an amazing woman. To this day, I remain unable to properly express how much Irene and Shawn will always mean to me.

When the student is ready, the teacher will appear. In my case, multiple teachers came forward. At this point, I'd only experienced male yoga teachers. My next yoga class introduced me to the first of many phenomenal female teachers. Of all the souls I have encountered in the yoga community, Renee Armen Deslauriers had the greatest impact on my early yoga practice. I consider Renee and Philip to be my yoga parents, the reference having nothing to do with age. They love and nurture everyone who enters RIPY. Renee always listens to what I have going on in my life. In the early days, I stayed after class, talking her ear off. I needed to talk about the impact yoga was having on my life, and she listened. During class, she offers a detailed explanation for every pose, eager to pass on her knowledge with a genuine passion. Keeping my addictive personality intact, I practiced yoga frequently. My RIPTA work schedule allowed me to attend class in the morning. Grief-stricken from the loss of my mother and the departure of my girlfriend and our dog, not to mention my having screwed up another possible relationship, I submerged myself in RIPY.

My Monday class was taught by Gayle Walsh. From the very beginning, Gayle offered me support and personal feedback. She never hesitated to point out her flaws and reminded us that striving for perfection is not necessary.

One time when I arrived late to class, I asked Gayle, "If I drive one hundred miles per hour, like a lunatic, trying to get to class on time, am I being a good yogi?"

"Only if you're aware of it," she replied with a smile.

She also managed to push my emotional buttons with her choice of topic on any given day.

I arrived at class one Monday morning and asked, "Are you going to push my buttons today?"

Her response: "Let's see what happens."

At times, Monday morning's class had only a small handful of people. Gayle helped me tremendously in those early days, allowing me to grow as a new yogi.

Tuesday morning's class was taught by yoga mom and the queen of RIPY, Renee. Wednesday morning's class was with Terry. Thursday mornings introduced me to Jess Gumkowski: the Yogi Triathlete. Every Thursday morning, her challenging class brought me to my knees. Jess wore a big smile throughout. Her philosophy pushed me to let go of my old way of thinking. To abandon the gym mentality. I gave her the nickname "the Terminator" because she is such a force of nature. She helped me go from enduring class to being "in flow." I met several triathletes at RIPY. A different breed of incredible athletes.

One morning, I doubled over in class. I may have experienced a panic attack or an anxiety attack. The day before, I had had my first hypnotherapy session with a new therapist, Kathy. A connection between the two events seemed very possible.

As I stood there doubled over, Jess walked up and casually asked, "Are you OK?"

I told her I couldn't move. I felt frozen or stuck. She asked if I could make it to the lobby.

"I think so," I replied.

I felt like an idiot having to leave a room dominated by super-yoga girls. I sat in the lobby, enjoying the cool air—a stark contrast from the extreme heat of class. I tried to process what had just happened. Jess came into the lobby. She got down on one knee directly in front of me, and placed her hand on my leg.

"You OK?" she whispered.

I began to weep. I had no control over it. I shared my hypnotherapy experience with her.

"Ooh," she said, "I see." She told me she wanted me to feel everything that was happening to me. She seemed excited for me. "Just feel all of it," she said. So I did.

She told me to stand up or lie on the floor, whatever felt right.

"Take as long as you need," she instructed. I told her I couldn't return to class. Not today.

She told me everything was fine, then returned to the studio, picked up my mat, and returned it to me, sparing me a long walk and an unwanted trip back into the studio.

The following week I returned to class upbeat and ready to explain myself in detail to Jess. The lobby was full of yogis as she walked by.

"What's up, Brendan?" she asked, in her typical loving-life tone.

I shrugged.

She kept walking without bringing up the embarrassing ordeal of the prior week. We never discussed it again. I'm sure she would have been happy to rehash it if I'd needed to, but the way she dealt with it was fine with me. Jess and her husband,

BJ, published a cookbook, *YogiTriathlete Cookbook: High Vibe Recipes for the Athlete Appetite.* I love the book and use it often.

On Fridays, class was taught by Lori DeFusco Pagliaroni, the self-proclaimed "core queen." Between her frequent world travels, she guided us in yoga practice. Each Friday, I eagerly walk in to RIPY looking for Lori.

Once I locate the incredibly athletic teacher, who is half my size, I announce, "I'm ready for you!"

Keeping a straight face, and usually without making eye contact with me, she answers in a monotone voice, "I know you are, Brendan."

The exchange between the two of us is and always will be a tradition I look forward to whenever we cross paths. Lori's class represents the pinnacle of challenging poses and practice. Lori is the master of inversions, arm balances, Crow Pose variations, headstands, handstands, and everything in between. With her help and guidance, I learned to stand on my head and my hands—in my fifties. Lori helped me to understand that the "impossible" is quite possible.

BRENDAN HIGGINS

Photo courtesy of Kerri Stowik

Saturday morning's class was taught by Philip. Sunday morning's class was taught by Renee. That rounded out my week. I attended often. I developed a connection with all my yoga teachers. The weekly lineup of teachers has changed since the studio first opened, but the heartbeat of RIPY continues. Another teacher, one not in the weekly rotation but who impacted my early practice, is Masha Besedin. A super-yoga girl indeed. The first time she walked into class, with her shoulders back and her supreme confidence, I quickly nicknamed her "Xena: Warrior Princess." Masha always leads a challenging class with helpful feedback. It's impossible for me to identify a favorite teacher because I feel that way about all of them. In those early days, I had a crush on every teacher, male and female. The personal growth I've experienced within the studio is undeniable.

This is my favorite definition of love: "Extending oneself for one's own or another's growth." Followed by: "Love is not an emotion; it's an action." These words, shared with me by Irene Tomkinson, best describe what occurs in every class at RIPY. So who is my favorite yoga teacher? My conclusion is this. During each moment I spend in class with any given teacher, they are my favorite. Early on, the dynamics of yoga class felt complex and confusing. Between the extreme heat, challenging poses, and highly advanced yogis all around me, I often felt overwhelmed. I started making immediate adjustments to help myself. I moved to the front of class. Since I had been relentlessly comparing myself to advanced yogis, having a blank wall in front of me helped me to stop critiquing myself. Comparing my performance to that of others is a long-standing problem that I struggle with to this day. At RIPY, the walls are bare. No mirrors. Looking at my reflection during class is another surefire way to feel like shit about myself. Keeping myself in the front of the class cuts down on distractions a great deal. I quickly learned to hydrate often during class. I sweat so much, I become dizzy. Drinking as much water as I need to allows me to finish class and not pass out from dehydration.

The single most important change: I learned to breathe. This was my introduction to Ujjayi breathing. A basic explanation: breathe in through the nose and breathe out through the nose. An ocean-like sound is created by using the throat as a point of origin. A class that breathes together creates a synergy. A feeling of peace fills my heart when everyone is breathing together as one. It offers me a reprieve from a perpetually racing mind. In fact, it is the clearest my mind can get during the day. Once breathing becomes my focus, everything slows down. I begin to awaken as a human being, feeling more aware of each breath. In a single breath, anything is possible, which is a recurring message in class. It began to make sense. For example, if the thought *I can't hold this pose any longer* enters my mind, I replace that false thought with a new one: *I can hold this pose for a single breath*. Instead of *I can't stand the heat in the room*, I focus on a single breath, no longer thinking about the conditions in the room. Prior to this transformation, I'd tried to grind everything out in my attempt to endure situations and obstacles in my path. Although still extremely challenging, class started to get easier. The concept of flow entered my life. I began to attempt yoga poses I'd previously believed impossible. It's that powerful.

I said goodbye to the weight room once I started practicing yoga. The gym is filled with people walking around with headphones on, totally separated from one another. That environment no longer interested me. Attending yoga class, feeling the room breathing and moving as one, instantaneously became where I belonged. In the past, I would have snickered at the idea of practicing yoga over lifting weights. The timing was right to make a change. I maintained strength as though I'd never left the weight room. I experienced improved focus and coordination, far surpassing any period in my life when I'd considered myself in top physical condition. Other notable changes included weight loss, stamina, balance, flexibility, and a calmness that led to my making new friends with like-minded people.

My first year in the yoga studio, I attended four to six classes per week. The cast of teachers and yogis allowed me to grow as a person. I started to heal deep, painful wounds. It was an introduction to a new beginning and a new way of life for me. One of my all-time favorite thoughts to ponder was offered by Philip: "Allow people to be who they are without letting it affect you." In theory, I loved the suggestion, but in day-to-day life, I still work hard to accomplish it. I wouldn't be able to mention everyone I have practiced with by name. We all know who we are. After decades of teaching karate and wrestling, I welcomed the opportunity to be the student. Returning to the concept of remaining teachable while allowing others to lead.

Rhode Island Power Yoga is my forever yoga home. I still practice there regularly. The space and the souls who occupy it are forever in my heart. *Namaste.*

After five years of practicing yoga, I found myself continuing to struggle with my long- standing demons. I noticed some similarities between AA and yoga. For me, the most painful was watching others evolve and become free of the bondage of self while I continued to repeat the same things, expecting a different result. I was still struggling with anger, resentment, dishonesty, overeating, and sex addiction, and I was completely incapable of being in a healthy relationship of any kind. Sadly, the inner peace I yearned for continued to elude me. My new yogi lifestyle and longtime sobriety didn't seem to help me grow as a person. I stayed angry at people who were not even thinking about me. My struggle with rage and a racing mind that never shut off continued to effortlessly take me down to the mat. I needed to face facts. AA, self-help books, therapy, sex, women, and even yoga could not help me. I believed this painful way of life would always be my cross to bear.

CHAPTER

A Visit to Old Dominion: The Boogie Man Is Real

Every time I see a sign
To show me who I am
I turn around and head back down
The road of consequence
Am I ever gonna get myself together
Never ever

Electric Mary, "It's Alright"

On August 4, 2018, I embarked on the motorcycle journey of a lifetime. I rode in the pouring rain across four states. Eventually, sunshine and extreme heat replaced the wet weather. A meeting with my childhood hero, "Handsome" Jimmy "The Boogie Woogie Man" Valiant, was on the horizon. I desperately needed advice. My life remained in a state of confusion in spite of my efforts to find answers. My questions needed to be asked, and my heart was guiding me to Virginia to ask a total stranger for answers.

How do you determine the next right thing to do in life? How do you know it's the right decision?

The past few years had been filled with tragedy and heartbreak. My mother had disappeared from the planet without warning. Three weeks later, my girlfriend left, taking our dog with her. Shortly after that, I met someone new, but quickly screwed that up. A sucker for punishment, I entered into yet another new relationship, even though the doors from the previous ones were barely shut. I kept true to form. Against the advice of my inner circle of family and friends to take some time alone and regroup, I took an ill-advised leap of faith. I sold all my household belongings and moved in with my new girlfriend and her daughter—only eight weeks after we'd met. And eight weeks after moving in, we got engaged. Eight months after that, one year to the day we had met, we had a fairytale wedding.

After emptying out my bank account on a beautiful ring, lavish wedding, and honeymoon, I left the marriage. We had moved way too fast getting in, and just as fast getting out. We were married and divorced in the blink of an eye. You might think that as a result of my terrible track record with women, I would be fully aware that quickly jumping into a new relationship would have severe consequences for both parties. Instead, I dove right into the deep end. The only problem was, I didn't know how to swim. I was winging it the entire time. I was so naive, I thought an expensive wedding and a marriage certificate would, in some way, help build a healthy relationship. When I threw in the towel on the marriage, I began to feel despair on a regular basis. I was zero for life in relationships, and this was the final straw for me.

All I had was a crappy car, the clothes on my back, a Harley-Davidson, and my cat, Friday. I moved to a new town and rented a small house, though I had nothing to furnish it with. I slept on an air mattress that slowly lost air by morning. A truly symbolic way to start each day. The air was seeping out of my life. It would end the way most of my wrestling matches had ended—with me flat on my back. I lived in new, unfamiliar surroundings and felt like a stranger to myself. I gained fifty pounds and came down with pneumonia. I'd never felt this sick in my entire life. I was afraid to fall asleep at night. On the news, they were talking about people dying in their sleep from the flu. I felt like a candidate for such a departure. But it was also the first time I'd welcomed the idea of not waking up. A fleeting thought at first, but it would be back again to visit.

It took me months to recover from pneumonia, all while living in a house without furniture. Through it all, I continued to work as a bus operator for the Rhode Island Public Transit Authority. A job I'd grown to intensely despise. I'd badly needed this motorcycle road trip.

As I continued riding, a sign ahead read, "Welcome to Virginia." "Rock 'n' Roll Fantasy" by Bad Company played in the wind. I raised my hands over my head in a gesture of victory as I crossed the state line. My first order of business was to ride to Richmond to meet my best friend, Jeff Katz. In 2000, Jeff and I had parted ways after the death of our dear friend Tony Rumble. Jeff had moved away from Boston to take a new job in Las Vegas. We lost touch after that.

In 2004, thanks to a new thing called social media, we reconnected. At the time, Myspace was all the rage. I found my old buddy in good health, alive and well. He and Heidi had three children: Harry, Julia, and Joe. Making matters better, he had moved back to Boston. We made plans to get together; I couldn't wait to see Jeff and Heidi and meet the kids. One visit turned into another. We resumed our friendship and became closer than ever before. It was as if no time had passed at all. I would travel to Swampscott, Massachusetts, to visit them, and they would come to Rhode Island. During our visits, we'd exchange television and movie recommendations. Jeff and Heidi welcomed me into their family with open arms and hearts. Jeff and I had lived through exciting times together in the wrestling world, and we took effortless strolls down memory lane. Telling someone a story is vastly different than two people chiming in, back and forth, telling stories they've lived through together.

We always ate well. Jeff is a master in the kitchen. I would supply desserts from the countless bakeries around Rhode Island. At times, I arrived alone, while other times, I came with a new girlfriend, eager to introduce her and gain approval from the Katz clan.

Brothers from another mother—me and Jeff Katz in Potowomut, Rhode Island

In 2014, I was inducted into the New England Pro Wrestling Hall of Fame. When I became aware of my upcoming induction, I wanted Jeff Katz to induct me. In 2019, I returned the favor, inducting my dear friend Jeff into the New England Pro Wrestling Hall of Fame for his contributions to the business. We'd joined an impressive list of wrestling legends, including the man we were about to pay a visit to: "Handsome" Jimmy Valiant.

Jeff had accepted a job with WRVA Radio in 2012, taking on the ultimate commute from Boston to Richmond, Virginia. The rest of the Katz family had stayed in Boston, living day-to-day life. Jeff spent long periods of time away from his family. He confided in me how much he missed them. Heidi held down the fort with a true indomitable spirit. Their love and strength as a couple are impossible to put into words.

I pulled into Richmond at 8:00 p.m., a few hours later than I'd estimated. I felt exhausted from the journey. I stepped into an air-conditioned hotel lobby, checked into my room, and took a much-needed long shower. Jeff met me at the motel. His oldest son, Harry, was in town, visiting from Boston to spend time with his father. He was a welcome addition to our trip to Shawsville the next day. Harry is a tall, handsome young man who, at the time, was entering his senior year in high school. He is both athletic and academically brilliant. Young Mr. Katz holds zero interest in professional wrestling. Perhaps even considers it foolish. Nonetheless, spending time with the Katz men was just what the doctor had ordered for me. I was delighted to park the motorcycle for a spell and ride shotgun with my buddies. I fell into their car and adjusted the air-conditioning vents toward my face.

Jeff as an on-air radio and television personality is nothing new to me. After all, he is well-known around the country. He also makes frequent television appearances, as well as appearing in print. What I didn't know was that Jeff had taken over the airwaves in Richmond. His show has high ratings, and both Harry and I were about to find out just how much popularity Jeff enjoys in the River City. The situation fascinated me, mainly because while Jeff is from Philadelphia and holds strong ties to Boston, he is somehow able to captivate Richmond, the capital of Virginia. My guess would be that it's his honesty, along with the A-list guests he delivers, that keeps his loyal audience tuned in and coming back for more. His popularity in the South is undeniable.

Dinner quickly became our priority. We sat outside on a gorgeous night with no wind and temperatures in the eighties. Jeff explained how the restaurant came to be, providing a brief biography of the owner, a back story on the décor, and then rounding out the story with information about the development the building sat on. The story added to the experience. It felt peaceful being with these guys. My guard was down. Nothing to defend or explain. Just a moment in time with people I loved.

It didn't take long for father and son to engage in semi-heated conversation about politics. Harry is ready and eager to share his liberal views. Jeff is willing to share his conservative opinion if prompted, but he's not necessarily looking for a fight. Even though the two completely disagree, Harry is a chip off the old block. I always agree with Jeff. I very rarely see things in a different light. On and off the air. In the end, they both agreed: no politics during dinner. Although Harry would seem to forget about the truce. The back-and-forth between the two provided some quality entertainment. We enjoyed a great meal and dessert, and after dinner, we took a stroll. Jeff seemed to know more about the area than the natives do. It was a great way to spend my first night in River City.

After logging 522.4 miles earlier in the day, I was ready for some shut-eye. A 202.4-mile ride awaited us the next morning. Starting that evening, Jeff rang every drop out of each day I spent in Virginia. He made sure I took in every possible experience. I can never properly express what a generous host and friend he is. And to top it all off, the very personal experience of spending time with my childhood hero, Jimmy Valiant, was less than twelve hours away.

Jeff had no knowledge of my plan to speak with Boogie on a personal level. However, he was very aware of the unpleasant chain of events in my life, which had toppled over like dominos. As far as he knew, this was a trip down wrestling memory lane. For me, it held a much deeper meaning. I needed direction in my life. I had shut down after my divorce; having turned off my emotional light switch, I was struggling to find a way to turn it back on. My emotional state was slipping with each passing day. It involved taking a risk, but I believed Jimmy Valiant would be open and available for a personal conversation with me. Then again, he might say, "Thanks for stopping by," and that would be it. I wouldn't know until I was face-to-face with him. Perhaps the answer was as simple as having hope. The time had arrived for the final leg of the journey.

The morning of August 8, 2018, I woke up in my hotel room before the alarm sounded. I felt rested, excited, optimistic, and hopeful. I arranged to meet Jeff and Harry for breakfast at River City Diner—conveniently connected to the motel. This made it possible for me to go from my room to the air-conditioned diner without stepping outside into the near one-hundred-degree Southern heat. A wrestling reference came to mind as I entered this classic diner. When I watched wrestling as a child, legendary promoter and announcer Vince McMahon would occasionally shout out, "And there's trouble in River City!" during a high spot or after a hot tag during a match. A fond childhood memory indeed.

A motorcycle mounted above the booths caught my eye as I entered from the side door. I fell in love with the diner with each step I took. A server greeted me with a smile. I asked for a table for three. She led me to a booth, passing movie posters, vinyl records, and album sleeves on the walls. Our server was tall and thin with long dark hair; her Southern accent made me smile and feel safe. She called everyone sugar, sweetie, honey, and baby. She made this Northerner feel safe and welcome. She was perfect in her role. Jeff texted: *Ten minutes away,* while my new friend poured me a cup of coffee. I decided to fill her in on our plans for the day.

"Guess what I'm doing today," I offered.

"Do tell," she said as she shifted her hips to the side and crossed her arms.

"When my friends arrive, we are driving to Shawsville to attend a seventy-sixth birthday party for "Handsome" Jimmy "The Boogie Woogie Man" Valiant. Do you know who he is?" I asked.

A bright Southern smile spread across her face.

"Yes, of course I do. As a young girl, I worked the concession stand at Richmond Coliseum." She recalled seeing "Nature Boy" Ric Flair battle Ricky "The Dragon" Steamboat to a one-hour draw. She recalled working many concerts and meeting lots of celebrities, like Billy Gibbons, Dusty Hill, and Frank Beard from the legendary ZZ Top—one of my favorite bands. "Jimmy Valiant is such a kind person," she continued, "he was so nice to me."

Jeff and Harry walked in, and I waved them over. Jeff was in good spirits, and Harry had the demeanor of a teenager who was ready for breakfast. I notified Jeff that my new friend knew the birthday boy. Jeff smiled. Like me, Jeff had spent years in and around the wrestling world. He is also a fan. We'd both grown up loving the infamous Valiant Brothers— Jeff in Philly, and I in Providence. Our server recognized Jeff's unmistakable voice from the radio. She mentioned she would know that voice anywhere and was happy to finally put a face to it.

I suggested to Jeff that he book Boogie as a guest for his radio show when we meet him, but it turned out, Boogie had already been a guest on *The Jeff Katz Show*—multiple times. Boogie's popularity is still strong to this day. We were about to experience *that* firsthand. The couple in the next booth caught wind of our conversation and offered a heartfelt story about meeting Boogie, telling us of his kindness toward them. Soon, what felt like the entire diner and staff joined in, offering stories of the wrestling legend. A buzz filled the air. A man sitting at the counter summed it up, proclaiming, "Jimmy Valiant *is* the South!" He delivered his message with authority, as if questioning his statement might land you in the parking lot with him in a confrontational manner. I couldn't have agreed with him more. Goosebumps covered my arms. The fans had spoken. It occurred to me that none of this would be happening if I hadn't jumped on my bike and headed south. Throughout this entire magical moment, Harry never looked up from his menu. He seemed unaware and uninterested in the events unfolding around him. There was a sharp contrast to our agendas for the day. The reaction in the diner to the name Jimmy Valiant fascinated me. Mainly because Jimmy had been semiretired and out of the national spotlight for at least twenty years. The only way to describe the man: a true legend.

As we enjoyed a hearty breakfast, I decided to show Harry a YouTube video of "Handsome" Jimmy Valiant during his prime in 1979. In the video, a shirtless "Handsome" Jimmy with a handlebar mustache was being interviewed by announcer Lance Russell in Memphis. He began saying, "Woo, *mercy, daddy, mercy,* 'Handsome' Jimmy feels good today!"

"Oh my God . . . oh my God," Harry repeated. He found the video silly and pointless.

Unlike his father, Harry has no interest in wrestling. His indifference is fine with me. Early on in life, I became aware that most people did not understand my passion for wrestling. I stopped being offended by it long ago, and instead, I embrace my allegiance to the sport. I was happy to have Harry along for the ride.

After breakfast, I asked our server for the check. Jeff's hospitality the night before had made me want to pay for breakfast.

"Oh, it's been taken care of," our fellow "Handsome" Jimmy Valiant fan said. She pointed to the owner, over in the corner. This was our second meal on the house. I could get used to this. I gave our server a worthy tip and a hug. She'd made our pre-trip meal special. Even though I'd never formally introduced myself, she wanted an autograph from yours truly, Knuckles Nelson. The last time I had signed one was over twenty years ago.

Everyone at River City Diner took great pride in their work. I was impressed from start to finish. And even more so when I became aware of the Jeff Katz Milkshake. Yes, my friend has a decadent delight named after him on the diner's menu. It consists of vanilla ice cream, Heath Bar crumbles, caramel, whipped cream, and a cherry on top. I had to try one. I highly recommend indulging if you find yourself in Richmond.

"Jeff, this milkshake is named after you," I said in between sips.

He shrugged it off without a word. I thought it was cool.

Jeff had reached out to Angel Valiant in advance to verify that Jimmy would be home for our visit. "The Boogie Woogie Man" still makes weekly public appearances around the country.

Fortunately for us, he would be home on August 5. Over breakfast, Jeff told me about the phone conversation with Angel. He'd let her know that I was a longtime fan of her husband's and a former pro wrestler myself. Jeff explained to Angel that my ring vest had been inspired by her husband. The vest had stars covering the front, with "Bad Co." airbrushed on the back. I had matching kneepads with stars, imitating the Valiant Brothers. Angel promised to tell her husband of our upcoming visit. Once I knew they were expecting us, I was ready to ride.

We said goodbye to everyone in the diner. We'd shared a moment in time together, so I made a point to acknowledge each person while walking out.

The Jeff Katz Milkshake

As I stood in the parking lot of the diner, the sun beat down on me with intense heat.

"Are you sure you wouldn't rather ride in the car?" Jeff asked.

I smiled.

"No thanks, I have to arrive on my bike." I explained to Jeff and Harry that I needed to complete the ride to Shawsville on my Harley. Jimmy is a lifelong biker—a Harley man through and through. Arriving on two wheels was my personal tribute to him on his seventy-sixth birthday. With that, our small convoy left the parking lot.

During the past several years of my life, my existence had been reduced to putting one foot in front of the other in mundane repetition. Today felt different. Excitement and hope filled my entire body. Once I hit highway speed, the wind felt like a giant blow-dryer. Virginia is a *helmet required* state, which makes for a sweaty head. I prefer to decide for myself whether or not to wear a helmet. Nonetheless, with Rusty and Electric Mary coursing through my speakers, it was time to keep the shiny side up and the dirty side down.

This personal journey to meet Boogie led me to ask myself, *Why him?* And here's what I came up with: Wrestling is my earliest television memory. As an adult, I became a professional wrestler. My travels landed me in locker rooms all over the planet. It never fazed me to be alongside the top names in wrestling: Ric Flair, Hulk Hogan, Stone Cold Steve Austin, The Rock, Shawn Michaels, Triple H, and everyone else from that era. They were just "the boys," but with much bigger bank accounts. But something different was unfolding. The small boy still somewhere inside me wanted to talk to "Handsome" Jimmy Valiant. Without realizing it, I'd gone back to the first person that I—all on my own—had thought was cool. Not someone my father or my peers had liked. This was *my* guy. And I wanted to see him again after all these years.

Leading up to the trip, I watched old Valiant Brothers matches. I watched "Handsome" Jimmy in singles matches from the '70s. I viewed "Boogie Woogie Man" matches from the '80s. I relived his incredible feat of transforming himself from *hated bad guy* to *beloved fan favorite*. In the '80s, his popularity rivaled that of anyone in wrestling history.

I grew up in a non-wrestling household, yet I became obsessed with wrestling at an early age. Every Saturday morning, along with neighborhood friends, I watched faithfully. The exact same program ran on two different stations—once at 11:00 a.m. and then again at noon. After the first program had ended, my friends would bolt from the house to play outside. I would try to explain that wrestling was about to come on again. They would respond that it was going to be the exact same show we had just watched. They opted not to, but I always stayed inside to watch again. The obsession was already taking form. Wrestling magazines, stacked high in my bedroom, kept me up to date on wrestling promotions across the country and around the world. My father's heroes were Ted Williams and John Wayne. He never understood my admiration for "Handsome" Jimmy Valiant, even questioning if I was a homosexual for loving him so much. I didn't care. The Valiant Brothers personified cool. They wrote catchphrases on their ring attire, with sayings like, "The End" on their behinds and "First-Class Male" on the back of their jackets. The words "I AM A" inside a big star summed it all up. My personal favorite: "Lay Down Sally" written on the back of Jimmy's tights. A song made popular by Eric Clapton, it contained my grandmother's first name.

As a kid, I would take school clothes, just purchased from Sears, and enhance their appearance with a magic marker, drawing and filling in stars down the side of my pant legs. Then I would write phrases on the back of my pants and shirts. My parents were not impressed with these modifications. During that awesome period of my life, my neighborhood friends enjoyed wrestling too, including Bob Boie and future state representative, my motorcycle mentor, Bob Quattrocchi. The latter, Bob Q., was my first wrestling opponent. We engaged in a bitter feud—one battle after the next, all taking place on his parents' front lawn. I would go home exhausted, and at times, bloody and bruised. I'd have to explain my condition to my mother. As for the importance and influence of Jimmy Valiant, watching the old matches prior to my trip to Virginia brought to my attention that he was just being himself. Maybe that is the reason he so powerfully affected my life. I always bore the burden of caring what others thought of me. If I liked a girl in elementary or junior high school, I wanted my friends' seal of approval that she measured up to standards. I was always looking to find out what others thought was cool. Except when it came to wrestling. It was not possible to take that away from me. If you didn't like wrestling, I felt a disconnect from you. Jimmy Valiant simply did not care what anyone thought of him. Until I spend time with him—or should I get to spend any quality time with him, it will remain speculation.

On the road to Shawsville, Harry paid tribute to Boogie without realizing it. He reclined in his seat, sleeping the entire ride. Something Boogie is known to do. Jeff is not a biker. He didn't know I wouldn't be able to travel at high speeds on my touring bike. Without meaning to, he quickly left me in the dust. I pulled over and called him. I explained he should drive on, and I would meet him at BWC. Right after I hung up, I lost phone service for the duration of the ride. The bulk of the ride from Richmond to Shawsville is along Route 81. You drive one hundred miles into the middle of nowhere; then you drive another one hundred miles. The anticipation continued to mount. As fate would have it, I traveled the final leg of the trip alone.

The entire adventure easily could have been one of those things you discuss but never end up doing, but Jeff's presence in Richmond had transformed the idea into reality.

I'd mentioned the idea to him, and he'd said, "Sounds like fun, when are we going?" Typical Katzman.

I stopped for gas in Buchanan, Virginia. All that was missing from this scene were tumbleweeds rolling by. I coasted down the exit in the relentless heat. The air was thick. I pulled into the only gas station for miles. The gas pump offered regular fuel. Mid-grade and premium were not options. I only run premium in my bike. Unfortunately, I had little choice here. I walked into the convenience store to pay for my inferior gasoline, and inside I found a mini flea market. New England Patriots items lined the walls. I looked around, used the restroom, and returned to the bike to pump my gas. As I walked toward the pump, I noticed the car in front of me had Rhode Island license plates.

"Is that a Rhode Island plate?" I asked.

The young girl standing outside the car did not reply. Perhaps my biker appearance had rattled her a bit.

"I'm from Rhode Island too," I said softly. I asked what she was doing so far from home.

"Today is Jimmy Valiant's birthday, and I'm going to his party!" she said enthusiastically. Just kidding—she didn't say that.

Just then, another car with Rhode Island plates pulled

alongside us. They were together. The woman driving said hello. They lived in Newport, the next town over from me. They knew the street I lived on, Oliphant Lane. Turns out, this mother and daughter team were making their own journey, moving the young lady to college in rural Virginia.

With fifty miles to travel, I said goodbye to my new friends from the Ocean State. I wished them luck on their adventure. I returned to the highway, surrounded by beautiful scenic countryside and incredible, majestic mountains. As I rode, it struck me that people in the area live so far off the grid. How do they do it? Where do they shop? How far is the commute to work? What if they need premium gas? I observed a quality of life around me that many people never consider, but that others dream about. In the right situation, with the right person, it could be a very desirable lifestyle.

A highway sign for Shawsville appeared and a *child on Christmas Eve* vibe filled my body. I was so close. My back ached from the two-hundred-mile ride.

As I cruised into Shawsville, the Christmas Eve feeling turned to Christmas morning euphoria, and it reached every bit of my essence. In a world with no coincidences, the song "Long Way From Home (Do Me)" by Electric Mary began to play. Rusty, as always, was keeping me safe and providing perfect companionship and the musical soundtrack of my life. As I turned onto Alleghany Springs Road, I felt at peace. I shared an unexpected moment with a teenage girl walking along the side of the road. She had long dark hair and was dressed in jeans and a tank top. She offered me a big wave and a show-stopping smile as I rode past. Devoid of fear, she welcomed me to her town. I drove along the winding country road at a low speed, with my right hand on the throttle and my left hand on my leg. It was time to take it all in. Mother Nature was generously presenting me with so much to observe and appreciate. I was completely in the moment. My breathing was deep—my awareness, locked in. The bike purred along, and Rusty continued singing. It was a blessing to learn that such moments in life can be captured in one's memory, and it will live on for me as one from which I'll continue to draw strength.

I arrived at my destination: 2916 Alleghany Springs Road. I stopped in the middle of the road and turned off the bike. I felt total serenity as I looked up at the only place in the universe I wanted to be. The live view was identical to that in the photos and videos I'd watched building up to this moment. I flashed back to Mount Saint Charles Academy in the 1970s. The first time I'd been face-to-face with my childhood hero. Now, forty years later, I felt hopeful that I would be able to spend some time with him.

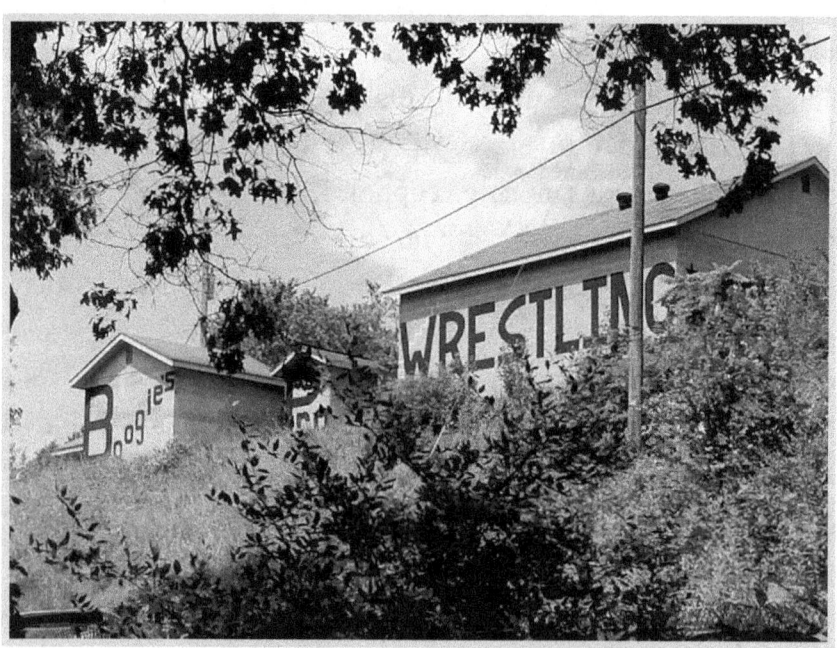

Boogie's Wrestling Camp Hall of Fame and Museum

My arrival at BWC

The driveway had a steady incline with a white sign welcoming all to Boogie's Wrestling Camp Hall of Fame and Museum. I parked next to a vintage trike belonging to Boogie. Cars lined both sides of the driveway. A van with a film crew unloaded their equipment, ready to film the events of the day. Along a tall concrete wall, a variety of unique vehicles belonging to the wrestling legend were parked on display for all to explore. A motorcycle, a dune buggy, a white limousine, and the famous Boogie Wagon. A tricked-out station wagon with yellow flames covering the hood and lettering across the windshield: *BOOGIE WAGON*. A plaque on the wall in front of each vehicle provided descriptions. The limo had New York plates and *Valiant Brothers* written in white letters across the back window. I touched the side of the car, sliding my hand gently along it as I walked from back to front. The stories this baby could tell.

I noticed Harry walking down the stairs leading to the campus. Young Mr. Katz is a good sport. He's not a wrestling fan at all, but he could see how important this day was for Uncle Knuckles. At my request, he'd taken photos of me in front of each of the vehicles. I asked him how the ride went. He shrugged. I understood the two of us had different mindsets. I was happy he'd come along despite his indifference to wrestling.

The time to meet my childhood hero had finally arrived. I focused on every detail as I descended the stairs. Before my foot touched the bottom step, which led to the walkway, I noticed a plaque that read, "Boogieland." Happy, friendly people lined the walkway. Wrestling students; family members; friends; a film crew; and, of course, fans, had all gathered to celebrate Boogie's seventy-sixth birthday. The mood in the air was peaceful and inviting. A welcome change from my usual day-to-day life in public transportation. I felt calm and accommodated with each step forward.

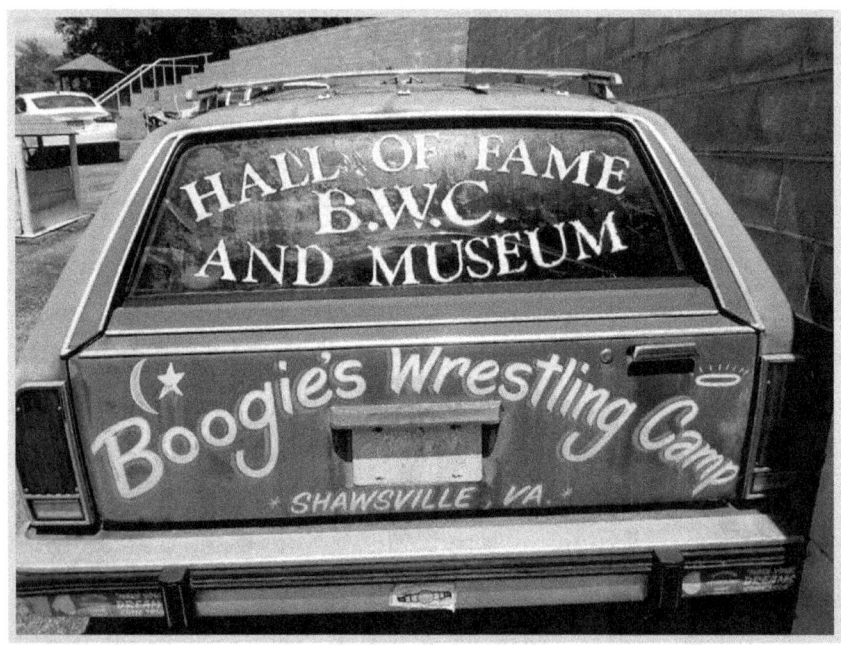

Welcome to BWC!

Suddenly, I heard a familiar sound—loud and powerful, like a shotgun blast. It was the unmistakable sound of someone taking a bump in a wrestling ring, and I was moving directly toward it. I said hello to everyone in my path, making eye contact and offering a handshake. Harry led the way. Wrestling camp was in session. I walked inside the main building. The outside temperature was over ninety degrees, but it felt like air-conditioning compared to the heat inside the building. The ring was full of aspiring talent. Male and female youngsters mixed with grizzled veterans. Outside the ring, a busy scene was unfolding, with a camera crew filming the day. A large birthday cake sat on a table to my left. Dozens of people were milling about. Some were watching practice, and others were engaged in friendly conversation. I looked down at a large red star at my feet. Inside the star, the words "I AM A" were written in white letters—a classic Valiant Brothers catchphrase usually found on the back of their tights and ring jackets. The familiar words were a sight for sore eyes. Without warning, Jimmy Valiant appeared; he stood right next to me.

I extended my hand and said, "My name is Knuckles Nelson. We met a few months ago in Rhode Island. You invited me to visit your wrestling camp, so I rode my Harley-Davidson from Rhode Island in tribute to you on your birthday."

Without saying a word, Boogie put his hand on the back of my neck and hugged me. I would come to discover this is called the Valiant Neck Hug. His embrace felt safe. I held back tears. The word that best described me at that moment: *broken*. The hug from Boogie helped me begin the transition from lost soul to a man on the mend.

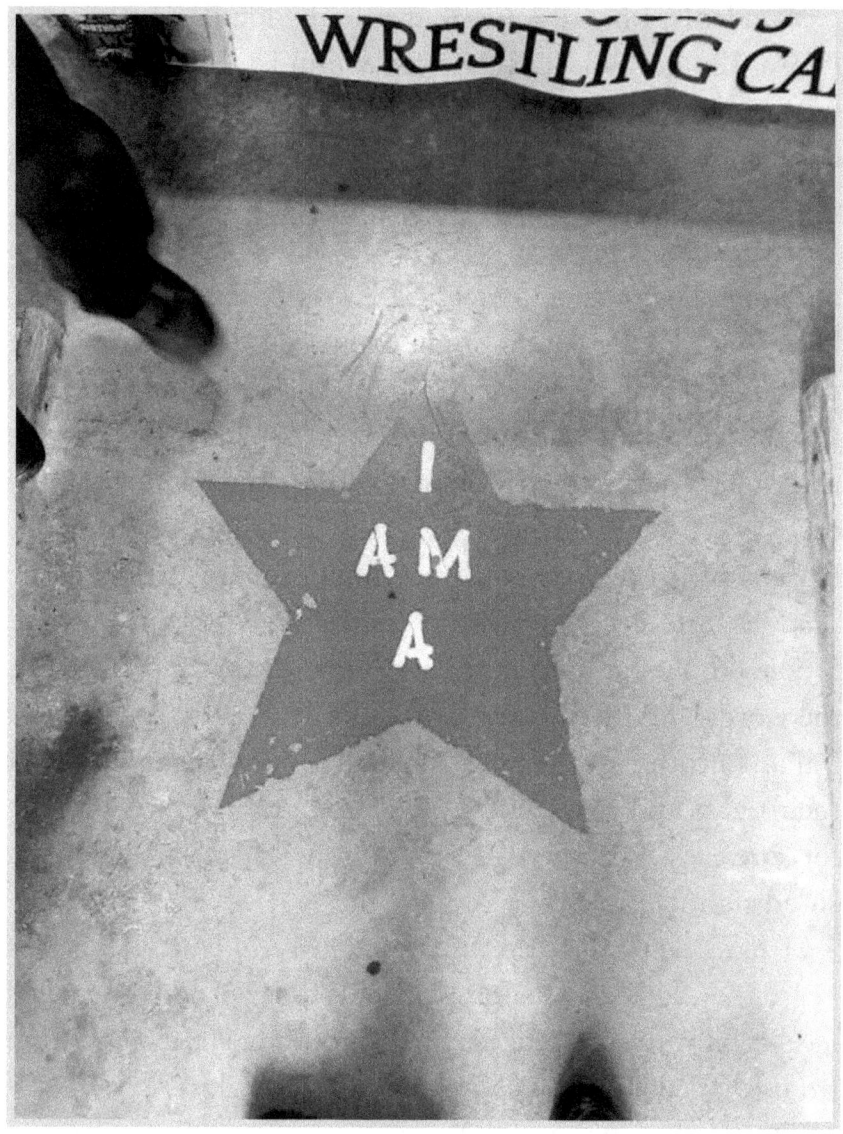

"I AM A [STAR]" is written on the floor inside the entrance to BWC.

Boogie turned to his wife, Angel, and said, "This is Knux. He rode his Harley all the way from Rhode Island to wish me a happy birthday."

Angel smiled.

"Welcome," she said.

I felt like I was home.

Many guests were vying for the birthday boy's attention. Quite understandable when you consider his status as wrestling royalty—a pioneer in the sport and a true living legend. Being the consummate host, Boogie wanted to make sure all his guests were attended to, so I backed off a bit from bogarting his attention. I noticed Jeff and Harry on the other side of the ring and made my way over to join them. Jeff appeared to be fully enjoying himself, offering tidbits of advice to the students in the ring. We stood in agreement that our decision to drive to Shawsville was a good one. I told Jeff I believed the "Boston Bad Boy," Tony Rumble, was smiling down on us that day. Jeff smiled in agreement.

With Boogie sidetracked with well-wishers, we began our sightseeing tour of BWC. The building that housed the wrestling ring displayed thousands of photos, filling each wall from floor to ceiling. Two rows of bleachers surrounded the ring, allowing the wrestlers to perform to a live audience. Thousands of different-colored signatures from past visitors covered the wooden benches. A great way for people to remind Boogie who'd stopped by for a visit. I left a message too: "Knux Was Here, 2018."

We walked outside, and Jeff commented on the replica of the Statue of Liberty, a reminder that Boogie is known as "The Boy from New York City." A pole full of street signs with great names, like Shooter Street, stood next to the statue. Under a gazebo, Boogie's family and friends spent the day relaxing while trying to beat the heat. With four additional buildings to explore, we took our time to soak it all in. It was a walk down memory lane, filled with rich history and culture from the world of professional wrestling. Inside one of the museum buildings, items ranged from wrestling boots, trunks, and title belts to awards, and literally thousands more photos. There is nothing quite like Boogie's Wrestling Camp anywhere on Earth. To properly see everything takes hours. The combination of Valiant Brothers and Boogie Woogie Man memorabilia is a testament to a great wrestling career. Many champions grace the history books of professional wrestling. A poster on the wall containing an image of Boogie in his prime summed it all up for me. The words on the poster: "Jimmy Valiant, the King of Champions."

As a former promoter and trainer, I noticed several noteworthy details about BWC. Answering the question, "Who trained you?" with "I was trained by Jimmy Valiant" is an impressive credential. The name carries a lot of weight in wrestling circles. I worked in some unsafe wrestling rings over the years, but the ring at BWC is in top condition. A separate building fully equipped with lighting and backdrops is used for professional photography. The students also have the luxury of having an in-house television studio, giving them the opportunity to work in front of a camera.

The entire campus is immaculate. I asked Angel if the students take care of the maintenance for BWC.

She smiled and said, "No. Boogie does everything. He drives the neighbors crazy cutting the grass early in the morning. Everything you see, right down to the photos on the wall, is Boogie's handiwork."

Wrestling schools can be tough. Only the strong survive. It's sink or swim. During my era, some trainers would take a new student's money up front and then beat the shit out of them to test their threshold for pain. If they doubted the prospect had what it takes to survive wrestling training, they would physically punish them in an effort to make them quit. Jimmy and Angel prefer a different approach. The entire operation is based on the Valiants' personal philosophy of love. I witnessed firsthand the loving environment they have created. The tuition is extremely affordable. The trainers are highly skilled. A WWE Hall of Famer constantly oversees everything. Everyone is family. In fact, I was amazed how quickly I felt like family at the camp. That is what makes it the most unique wrestling training center on Earth. The motto on the wall is crystal clear:

> *Can the dream become reality?*
> *Only you can make it happen!*

In his chosen profession, Jimmy has known great success. From 1964 until today, he has competed in over ten thousand matches and traveled millions of miles. He makes himself available to anyone seeking his advice and guidance, in and out of the ring. During my visit, I experienced his love and kindness up close and personal. After exploring Boogieland, I returned to my bike to grab a couple things. Inside my travel bag was a gift and a birthday card for my childhood hero. I'm not sure how anyone else would've handled the situation, but I would never arrive at a birthday party empty-handed. Back home, I'd picked out a pair of round Steamship sunglasses in black and a birthday card. Jeff, Harry, and I all signed the card. In addition, I'd brought an Ocean State Harley-Davidson T-shirt for my fellow biker.

I felt confident the moment would present itself for me to give Boogie his gifts. I walked back inside the main building while wrestling practice was still in full swing.

From across the room, Boogie yelled, "Knux, come sit with me!"

He rose to his feet as I walked toward him. He told me how impressed he was that I'd ridden my Harley all the way from Rhode Island just to wish him a happy birthday. As a longtime biker, he understood the scope of such a long ride. My personal-tribute journey had struck a chord with Boogie.

First, I gave him the black-and-orange Ocean State Harley-Davidson T-shirt. I explained to him the location of the dealership. Next, I handed him his card and colorfully wrapped gift. He struggled to open both packages with his massive hands. After a few rips, he managed to get them open. He laughed as he removed the cool shades from their case.

He turned to Angel and said, "Show him."

Angel reached under the counter and produced a pair of broken glasses. We all laughed. Boogie liked the glasses I picked out for him.

Angel confirmed this by saying, "Oh, they are definitely *you*."

In true Valiant Brothers style, Jimmy put on the shades. Once he had them on his face, he looked up to the heavens, placing his hands on his hips—his decades-long personal trademark. I captured the moment with a photo. A moment I will always cherish. I had traveled a long distance hoping for a good experience, and the day continued to unfold perfectly.

"Handsome" Jimmy Valiant
(Photo courtesy of Jimmy and Angel Valiant)

Jimmy Valiant sporting his new sunglasses, a gift from his biggest fan

A VISIT TO OLD DOMINION: THE BOOGIE MAN IS REAL

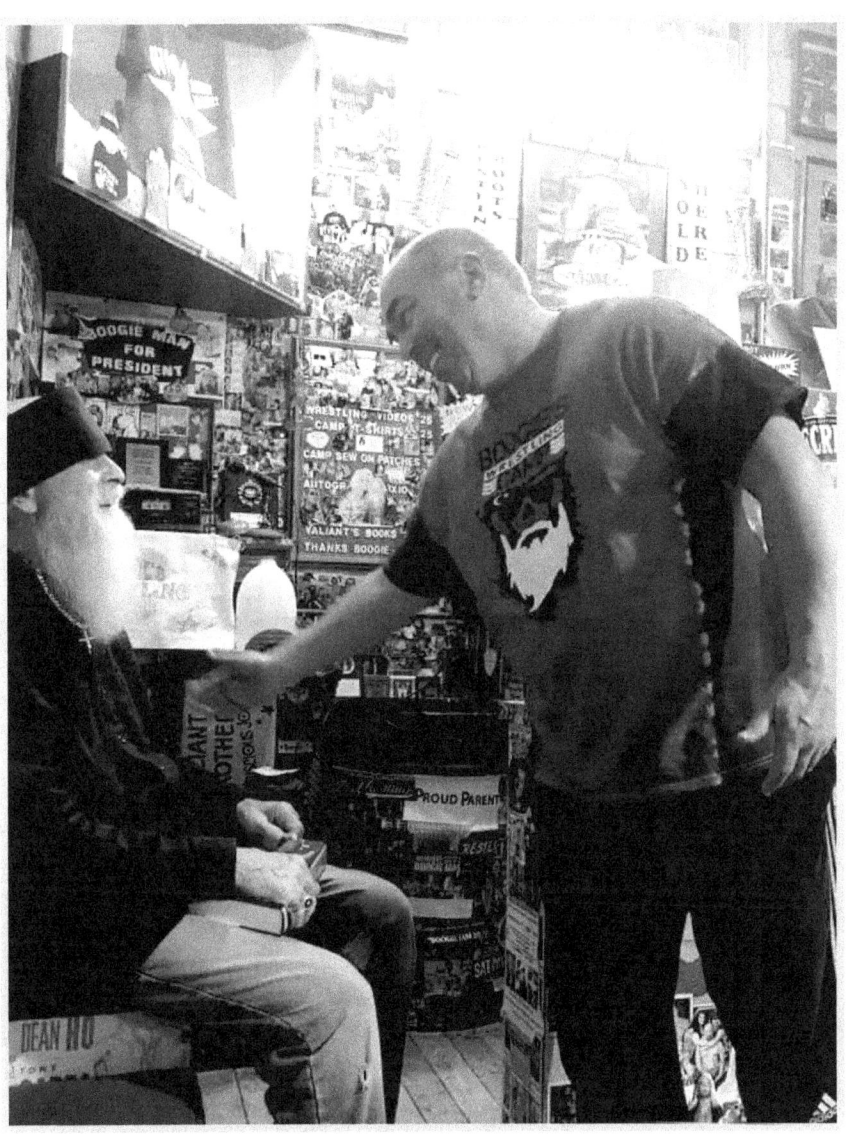

Sharing a joke with Jimmy

Spending time with Jimmy Valiant, learning from the master

Me and "Handsome" Jimmy Valiant

As I wanted to support BWC, I purchased every item available: a fiftieth-anniversary DVD, a tie-dyed BWC T-shirt, and a hardcover autobiography book titled *Woo . . . Mercy Daddy! Welcome to My World: The Jimmy Valiant Story.* Jimmy signed my copy of his book:

> *Brendan*
> *"Knux"*
> *Best in Wrestling*
> *Woo Mercy Daddy*
> *Love Ya, Brother*
> *Jimmy Valiant*
> *2018*

I'm not one to collect autographs. In fact, this is my only one. I will cherish it always.

This felt like the right time to ask my questions. I looked in Boogie's eyes for the first time in forty years.

"Can I ask you something?" I said.

"Sure, brother, go ahead," Boogie replied.

"How do you determine the next right thing to do in life? How do you know it's the right decision?"

He placed his hands in prayer in front of his chest, moving them forward and back a few times. He put one hand on the back of my neck. Before he could answer, I explained that my life had become quite difficult. I told him of death, heartbreak, and loss. He could see I was deeply troubled. He kept his hand on my neck the entire time I spoke. Wrestling practice surged on around us. He let me get it all out. Once he was sure I'd finished, he paused for a moment. Then he spoke.

"Knux, I want you to forgive. Forgive everyone for

everything you feel they have ever done to you. Once you do this, I mean *really* do it, everything else will fall into place. I can honestly say I have forgiven everyone in my life. That doesn't mean they have forgiven me. I have no control over that." He also told me to start relying on God when making decisions. I let that one go in one ear and out the other. "It will take time, brother. I know you can do it. That is the answer," he concluded.

As we stood there, the memory of my first face-to-face meeting with Jimmy entered my mind. I, a small boy, and Jimmy, in the prime of his life.

I started to feel lighter. Fear lifted from my mind and body. A shift was occurring.

I looked at Boogie and said, "Thank you."

I wanted to tell him more about myself. I talked, and he listened. It was awesome. He welcomed my stories about wrestling and life. When I consider the number of people in attendance that day, I recognize how fortunate I was to have gotten so much one-on-one time with Boogie.

I showed him photos from my past. There were two photos that I wanted him to see. The first was from my wrestling days, with my long flowing hair and ring vest covered in big white stars.

"Who am I trying to be?" I asked him.

He stared at the photo. He really looked at it. He smiled as he passed it to Angel, asking her to look at it too.

"That's cool, Knux," he said warmly.

The second photo was a more recent one of me in front of Mount Rushmore, my hands in fists, with my thumbs out, pointing to the back of my shirt. One was pointing over my shoulder and down my back, and the other was pointing up at the small of my back. Just like the Valiant Brothers did in the '70s to highlight whatever cool saying they were sporting on the backs of their jackets. Boogie also did the pose, pointing to the writing on the back of his shirt. I could see how much he appreciated my photo. Funny thing is, when that photo was taken, I'd instinctively struck that pose. Totally unplanned. I also copied that gesture for years in the ring.

Striking the Valiant Brothers pose

As I've mentioned, my buddy Rusty from Electric Mary is also a wrestling fan. He came up with a brilliant idea for a wrestling gimmick. I shared it with Boogie and Angel, but will keep it under wraps until a worthy candidate is chosen. They agreed it has potential. I feel that if a young up-and-coming wrestler from BWC were looking for an idea to jump-start a career, maybe this one can help. Seeing the idea come to life would please Rusty as well.

Everyone now gathered around the cake to sing "Happy Birthday." Boogie quickly shifted attention from himself by explaining that his wife's birthday was also right around the corner. He'd made his birthday secondary to hers—a typical, selfless act from Boogie. He requested we sing "Happy Birthday" to Angel rather than to him. We compromised and sang to both of them. The large rectangular cake had the words "Happy Birthday" written in red on top of the vanilla frosting. BWC family member Big Al made a heartfelt special dedication.

Boogie is a wonderful host. Even as a man highly decorated in the wrestling world, he took the time to make sure every person in attendance received a piece of cake. He treats everyone the same, like a family member. Angel fed her husband a piece of cake from her fork. The love they share was on full display.

The birthday celebration at BWC with Angel and Boogie

The vibe at BWC reminds me of that in yoga class. Everyone is kind to one another, and peace and love fill the room. The Valiants have the trust of everyone. Jimmy Valiant continues to give back to the sport of wrestling, passing along his wealth of knowledge and sharing stories from his Hall of Fame career. The afternoon I spent at BWC was splendid in every way. Leaving was the last thing on my mind. I felt like I belonged there. My connection to wrestling had been lost long ago and was getting smaller in my rearview mirror, but during my visit to BWC, it started to come back into focus. The connection was rejuvenated by my having spent just one day at BWC. And this went beyond wrestling. It felt more like an awakening. A man I'd admired my entire life but had not known personally just four hours earlier welcomed me to the fold instantly. And he never asked for anything in return.

The time arrived to say goodbye. We had a long ride back to Richmond ahead of us. Jeff and Harry thanked everyone as we walked outside. I felt very emotional. I knew exactly what to say to Boogie. The words came from my heart as the BWC family stood around us.

"Thank you for everything. You are my favorite wrestler, then and now."

I turned to Angel and hugged her, thanking her as well.

I turned back to Boogie. I asked him to think of the one person he would most like to meet and spend the day with. I could see he had someone in mind, but I didn't ask who.

I explained, "That is exactly what I just did." My eyes filled with tears.

Over his shoulder, family member Dee Moody sighed lovingly at my comment. Boogie hooked my neck with one hand and hugged me with the other.

"Be safe riding home, Brother Knux. I really appreciate

your coming all this way to wish me a happy birthday. You are always welcome here. Please drop us a line when you get home safely."

I realized, standing there, that my decision to make this journey had been a wise one. The advice Boogie had passed on to me made every mile of the trip worth it. The rain, the heat, going the wrong way over the George Washington Bridge, losing Jeff and Harry on the highway—all worth it. It was fate. From the moment I had ridden into Shawsville and been greeted by the young girl on the side of the road, this trip had helped begin the healing process of a very broken man. On that day, Jimmy Valiant had no idea a man in desperate need of advice would arrive at his door. Fifty-two weeks a year, people visit BWC. I hope all of them enjoy the experience even half as much as I did.

Before I left the circle of BWC family members, I said goodbye to everyone. The group had witnessed the moment I'd shared with their mentor. I sat on my motorcycle and put my hands on my hips. I looked up at BWC and made a promise to myself: *I will practice forgiveness*. The personal inner peace I so longed for had found its missing ingredient. I'd heard about forgiveness at AA meetings, in yoga classes, and within the pages of *A Course in Miracles*—but in order to have it sink in, the message needed to be delivered directly to me by my childhood hero. I couldn't have imagined anything more healing coming out of this visit. It was beyond my expectations. It also marked the beginning of my close friendship with Jimmy and Angel Valiant. I'd arrived that day unsure of who I was, but I left with an open heart and a new lease on life. A changed man. A BWC family member.

A VISIT TO OLD DOMINION: THE BOOGIE MAN IS REAL

Thank you, Jimmy Valiant, my childhood hero. I love you, brother.

River City

I am the one
To shake and stroll
Thy will be done
I am the one
I am completely in my world
I introduce I am complete

Rusty, "Busted"

THE FEELING OF HOPE ACCOMPANIED ME BACK TO Richmond. I thought the adventure was over, but there was more to come. I felt a level of inner peace for the first time in a long time. Years earlier, after having competed in a wrestling match, I'd experienced a similar feeling. Now it was like an old friend paying me a visit. Every inch of my being felt relaxed.

This time, Jeff stayed with me on the drive. Harry resumed his tribute to Boogie by reclining his seat and going to sleep. I rode my Harley with the music off, reflecting on the day at BWC. Boogie's kindness and advice had given me plenty of things to consider for the future. A blueprint that would hopefully present me with a new experience in life. Prior to all the disappointments of the last few years, life had been good. I now felt optimistic I could resume a happy life.

On the road, my thoughts returned to home, with unresolved issues and a job I hated all taking up space in my head. I wanted to practice forgiveness. I formulated a plan to get the ball rolling. After two hours on the road, we arrived at the motel. I parked the bike, eager to return to air-conditioning. All three of us had the HHs—the hunger horrors. Jeff suggested Mission BBQ for dinner, a fine choice and my first visit to the popular chain restaurant.

Harry had kept quiet most of the day, starting at breakfast. I knew wrestling was not his cup of tea, but still, I had hoped he would enjoy himself. I asked what he'd thought of our adventure.

Without hesitation he said, "It was sad. The whole thing was sad."

I took no offense to his disconnect from the day's events. After all, I have defended my love of professional wrestling my entire life. Harry had experienced the day through a different lens.

In contrast, Jeff and I had thoroughly enjoyed our visit to BWC. The two of us can conjure up an obscure memory from our past with just a word and know exactly what the other is referring to. It doesn't matter if we are alone or in a group of people. We can make eye contact and share a smile, knowing we are thinking about the same thing, while those around us are not aware of it. Today had added to a long list of mutual memories from our past. We have shared some amazing periods of our lives together.

Left to right: Jeff Katz, Jimmy Valiant, and me

Back at my motel, I had a phone call to make. I wanted to share my experience with someone who understood from a wrestling point of view. Someone who also admires "Handsome" Jimmy Valiant. That person was the one and only Elwood "Big Woody" Apt—no detailed explanation was needed. He understood that my meeting with Boogie had meant a great deal to me. It would have been the same for him. I had extended to Woody an offer to join us, but unfortunately, it hadn't been in the cards for him to attend. We spoke for a while, with me doing most of the talking about my visit to BWC. It was the best I'd felt in a long time.

Jeff returned to work at WRVA the next day, and I was looking forward to hearing him on the air. I was hoping he might have a chance to mention our adventure. I found myself on my own for the day, so it was time to locate a yoga studio. I searched online for hot yoga studios near me. A dozen popped up. A studio, minutes away, offered the class I desired: heated vinyasa flow. I love riding my Harley to yoga class. In Rhode Island, I strap my mat on the back of my bike, and the ride always clears my head in preparation for class. The ride after class is a treat for me, moving along in the wind after sixty to ninety minutes in extreme heat.

When I arrived at the studio, a tattooed yogi greeted me at the front counter. I love the curious looks I receive when I walk into a new studio dressed in biker attire: jeans, Harley-Davidson boots, a tank top, and a skullcap covered in flames. Far from a yogi look. She asked if I wanted to try a class.

"Yes," I responded.

She asked if it was my first class.

"No. I practice regularly," I said.

I filled out the necessary paperwork, and she led me to the changing area. The studio had a futuristic feel with flashy neon lights and loud, annoying music. I love loud music, just not in yoga class. This is my personal preference, and it's not shared by everyone. My inner voice commented, *This must be what yoga will be like in the future.* I changed into my shorts and prepared to flow.

I take on more of a yogi appearance when I'm barefoot and shirtless. On my feet, I have a tattoo of yin and yang—half on each foot. When I bring my feet together, the symbol becomes complete. On my back, the Sanskrit symbol for the word *breathe* starts at the base of my neck and runs all the way to the bottom of my back. A reminder to breathe is so important to me, I decided to write it on my body permanently. My friend and tattoo artist Jes Swisher of Marco's Tattoo in Wakefield, Rhode Island, is always ready to create a work of art that will permanently mark my body.

The class was filled with awesome yogis. Everyone kept to themselves. I picked a spot in front and set up my mat. The room was full of mirrors. Ugh. I hate having mirrors in class. I turned to the woman next to me and asked if the music would continue playing during class.

"Oh, yes," she responded, "only louder." She warned me that this would not be a calm, gentle yoga class.

The only other male in the class was directly behind me. He was much taller than me.

"I hope you're ready to sweat," he offered.

In true un-yogi fashion, I took all the feedback as a challenge. I prepared myself to bury them with my conditioning. As The Rock would say, "Just bring it."

My yoga home offers a vastly different philosophy. Rhode Island Power Yoga is devoid of gimmicks. The walls are bare. Neon lights, loud music, and mirrors are replaced with steam, heat, and sweat. Without warning, in this futuristic yoga class, my ego gained momentum. My focus shifted to proving myself.

I wanted to show everyone what I could do. Instead of joining the class, I wanted to dominate class. It's amazing how quickly the ego kicks in and wants to run the show. All my true yoga training back home was temporarily placed on pause. Instead, Knuckles Nelson emerged from the shadows—ready, set, yogi!

As promised, the music increased in volume as the class began. My surroundings felt more like a nightclub. Right down to the *hot* hot yoga teacher leading class. As usual, the room was dominated by elite female athletes. The atmosphere felt more like a spin class. The pace was too fast—moving from pose to pose without one second to hold it and feel it. I fell behind quickly, but after a few minutes, I caught on to the rhythm of the class. The tall man behind me dropped to his knees, totally gassed. My ego looked down at him, thinking, *Oh, poor baby. I hope you're ready to sweat!* The entire experience had little to do with yoga and everything to do with separation and ego. It was also self-inflicted. If I remain in flow, I can center myself in any situation. But I chose not to do so on this day. Surprisingly, I finished class in good condition. This appears to be one direction yoga is heading. It is not for me. The cost to drop in: $25.

At 3:00 p.m., I turned my motorcycle radio dial to 1140 WRVA-AM. *The Jeff Katz Show* now replaced the music usually coming from my speakers. I still get a kick out of knowing Jeff on a personal level and then listening to him on the air. In wrestling terms, I'm a big "mark" for Jeff Katz. The person on the air is the same as the person off the air. A truly authentic, patriotic American. As a former Philadelphia police officer, he supports law enforcement like no other. A genuine person always, Jeff is unafraid to share his opinion. A quality I admire greatly. Jeff came on the air and right away told his audience about our trip to BWC. He mentioned my name often. Without realizing it, Jeff offered me a chance to keep my wrestling persona alive twenty years later by referring to me on the air as Knuckles Nelson, a name I had put to bed two decades earlier. It felt good to have my former life briefly brought out of retirement in 2018.

After that, wherever I went during my stay in Richmond, someone inevitably would say to me, "You must be Knuckles Nelson." I listen to Jeff's show back in Rhode Island, but in Richmond, it had a special feel to it. I frequently asked people around town if they listened to the show, and my census concluded, *yes*. The people of Richmond are indeed listening to my good friend. After the conclusion of the show, Jeff picked me up for another adventure in River City. He suggested a visit to the Virginia War Memorial. Harry decided to sit this one out.

Visiting the VWM was a humbling experience. The detailed account of history is impossible to put into words. Jeff held true to form, providing a wealth of knowledge as we explored. Little did I know as we toured the grounds that I would soon be returning to the VWM a second time, where I would find my personal inspiration to write this book.

Another evening of Southern heat fell around us, and more VIP treatment awaited us. This time, at the Backyard Grill. During my stay in Virginia, my Rhode Island accent presented a language barrier. Tonight, it would be no exception. In addition, this night just happened to be the only occasion on which I decided not to wear a Harley-Davidson T-shirt. Instead, I opted for a pink V-necked T-shirt, a decision I paid for over the course of the evening. Harry joined us for dinner. The three of us were seated by a young lady with a strong Southern accent. While the server was taking our drink order, the front door opened. A man walked in, and I immediately knew he owned the establishment. I'd heard about John Harper in the past; Jeff had mentioned him often prior to my visit. I felt like I already knew John. He was a colorful character who looked like he was straight out of central casting. And talk about accents! I liked him right away. If I hadn't known who John was, I might have assumed he was the manager of the restaurant. He worked the entire time, making pit stops at our table to ensure we had everything we needed, only to be called away to resolve other issues. He worked the room effortlessly. This became the second restaurant to feature a menu item named after Jeff. River City Diner offers the "Jeff Katz Milkshake," and before it closed recently, the Backyard Grill not only offered "The Katz Sandwich," a phenomenal brisket sandwich, it also offered a second item, "The Katz Burger." Harry started to catch on to his father's celebrity status in Richmond. He kept quiet, but his face gleamed with pride. Who wouldn't be proud? Having items on a restaurant's menu named after your father is pretty freakin' cool.

Jeff Katz proudly showing off menu items named after him.

Our server was struggling with my regional accent. John revealed to us that while they were in the kitchen, she'd told him in a worried tone, "I can't understand the guy in the pink shirt." He double-checked my food order to make sure it was correct. John personally served our appetizers—fried green tomatoes and mac 'n' cheese cakes—all the while making sure his establishment was running smoothly. At one point, John sat down with us.

"Have you ever visited Rhode Island?" I asked him. He seemed amused by my accent. (It's not New York and it's not Boston. It's a slang all its own.)

"Nah," he said. "I've never been north of the Mason-Dixon Line."

I was stunned by his response, but I did my best to conceal it.

Once John had left the table, Harry decided to share with me his opinion of the Confederate flag. Harry explained that the flag was a symbol of hatred.

He added, "The South lost the war, and they need to get over it."

I asked him to please keep his voice down. He had no intention of lowering his voice. In fact, he raised it after my request. Like father, like son. Somehow, I managed to change the subject. I told him how much I regretted my choice of shirt for the evening. Harry told me that at my size, I can wear anything I want without repercussions.

Several WRVA listeners lined the bar. John requested that Jeff come over to meet some of them. Harry and I tagged along. The subject turned to wrestling, and just like that, Harry was out of the conversation. I took the opportunity to share a great Jeff Katz story from our wrestling past with the folks gathered at the bar: In 1999, the National Wrestling Alliance held its fiftieth anniversary show in Cherry Hill, New Jersey. Jeff served as ring announcer for the evening. Dressed in a suit and tie, Jeff fell victim to a vicious attack by Abdullah the Butcher with a metal table fork. Abby, as we called him, zeroed in on Jeff's forehead, ready to carve it up. Jeff hadn't been informed that the attack was to come, and he appeared shaken. Luckily for Jeff, the late, great Harley Race interjected. The seven-time world champion saved Jeff from certain, permanent scarring at the hands of Abby and his metal fork. To this day, Jeff has never understood the reason behind the attack. The patrons at the bar listened closely to my story. They seemed perplexed that a wrestler would carry a table fork with the intention of inflicting bodily harm. Wrestling fans know this is business as usual. I located a photo of the four-hundred-pound madman from the Sudan to enhance my story. The photo, displayed on my phone, shocked the small gathering—a bloody Abdullah holding a fork. Only my friend Gino Martino has a harder head than Abby. Jeff came out unscathed if not a little shaken.

Holding true to form, our dinner was on the house. The VIP treatment felt amazing. Jeff's impact on the city of Richmond is undeniable. The generosity of John's and Jeff's other friends around town made for a special time when I really needed a lift in spirit. As we left the Backyard Grill, John assured me it is perfectly OK to wear a pink shirt. He told me he always wears one to his daughter's volleyball games. The Backyard Grill gets a big thumbs up from Knuckles Nelson.

After dinner, Jeff introduced me to frozen custard. It's sort of like soft ice cream, just more delicious. We took a stroll through the shopping complex and enjoyed our dessert. As we walked along, I told Jeff I liked his friend John. I revealed how surprised I was to learn he'd never been north of the

Mason-Dixon Line. Jeff laughed and explained that John owned a chain of fast-food restaurants. He most definitely had been north of the Line and everywhere else. John is a good ol' boy, but also a successful businessman. The joke had been on me.

The following morning, I received my long-awaited VIP tour of the WRVA radio station. Jeff showed me around the station and introduced me to staff and coworkers. Wall-to-wall swag lined Jeff's office. Right away, I noticed a piece of canvas from Mid-Atlantic Championship Wrestling, complete with bloodstains. Every time I commented on an item, Jeff would ask, "You want it?" I left that day with a copy of Tom Brady's *The TB12 Method: How to Achieve a Lifetime of Sustained Peak Performance,* a WRVA travel mug, and a beautiful black leather FBI portfolio from the Richmond office. Everything except the bloodstained piece of canvas was fair game. The legal pad inside the FBI portfolio would one day contain the first pages of this book. Jeff made sure I did not leave empty-handed while he appeared indifferent to the items. Jeff felt the *TB12* book could be passed along to my father, a New England Patriots fan. Upon leaving the studio, I felt like I'd been on a game show.

I spent the rest of the day riding my motorcycle around the area, making a stop at Steel Horse Harley-Davidson. I purchased a T-shirt to commemorate my visit. This was the only day that I missed Jeff's show. Jeff called me after the show ended to see if I had any interest in returning to the Virginia War Memorial. He told me a veteran named Craig Rossi had been a guest on the show earlier in the day, while I'd been tooling around town on my bike. Jeff liked Craig and wanted to hear him speak at the VWM. I had no idea who Craig was, or what would be the subject of his lecture, but I gladly tagged along. On the ride, Jeff brought me up to speed. Craig is an author. His appearance on Jeff's show was to plug his new book *Craig & Fred: A Marine, a Stray Dog, and How They Rescued Each Other*.

We arrived at the VWM to a standing-room-only crowd. Craig stood onstage, presenting a slideshow on a large video screen behind him. One remarkable photo after another appeared as he spoke to a captivated audience. The photos took me directly into the heart of his incredible story of meeting a stray dog in a war zone. Craig's story mesmerized the audience, but it is his to tell, so I highly recommend looking him up on social media and YouTube. With his calming voice and movie-star looks, Craig had my full attention. After a while, he invited the real star of the show to join him onstage. Fred the Afghan dog appeared to enjoy his fame and popularity. After I'd heard Craig's story of survival and love, I realized he deserves every second of it. Seated next to me were two women dressed to the nines. As the dog made his way onstage, the ladies jumped to their feet, crying out, "There he is!" and began taking photos. Fred has fans.

The first thing Fred did onstage: two yoga poses—Upward-Facing Dog and Downward-Facing Dog. Craig is from Virginia. He appeared quite proud to speak in his home state. His story was so emotional, it was impossible for me to control the tears rolling down my face. A tough-looking fellow biker sitting alongside me was also wiping away tears. At one point, Fred needed a bathroom break. Craig's assistant led Fred up the aisle toward the exit. He stopped right in front of me. Fred sniffed my hand and gave it a lick. Craig continued to speak and then took some questions from the audience. He shared the personal experience of his life, which had taken twists and turns he'd never anticipated. The idea to write a book had never crossed his mind until he finally just sat down and wrote it. The more he shared, the more clarity I felt. It was similar to that first time I'd heard Jimmy Valiant speak, back in Rhode Island. The most profound moment I'd ever experienced occurred while I was sitting there at the Virginia War Memorial. I realized a book lived inside *me* as well, and it needed to come out. I was going to tell my story. The door opened, and I walked through it.

The event concluded with Craig inviting the crowd to a book signing in the lobby. A line quickly formed, stretching around the corner. I wanted to meet Craig, but it seemed unlikely with the number of people already in line. Jeff and I had sat separately due to the size of the crowd, and when we reunited, I asked Jeff his thoughts on Craig's presentation.

Jeff smiled and said, "It was great!"

Meanwhile, Craig, Fred, and their entourage moved toward the lobby.

As they passed us, Jeff said, "Craig, it's Jeff Katz!"

Craig stopped in his tracks.

"Hi, Jeff!" he said. "Walk out with us."

Turns out, I would meet Craig after all. My VIP tour of Richmond continued. We passed the line and headed to a private area. Craig thanked Jeff for his having had him on the show earlier in the day. We then took a photo with Craig and Fred. I told Craig how much I enjoyed hearing his story, but I left out the part about how he had inspired me to write a book. The truth is, the idea was so new and powerful to me, I had no idea how I would proceed. We hung out in the lobby for a bit, and Jeff greeted some of his listeners who were in attendance. One listener asked if I was Knuckles Nelson. I smiled and backed off to the side as Jeff held court, talking about Richmond's current events and politics.

Jeff Katz with Craig Rossi and Fred the Afghan dog

As we walked to the car, a man behind us said, "Man, that was some story. I really need to buy a dog."

I looked back and offered, "Adopt one, brother."

He smiled and replied, "Yes, of course."

Jeff had done it again. I'd had another fantastic time with the Katzman. With Harry staying in for the evening, we had a chance to catch up over dinner. I never fully revealed what was going on with my mental health, but I did offer some of what had transpired in the recent past. Jeff, in turn, shared with me that spending long periods of time away from his family was taking an emotional toll on him. We've always shared our thoughts and feelings with each other. I consider Jeff Katz to be my third sibling, after my brothers, Kevin and Jeff.

Harry stayed home watching *Animal House* for the second time, preparing for his upcoming enrollment at Stanford University. He joined us briefly via text, inquiring about a possible to-go order.

Jeff and I had our time to gab and Harry was hungry. As we drove back to my motel, a shift continued to take shape inside me. I didn't feel the need to share it. Probably because I wasn't sure of what exactly I was feeling. In the motel parking lot, Jeff started to run down the possible activities for the following day. I had a whole week before I had to return to work. I told Jeff that I might start my ride home in the morning. Jeff seemed a bit surprised.

"OK, if that's what you want to do," he said.

I told him I wasn't sure yet and needed to sleep on it. I promised to update him in the morning. Just in case, I thanked him for his incredible hospitality. I felt so much gratitude for everything. Jeff had made my stay in the River City one for the ages.

I had arrived in Richmond a tired, discouraged man, and my life became fully recharged in less than one week. Jeff may not have realized it, but he'd shown me the time of my life. Everything had lined up perfectly. Jeff's presence in Virginia had been the deciding factor for me to make this trip in the first place. Like Jeff always says, "We are brothers from another mother."

I went to sleep that night with complete confidence that I could put my story on paper. Inspiration appeared all around me. My time in Virginia had opened the door. My life as a spiritual seeker had taken many twists and turns, starting at age twelve at New England Tae Kwon Do in Warwick, Rhode Island. Alcohol and drugs had thrown a blanket over my growth until I found sobriety at thirty-eight years old. My years in recovery had always felt incomplete. Discovering yoga had guided me further, but had also felt incomplete. Everything had felt incomplete because I'd never managed to figure out why I felt inner conflict—regardless of all I'd turned to in my attempts to fix myself.

I have no shortage of quality people in my life to turn to for advice. Jeff Katz, of course. Heart-to-heart conversations with Bob Quattrocchi in his garage while he works on my motorcycle, preparing me for my adventures. My godfather, Joe Gliottone, has throughout my life provided me with solid advice. My friendship with Electric Mary's lead singer, Rusty, from the other side of the planet, has also given me hope. My inspirational visit and new friendship with Jimmy Valiant rejuvenated my fading spirit. It had all led me to this moment. With each breath I took, I felt I was getting closer to the truth. There is nothing worse than false hope; I knew all about that. I was excited about learning the potential answers to my long-standing questions. Could writing a book unlock those answers for me?

Righteously Reborn

When the stars tell me
Who I should lose
Will I be wise enough

Rusty, "Stars"

THE TIME HAD COME TO SAY GOODBYE TO VIRGINIA. I had a long motorcycle ride back to New England ahead of me. Life with renewed purpose and meaning entered my heart. I was ready to practice forgiveness. Writing a book appeared on the horizon and dominated my thoughts. With my keepsakes from the trip safely packed away, my Electra Glide purred as I left the motel parking lot in Richmond. Arriving or leaving a town on a motorcycle reminds me of riding in on a horse in the Old West. Men offer a nod of approval, while women give a wave and a smile. It's the most freedom I have ever experienced. It can't be put into words. It must be experienced to be fully understood.

At one point, however, I questioned if I'd make it home at all. On Interstate 95 North in Maryland, a car transporting four teenagers was riding alongside me. I was in the middle lane of the three-lane highway. They were in the lane to my left. Without warning, the car swerved into my lane. The young man driving was holding the steering wheel with his left hand and a cell phone with his right. In the front passenger seat, his female copilot realized the situation, and grabbed the steering wheel and turned it counterclockwise, moving the car out of my lane. I began to move over to my right to avoid being struck by the car, but the car on my right sped past me so close, I could've reached down and touched the hood. This all happened in a matter of seconds. Up ahead, traffic in my lane and the lane to my left had slowed to a near stop. I maneuvered quickly to the right, avoiding the car in front of me. I needed to steer right again into the breakdown lane to avoid rear-ending another car in the inside lane. I lost control of the motorcycle and prepared to crash. I thought, *This trip has given me a new lease on life, and now it's going to end like this?* In the blink of an eye, I gained control of the bike. From beginning to end, the entire ordeal lasted only about five seconds. I coasted in the breakdown lane to regain my composure. Then I turned my attention back to the car full of teens that had caused the near-fatal nightmare. They all looked to be in shock, completely aware of what had happened. I drove away, avoiding conflict and hoping the experience might have a lasting effect on them.

When I returned to my home state of Rhode Island, optimism trumped all negativity in my thoughts. From my earliest memories, I had struggled with anger. I'd maintained long-term grudges along with an uncontrollable temper. It had all gone untreated for decades. I'd felt convinced I would take to the grave these defects of character.

As another beautiful Rhode Island summer began to wind down, I had to get my head around the idea of returning to work. One morning, I sat down at my kitchen table, opened my new leather Richmond FBI portfolio from Jeff Katz, and stared at the blank legal pad inside. I began to write. I filled the entire legal pad. When I put pen to paper, it poured out of me. The title for my book came easily to me since wrestling had once consumed my life, and yoga had taken its place.

I filled six composition notebooks with my story. My favorite time to write is when I wake up. I like to sit with a cup of coffee and let it flow. I enjoy writing on paper with a pen.

It amazed me how easy it is for me to express my thoughts on paper. I do not write fiction. I write about what has happened, as honestly as possible. The entire process was free and easy. My life had a new purpose. I needed to build on what I already had down on paper and continue writing this book. I wanted to forgive everyone in my life for everything that I'd perceived they had done to me.

Prior to my day with Boogie, I'd had no intention of ever again contacting my ex. I decided to try something different. I sent her a text message apologizing for my role in our failed relationship. She replied, asking why I'd reached out. Why now? I told her that changes had occurred in my life, resulting in my wanting to apologize to her. Amazingly, she accepted my half-assed apology. I didn't know it at the time, but saying the words "I'm sorry" without elaborating on specifics or giving the other person an opportunity to add anything he or she needs to say is far from a proper apology. I still had a lot to learn.

A few days later, I stood in my yard, chatting with my neighbor Katie, a blonde surfer girl with a warm personality. We lived in separate houses on the same property. As we chatted, Katie told me I had company and nodded toward the driveway. I turned to see my ex pulling in. Her visit was completely unannounced, unexpected, and unwanted. I asked Katie to please stay with me; she chuckled, rolled her eyes, and opted to pass on the opportunity to meet my ex. She smiled and wished me luck.

My ex drove up the driveway in her beautiful silver and black Mustang convertible. She stopped and handed me a small bag of tomatoes from her garden—a garden that I'd created and had once called my own. She asked if she could get out of the car so the two of us might talk. I agreed. We sat on my patio for an hour, catching up. I told her about my new outlook and optimism. She brought me up to speed on her life. I knew our time together was over.

I didn't care for the unannounced visit, but I did feel closure afterward. I began to understand the immature reaction and feelings associated with the power of forgiveness. At one time in the relatively near past, I'd believed I could never forgive her, but miraculously, I'd now changed my mind. I still had a lot to learn about the process of forgiveness. Our polite interaction was short-lived, as future phone calls found us bickering, just like old times. I felt unhappy after speaking with her.

I kept Boogie apprised of my recent efforts. I told him about the setback with my ex. He reminded me that forgiving her was my job. That's it. He explained I had no control over her or anyone else, and no control over how they felt. In addition, I remembered my mother telling me that if she didn't like the way she felt after interacting with someone, she stopped interacting with that person. I decided to forgive my ex but also to cut ties with her. I kept moving forward, doing the best I could with my new direction in life. I adopted a mantra to remind myself when I'd slip: *What Would Boogie Do?* WWBD. Whenever I found myself in an uncomfortable situation, I'd simply think, *What Would Boogie Do?* The answer always came with ease.

Death paid another visit to my family. After a long life, my Aunt Phyllis passed away. As fate would have it, WWBD would be called upon in quick fashion. I'm the oldest of three boys. My brother Kevin is two years younger, and my brother Jeff is eight years younger. Kevin and I have always maintained a rocky relationship. We agree on very little. At one point, many years ago, Kevin decided to write me off for good. He made it crystal clear that he preferred as little contact with me as possible. For close to a decade, we respected his wishes. Looking back, I never tried to make things right with him, so it was more of a mutual agreement. While attending my aunt's wake, I found myself in the same room with Kevin. I stood in the long line, waiting to pay my respects to my cousins on the passing of their mother. My brother had already passed through the line and was sitting alone. I was heading right toward him. As the line inched forward, I asked myself, *WWBD?* The answer came swiftly: *Extend my hand, and let the chips fall where they may.* Once parallel with Kevin, I leaned over, offering my hand. He reached out, not yet aware it belonged to me. As we shook hands, I told him it had never occurred to me that Aunt Phyllis had come from such a big family. At the time, he and I were the only two in the room from our side of the family. Once he realized it was me, his facial expression changed to one of displeasure. It crossed my mind that maybe my reaching out to him was a bad idea. But instead, he began to smile, and said he thought the same thing. Relief filled my body. I love my brothers, and it had troubled me deeply over the years that the two of us had opted out of being brothers. This mutual decision had made life difficult for my parents and for my other brother, Jeff, who'd held no animosity toward either of us. By no means did I think a simple handshake would make everything hunky-dory between us, but it sure felt like a good start. My father arrived at the memorial service to see his two sons standing together. A moment he had long hoped to behold.

Once I'd adopted and embraced the WWBD philosophy, change happened quickly. Longstanding behaviors I'd once given up on felt possible to correct. Grudges washed away like magic in 2018. Change invaded my life. It didn't matter if I wanted it or not. My new outlook on life opened doors that I had believed to be nailed shut. A new and unfamiliar feeling of hope began to build momentum. My visit to Boogie's Wrestling Camp had amplified a message of forgiveness and transformed darkness into light.

I kept Boogie in the loop. He seemed to enjoy hearing from me. I told him of my progress. I keep in touch by phone and writing to him on Messenger. I told him about the experience with my brother Kevin. I wanted to share with Boogie my desire to write a book. His autobiography is phenomenal. I wasn't sure how he would react to the idea of my writing a book since he is so prominently featured in my story. But he made it easy for me. Without ever mentioning my recent interest in telling my story, he responded to one of my messages with this:

> Knux,
> You have a great writing style.
> You should consider writing a book.
> Everyone has a story to tell.

I replied, thanking him for his vote of confidence. I revealed to him how much writing I'd done since our time together at BWC. He told me how pleased he was to hear that and encouraged me to keep writing. His support fueled my desire to complete this book. My WWBD mantra was gaining momentum, and the time had come for me to bring it to work at the Public Transit Authority. I knew from experience it wouldn't take long for a situation to arise on the bus, and I would be able to see if my new outlook could translate to success in a real-time, real-life situation.

Jimmy Valiant maintains a close bond with wrestling fans; he embraces everyone. He refers to fans as his people, *the street people,* his brothers and sisters. During one of our recent conversations, Boogie reminded me that people who take the bus need me. They depend on me to drive them to their destination. Otherwise, they would have to walk. He told me that even the unpleasant individuals depend on me. Boogie speaks to me like I'm his brother. His words reach me every single time. So I stepped out of my comfort zone, going from being an all-business, unfriendly bus operator to employing a new approach of greeting every person who boarded the bus. It really didn't matter if they responded. To my surprise, almost everyone *did* respond. I began to tell passengers my first name. I lightened up considerably and developed friendly relations with my riders. A far cry from the unapproachable person they'd encountered in the past. A bus operator makes initial contact with the passengers long before they step aboard the bus. The first contact occurs as passengers stand on the sidewalk, looking through the windshield at the driver as the bus approaches. I started to smile more, doing my best to put passengers at ease before I opened the bus door. It influenced the atmosphere and mood on the bus in a profound way. Instead of, "Oh, look, it's that asshole driving the bus," I experienced smiles of relief and realized people were happy to see me behind the wheel. Why did I change my attitude? Because that's what Boogie would do.

For years I had gotten it wrong. I'd learned how to survive behind the wheel by not going the extra mile to be of service to my passengers. My decision to try and ultimately rely on the WWBD mantra enabled me to start getting it right. People from all walks of life ride the bus. A job that had once felt like I was wearing my shoes on the wrong feet became more and more tolerable. That is a remarkable turn of events. The experience further fueled my need to write this book. I never imagined feeling good about life again, let alone my job, yet here I was, feeling great.

After my mother died, I watched my father suffer the anguish of being alone, his soul mate taken from him far too soon. I stood helplessly watching as he tried to carry on without her. We all lost so much when my mother passed away. My father even lost his desire to live. I watched him carry on with a broken heart. I told my father of my plan to write a book. I showed him a rough idea I had for the cover. I revealed to him the book would be dedicated to his wife, my mother, Barbara Jean Branch Higgins. I know she was guiding me as I continued to tell my story.

The formula for inner peace was always inside me, patiently waiting for me to accept it. From my childhood experience in karate school, to sobriety, to yoga, and finally to meeting Boogie, the answers were always available. My experiences had led me to believe I needed to be in a great deal of pain before I could finally face the truth and accept it. Even then, I resisted—but this time, something felt different. As a child, I would enter karate school and look at the school pledge and the "Aims to Achieve" hanging on the wall of New England Tae Kwon Do:

Modesty
Perseverance
Self-Control
Indomitable Spirit

The words always stared back at me. I loved the military-like environment of karate school. I grew up in a loving home but was not disciplined very often. I was good at keeping my activities a secret. I picked up on how to be sneaky at a young age. I didn't realize it at the time, but I needed to be in the most structured environment possible. From an early age, my decision-making was terrible. Then I found karate. Finally, someone was telling me exactly what to do. I wanted to be the best martial artist possible. I took it all very seriously. At twelve years old, I learned the *New Oxford American Dictionary* definition of each of the "Aims to Achieve."

Periodically, the karate school would hold testing for students to advance in rank. The process involved a panel of judges sitting at a table, with students lined up in front of them. During one of my tests to advance to the next rank, a judge asked me what "perseverance" means. I stood at attention. My arms extended in front of me in tight fists. My eyes focused on the wall directly over his head as I recited the definition, word for word. "Perseverance is doing something despite difficulty or delay in achieving success, SIR!" Bam! I'd nailed it.

The judge sat back in his chair. He placed his hands behind his head and exhaled. He looked at the young boy in front of him. I stood at attention.

"Yeah, OK," he said, "but what does it mean to you?" I stood there silently. He continued, "That's great that you memorized the definition, but I'd like to hear, in *your* words, what it means."

This became one of my earliest life-defining moments. I couldn't tell him what it meant in my own words because I didn't know. It would take me decades to learn the answer.

At the beginning of my teenage years, I entered the world of addiction. A blanket was thrown over my soul. My moral compass would be broken for years to come. If today I were to cross paths with the judge from my childhood karate test, I'd finally be able to offer him my answer: *Perseverance means to never give up and to follow my heart always.*

CHAPTER 12

What a Difference a Year Makes

*Morning comes to greet me
With its shining yellow sun
Turning indiscreetly
Kiss the moon
Her work is done*

Rusty, "Slave"

It's been said that God will not put more on your plate than you can handle. For most of my life, I doubted this belief. I felt that God overloaded my plate on a regular basis. That was one of the many lies I told myself to get through each day. When I search my memory, spanning the entire course of my life, I realize I've always managed to find solutions to problems or challenging life situations that arise; I'm talking about the *making ends meet* kind of stuff. But emotional and spiritual issues have remained a work in progress for me, and at times, a mystery.

The past few years had presented new challenges and made me question if I even wanted to live. I felt overloaded most of the time. I protected myself with a monarch mentality—meaning, I had no interest in anyone's opinion other than my own. I crammed my beliefs down people's throats. I refused to listen to any opinion contrary to my own. I ignored almost everyone in my path. I removed people from my life without explanation or warning. It was a horrible, lonely way of life. Failed relationships, along with my poor physical and mental health, put me to the test. But, finally, things were looking up—or so I thought.

I had plenty to look forward to. Boogie was planning a trip to Rhode Island for New England Fan Fest 7. A longtime favorite musician of mine, Paul Rodgers, and his band, Bad

Company, were going to make a stop in Rhode Island for the first time in forty years, toward the end of the summer. I secured two front-row seats for the show. This marked the thirty-ninth time I would be seeing Paul perform live. The first time was also in Providence, at the Civic Center, back in 1979. My annual visit to BWC on Boogie's birthday was another event I was looking forward to. The highlight of the summer would be the wedding of my younger brother, Jeff. But before all this could unfold, I needed to jump over some hurdles.

It's been said, if you want things in life to change, try doing something different. For me, the things I resist the most turn out to be the ones that bring about profound, positive change. As 2019 got underway, I continued to struggle with being overweight. I'd failed to have any type of internal conversation with myself about changing my bizarre eating habits, and this told me I hadn't yet mustered the necessary courage to change. I kept stuffing my face like a pig and hating myself at the same time. I practiced yoga while carrying about fifty extra pounds. It hampered my ability to move my body in a manner I'd grown accustomed to. I felt like shit and compared myself to the elite athletes surrounding me in class. Prior to my gaining weight, my yoga practice had progressed to the point where I'd felt limitless in my body. Headstands and handstands had come with ease; I had even begun to feel a floating sensation. Once I gained the weight, I settled for my new body size and watched these exciting changes disappear. It felt like a plant growing just beneath the surface, ready to break through the soil, then suddenly stopping and going back down into the ground.

A typical New England winter set in. Cold weather and diminishing daylight provided the challenge of just getting through January, February, and March. I longed for spring to arrive. Northeastern weather can be brutal, with extreme conditions gradually intensifying for what feels like an eternity. They seem to take a greater toll on my physical and emotional state as I grow older. I was spending as much time as possible at Rhode Island Power Yoga, trying to manage the feelings associated with the cold winter weather while often complaining about it to those around me.

Finally, I decided to try something different. RIPY periodically offers classes and workshops on a wide range of topics. I attend most of the workshops and always learn something, if not *multiple* things. They've helped me continue to grow on my physical and spiritual path. There was one workshop I'd avoided, however: The annual Detox and Flow. This workshop solicits fear and doubt in me immediately. The program consists of a twenty-one-day cleanse with yoga, mindfulness practices, and diet, led by Erica LePore, ND. This workshop caused me fear and self-doubt.

The program combines RIPY's steamy hot yoga classes with mindfulness practices; a clean, hypoallergenic diet; and an all-natural supplement plan. It focuses on eating nourishing foods, free from chemicals and unlikely to trigger an allergic cascade of inflammation, disease, and cravings. By following diet guidelines set forth by Erica, the program helps people to discover that the food they consume on a regular basis could be interfering with optimum health. A combination of group support, a private Facebook page, and interaction with other participants in the studio opened the door a crack for me to peek in. Maybe, just maybe, I could do this. To properly follow the plan, I would need to give up coffee, sugar, and alcohol. Booze would be easy. I'd given that up a long time ago. But the other two presented a definite challenge. I had observed friends from the studio encouraging one another to participate. I quietly signed up, but with little confidence in my ability to follow the plan.

My living arrangement needed to change as well. My private cottage in Middletown had become unbearable due to construction activity and the conditions associated with multiple houses being built in my once-private surroundings. Around the same time that I signed up for the detox, I began to search for a new home.

The detox started with a two-hour in-studio orientation. The other participants in the room asked questions while they prepared to embark on the journey. I sat in silence, overwhelmed with information and strategies. The more I heard, the less confident I felt. Between the cost of food and supplements, and the rigid program guidelines, I questioned why I would put myself through this. But I went to Whole Foods Market, stocked up on food and supplements, and said to myself, *Here goes nothing.*

After the first week, I found myself following the detox with ease. I maintained a daily yoga practice to increase my chances of achieving my goal of weight loss. I kept my progress to myself, staying under the radar. The program participants had access to a private Facebook page, which I viewed every day, reading everyone's trials and tribulations. I saw friends in class and had brief conversations with them about the detox, but I had a hard time discussing the program because of my fear of failure. At the end of the twenty-one days, I had lost thirty pounds. I felt phenomenal. Summer was off to a great start. After the program was over, I decided to continue with a no-sugar diet. I also continued to abstain from coffee. These were two things I'd never considered possible prior to the detox. My confidence returned.

In June, Boogie returned to Rhode Island for the seventh annual New England Fan Fest weekend, taking place at the Crowne Plaza Hotel in Warwick. I arranged with promoter Joe Bruen to be Boogie's driver and handler for the weekend. I could hardly wait to pick him up at the airport. While I was waiting at the arrival gate, I noticed drivers holding up signs with the names of arriving passengers. I was sporting my tie-dyed BWC T-shirt. I told the other people who were waiting that the sign for my arriving passenger was my shirt. I made sure the busy terminal knew a WWE Hall of Famer was about to land in Rhode Island.

Once Boogie's plane had landed and he was inside the terminal, some folks gathered around us. They wanted to meet Boogie, and he took time to hang out. He signed autographs and posed for photos as I looked on.

Fan Fest offers wrestling fans a chance to meet and greet the biggest stars from the world of pro wrestling. This year brought a who's who to the Ocean State: Tully Blanchard, Arn Anderson, J. J. Dillon, Barry Windham, Paul Roma, Kelly Kelly, Bill Apter, Gary Michael Cappetta, Greg Valentine, the Honky Tonk Man, Tatanka, and the one and only "Handsome" Jimmy Valiant were all on hand for the weekend's festivities.

Another old friend from my wrestling days, Barry Darsow, would be in Rhode Island for Fan Fest. Along with his tag-team partner, Bill Eadie, the duo was known as "Ax" and "Smash" of Demolition. It would be my first time seeing Barry since our adventures in Japan almost twenty years earlier. The event hosts wrestlers from yesterday, today, and tomorrow. Vendors from all over the world converge on the Crowne Plaza

Hotel to display memorabilia and merchandise. Independent wrestling promotions display title belts and information on their organizations. The event kicks off with a VIP dinner, followed by the New England Pro Wrestling Hall of Fame Induction Ceremony.

Prior to the ceremony, Jeff and Heidi met us at the hotel. We all piled into my car to head to the VIP dinner. Boogie rode shotgun. I felt like a teenager with all my best friends loaded into the car. The dinner was held at the Thirsty Beaver Hometown Pub & Grub—a local spot directly across from the old Cranston police station and Atwood Avenue softball field. I played softball for years on that field as a member of the Player's Corner Pub team. The bar area of the pub was open to the public, and it was interesting to watch patrons' facial expressions as the Honky Tonk Man, Barry Windham, Greg Valentine, J. J. Dillon, Tully Blanchard, Arn Anderson, and, of course, Jimmy Valiant walked in. This was not your typical late afternoon at the Thirsty Beaver. After dinner, things really got crazy, with our crew going out for ice cream. I maintained my no sugar diet, but would never attempt to deprive those who were interested in a little dessert. I reminded Boogie that we still had the Hall of Fame Induction Ceremony on the schedule. He looked weary from a long day of travel, and I asked him if he was still interested in attending.

"I'd rather not, brother. I'm tired," he said quietly.

Boogie turned in while the rest of us attended the ceremony. This year saw two of my longtime friends being inducted: "Big Woody" and Jeff Katz. I'd been given the honor of inducting both.

Just prior to the Fan Fest weekend, I received word that Woody had been hospitalized. I was told his health was failing.

I decided to drive to Massachusetts and visit my old friend. I arrived at the hospital to find Woody bedridden. His hair and goatee had turned white since we'd last seen each other. As soon as our eyes met, I felt unconditional love for him. I leaned over the bed and hugged my friend. Another friend from our past, Terri, was in the room when I arrived. We all made small talk until I looked at Woody and started to cry. I told him I had met a lot of people over the course of my life, and he was one of the best friends I had ever had.

Terri said, "You know what, I'm going to leave you guys alone for a while."

We both asked her to stay, but she insisted on giving us some one-on-one time. Looking back, she was giving us time to say goodbye. We spent the next hour reminiscing—and boy, do we have some history together. It felt just like old times, with me reminding him of things he had long-since forgotten, and he, once his memory had been jogged, correcting me on my facts. Woody always had his facts straight. It was wonderful to revisit our friendship.

Woody started to laugh at one point and said, "You could be the kindest person I ever knew—but you could also be the biggest douche." Then he laughed in his infectious way. He always needed to get his belly laughs out in full, no matter the circumstances.

We laughed together like it was old times. We recalled one memory after another. I reminded Woody about the time his dog, Duncan, walked up to me while I was sitting in a chair, turned his back to me, and rubbed his ass against my leg, giving it a good, deep scratch. Then he walked over to Woody, jumped up on his lap, and stared back at me while Woody laughed uncontrollably. Woody petted Duncan and said, "Good boy, good boy."

The visit helped us both deal with the cycle of life, something that was rapidly winding down for one of us. We spoke about Tony Rumble and how well the two of them had gotten along. Woody told me that if I hadn't come to the seacoast in the first place, a lot of things would never have happened for him and others who also shared a love for pro wrestling and wanted to be involved in it. I felt honored that he felt that way. Woody was not an athlete by any stretch of the imagination, but he had natural charisma, charm, and personality. Those qualities made him an asset to any wrestling show. Whether it was in the ring or behind the scenes, he never forgot what Tony Rumble and I had passed along to him. Every locker room he ran maintained a professional atmosphere. He insisted on it. He respected a business that no longer held the same level of respect and privacy from the fans it had once proudly maintained.

I decided I would come back to visit Woody in a few days. This visit had been amazing, and I wanted more interaction with my dear friend while we could still have it. As I said goodbye, I gave him a hug and told him I would be back to see him soon.

As I started to stand up, he pulled me back down and whispered in my ear, "I love you, brother. Thanks for everything you did for me." He looked in my eyes and without saying another word, told me the end was very near. I walked out of the hospital determined to return. Woody died the following day.

Woody was one of the kindest men I have ever known. We had so much fun together in and out of the wrestling world. During my less responsible days, he made sure I had a ride to my scheduled wrestling shows. He was a master chef and regularly prepared meals for us to enjoy. I have fond memories of dining at his house with his grandmother and his wonder dog, Duncan. To this day, his chili is the best I have ever tasted. We traveled to Fenway Park often. At near five hundred pounds, he would negotiate a seat right down near the field because he couldn't fit in the old narrow seats. He would settle into a large comfortable seat, look back at me over his shoulder, and give a shrug. Those were great times. We'd spend about ten bucks on a bleacher seat and another ninety bucks on beer. For years, we also traveled around New England, attending rock concerts.

The words to induct both Woody and Jeff Katz into the NEPWHOF came to me without effort. I had nothing written down or planned; it all just flowed from my heart. Each of them had, in their own way, a major impact on my life. Being chosen to induct my two closest friends on the same night felt like a once-in-a-lifetime honor. I've become a better person thanks to having known them both.

After the HOF ceremony concluded, I returned to my hotel room and fell asleep with ease. In the early morning hours, the phone rang. I answered it, but there was no one on the other end, so I hung up and drifted back to sleep. Then a knock on my door woke me up again. I looked over at the clock. It was 4:45 a.m. I answered the door, and there stood Boogie in the hallway. He was in great spirits—clearly an early riser.

"Brother, I need some water," he said. I quickly fetched my Trader Joe's cooler bag filled with water and snacks and told him to take it back to his room, which was directly across the hall. I could hear the sound of the television coming from Boogie's room. I think he wanted some company, but I was still in need of sleep, so I went back to bed.

Later that morning, I took Boogie to breakfast at Jigger's Diner in East Greenwich. Boogie ordered Corned Beef Hash Benedict. He told me he never ordered anything like that at home. I ordered the same dish. We enjoyed a wonderful meal and conversation. Boogie told stories of wrestling in Rhode Island and the surrounding area. He has a remarkable memory, with stories spanning over forty years. I continue to cherish every moment I get to spend with him.

The most noteworthy memory I have from the Fan Fest is the mutual love and admiration between Boogie, his peers, and the fans. All the legends in attendance received warm welcomes from the fans, but it was different with Boogie. Everyone seemed to have an extra-special affection for him. Over the course of the day, wrestlers and fans alike paid respect to Boogie, visiting his table to receive a Valiant Neck Hug, a photo, an autograph, or an opportunity to chat with the WWE Hall of Famer.

My father even stopped by to meet my childhood hero in person. It was a special moment for me to have my two heroes together in the same room. They hit it off right away. Since they are not so far apart in age, they shared stories about life during the years before I was born. It was the highlight of the day for me. Boogie, who always takes a genuine interest in people, asked my dad questions about his life. I remembered him doing the same thing at BWC, but it gave me the best feeling to see him engaging with my father on a personal level. I was honored to be alongside Boogie all day. He posed for photos, and I served as photographer. Taking a photo of my father with Jimmy Valiant was a symbolic moment for me, an extremely special one that I will always cherish.

My two heroes together: Jimmy Valiant and my father, Robert Higgins—a very special moment

My childhood friend, Rhode Island State Representative Bob Quattrocchi and his wife, Edwina, also stopped by to meet "Handsome" Jimmy.

WHAT A DIFFERENCE A YEAR MAKES

The Boogie Woogie Man visiting the Ocean State

After Fan Fest ended, I took Boogie back to the airport—and just like that, he was on a plane back to Virginia. I knew I would see him again in August for my next trip to BWC to celebrate his birthday.

A strange thing happened in the days following Fan Fest. I started to feel uncomfortable all the time. I became quick to react and had a short fuse. I felt angry on a regular basis. I began to experience conflict at work again. I felt hopeless—and the entire situation baffled me. I had made so much progress with personal growth, but for some reason, I was back at ground zero. My internal voice was telling me that nothing had changed in my life. I started to listen to my inner voice, which was falsely telling me I was kidding myself if I thought I had unlocked any answers to my lifelong problems. My level of discouragement and disappointment was off the charts. Self-help books, *A Course in Miracles,* yoga, therapy, AA meetings, forgiveness, and everything else I had attempted clearly hadn't worked. My thoughts turned to my failed relationship history. After a separation and divorce, I was back on my own again.

That's when I met Betsy. The two of us had many things in common. I remember thinking that with the right woman in my life, my problems with the anguish I felt inside would finally be resolved. But that would not be the case.

Unfortunately, nothing was resolved. In fact, I sank to a new level of depression and anxiety. It was brutal. The decision to resume my search for answers was not a hard one to make. I knew I had to at least try because I'd started to have thoughts of ending it all. The idea of taking my own life returned as a very clear option. I needed to find the answers to my questions. Except this time felt much different. Almost like an hourglass had been turned over at some point, and I was up against the clock to fix myself again. I feared that if I didn't find answers in a timely fashion, I would take drastic action against myself once and for all. The worst part was, I kept all of it inside. I still felt the need to single-handedly resolve my own issues. Although in the past I'd been open to asking for guidance, with the situation feeling this grim, I put up a wall around myself and turned to useless self-help once again. All the while, I never let on to those around me how terrible I was feeling inside.

If you want things to change in life, try doing something different. That's exactly what I did next.

Of the Electric Mary Persuasion

The lyrics for this chapter were selected by Rusty.

I was a blind man
Sitting in the eye of the storm
I waited for a while
Until I thought it was gone
But you came back harder
Than I felt it before
I was down, broken boned
Scattered on the ground
All on my own

———

Electric Mary, "Sorry Baby"

MY FRIENDSHIP WITH THE AUSTRALIAN ROCK BAND Electric Mary's front man, Rusty Brown, continued via social media, phone calls, and Messenger video calls. It seemed unlikely that the Marys would land on American soil anytime soon. I looked forward to talking to my friend on the other side of the planet whenever the opportunity presented itself. We would rank our favorite singers and our favorite wrestlers; it was a nice break from my routine. During one of our conversations, Rusty informed me of three concert dates Electric Mary had scheduled in Australia for the summer of 2019. He reminded me that I once told him that if they were going to play in his neck of the woods, he should let me know so I could try to attend the shows.

I was happy the band would be returning to the stage; they had just taken a year off to finish the album *Mother*. But I didn't know if the timing was right for such a long trip and adventure. A few weeks passed, and the idea of traveling to Oz lost momentum.

One evening, Betsy paid me a visit. She walked into my kitchen and immediately requested we talk. She told me that earlier in the day, she had attended a yoga class in which her teacher had read from the book *A Year of Living Consciously* by Gay Hendricks. The book offers 365 daily inspirations, and the reading for February 20 was titled, "Have an 'Out of Yourself' Experience." Betsy was deeply moved by the reading. She told me that she'd never strayed from her comfort zone and had always played it safe. But she wanted to change that. She wanted to attend the Electric Mary shows. The more she talked, the more convinced I became. I did have a history of taking risks, but that part of my DNA had been dormant for many years. I rarely stepped out of my comfort zone anymore. Suddenly, however, my adventurous nature was waking up, like a bear coming out of hibernation.

"OK, I'm in," I said.

We sat at my kitchen table and booked the trip on my phone. Rusty provided suggestions on where to stay and promised to meet us at the airport upon our arrival. When I confirmed our travel plans, Rusty said, "Grouse." The word is an old-school term used in Melbourne, meaning "cool." He educated me further, explaining that something *very* cool was referred to as "the grouse." This trip qualified as THE GROUSE. A face-to-face meeting with Rusty quickly became a reality.

Betsy and I counted down the months and days until our departure date arrived. Although I had traveled to Japan several times in the past, nothing could have prepared me for the grueling journey that was about to unfold.

We took a short drive to my father's house to catch a ride to the bus station. We said our goodbyes to my dad in the bus terminal parking lot and jumped on a Peter Pan Bus in Providence, which delivered us to Logan Airport in Boston. From there, we would fly to Los Angeles, and then on to Sydney, Australia. Then, after one more short flight, we would finally touch down in Melbourne, Australia. The home of Electric Mary.

One thing was undeniable: Betsy and I were about to learn all about each other. The good, the bad, and the ugly. We had taken trips together in the past, but nothing like this. The flight from Boston to California was a piece of cake compared to the long trip across the Pacific to Oz. We ended up with economy seats even though we had upgraded in advance. Little could be done about it once we'd boarded the plane. Being uncomfortable on a long flight ranks up there with *things that suck the most,* and the impending half-day flight amplified the experience. To complicate matters, I found myself seated next to the only man on the plane who was larger than me. We jousted for elbow room on the slim armrest, with me coming out on top. He spent most of the flight with a blanket draped over his head, like a ghost costume on Halloween.

After the sixteen-hour flight, we landed in Sydney, Australia, wiped out to the max. In the terminal, we limped along to collect our bags and clear customs before heading to our next flight, and ultimate destination—Melbourne. After a lost-luggage ordeal and a missing-passport scare, we finally made it. Welcome, Electric Mary fans, to Australia. The final leg of the journey would be a piece of cake. A short hour-and-a-half flight was all that was left to endure.

Once we were on the ground, it hit me that a face-to-face meeting with Rusty was about to happen. We staggered off the plane into a busy terminal. The seats in the arrivals section were full of travelers. A man sitting off to our left began to clap his hands together in slow motion as he rose to his feet: Rusty. To my surprise, he is quite tall, standing eye to eye with me. I dropped my bags and extended my arm out with my fist facing down and thumb extended to the side. This is the Rusty trademark and his personal tribute to the '70s rock band Slade. It's the same gesture they used in their heyday. He smiled, returning the gesture. I embraced Rusty with a hug. After two years of phone conversations and online banter, we were finally face-to-face. A very emotional moment, one I will never forget. He gave Betsy a big hug, and a kiss as well. Betsy loves Electric Mary as much as I do. She is a superfan. This was a very emotional moment for her too. After all, she'd given me the kick in the ass that I'd needed to make this dream trip happen. Being met at the airport by Rusty was an extra-special experience for us both.

The incomparable Rusty Brown
(Photo courtesy of Chowie Photography)

Rusty completely took over from there. He offered to drive us to our hotel, but I opted for a rental car. I realized later that I should have taken him up on his kind offer. Before we parted ways, Rusty guided us to our hotel in St. Kilda. He is no stranger to the road after years of touring with his band, and he knew we needed to rest. Betsy and I collected our bags and moved on to the rental car office, getting a huge SUV that we really didn't need. It was time for my introduction to driving with a steering wheel on the opposite side of the car. The gearshift is still in the middle, but I kept reaching for it with my right hand, banging my hand into the car door. The turn signal is also on the opposite side of the steering column, causing me to frequently turn on the windshield wipers.

The next day, Electric Mary would take the stage at the infamous Corner Hotel, a venue Rusty had rocked countless times in the past. The Marys are from Melbourne, so that's their home base, and the fans show up in force to support the band.

At the hotel, I presented Rusty with a few T-shirts from America. A Bad Company shirt with the logo from their debut album. A shirt with a pair of brass knuckles on the front. A "Macho Man" Randy Savage shirt from the WCW days. And a Movin' On shirt from a local cover band back in Boston; they are all big fans of Electric Mary. In addition, I gave Rusty a pair of motorcycle goggles with spikes across the top. After a short visit in the parking lot outside the hotel, he left. As he drove off, I looked back to see him wearing the goggles.

I was exhausted but eager to explore St. Kilda. We decided to venture out on foot and walked a few blocks to Acland Street, a busy road filled with shops and restaurants. The train runs in both directions in the middle of the road. We walked along the sidewalk, taking it all in. Birds filled the trees, making loud, unfamiliar sounds. You would have been hard-pressed to find two more touristy-looking people walking the streets of St. Kilda that day. We wanted to eat something other than airline food and decided on Abbey Road Café, a Beatles-themed establishment. The walls there are filled with classic rock 'n' roll memorabilia—not exclusive to the Beatles, but to all music from that era. The place felt perfect for our first meal in Australia. Afterward, we strolled along, completely enjoying our new environment.

Later that night, I made the unwise decision to drive back to the airport by myself to exchange the rental car for a smaller, more affordable one. Having a giant SUV for my first experience in Australia seemed a bit extreme. After all, I'm not Jay-Z. I programmed the navigation device and headed out on my own. I lost internet service quickly and found myself *really* on my own. I attempted a right-hand turn, and to my horror, two lanes of oncoming traffic sped toward me. Right turns aren't permitted on a red light in Australia. I pulled over to the curb to regroup. I sat with my head in my hands for a moment. It occurred to me I'd been awake for over thirty hours and had no business being behind the wheel, regardless of the side of the street I was driving on. There was no reason I couldn't exchange the car the following morning.

I was up and wide awake at 3:00 a.m. and would not be falling back to sleep. Instead, I scrolled through my phone as the sun seeped through the cracks of the hotel curtains. Later that night, I would come to regret the lack of sleep. That day, we ventured out to continue exploring St. Kilda. We poked around, passing time until Rusty returned. Once Rusty joined us, we went back to Abbey Road. An appropriate place to have lunch with a great rock 'n' roll singer. It was wonderful to be face-to-face with a man who, like Jimmy Valiant, had impacted my life in such a positive way. His music had inspired me and quite possibly saved my life. The lyrics he'd penned years ago had helped me to keep my chin up during challenging situations. His songs inspired me to live life on life's terms.

Prior to arriving in St. Kilda, I'd asked Rusty if I could introduce the band if I ever traveled to Australia. I'd also asked him if they would be playing, "The Way You Make Me Feel," the song that mentions yours truly, Knuckles Nelson. "Yes and yes," he'd replied.

While sitting in Abbey Road Café, I scanned the room. With all the Beatles memorabilia around, it felt like I was about to begin a "Magical Mystery Tour" of my own. Rusty told me to go find his photo on the wall, and off I went. I looked high and low, but I could not find him on the wall.

I returned to the table, only to be told, "There *is* no photo of me in here." Uncle Rust Bucket had pulled a fast one on me.

Rusty looked across the table at me and said, "I reckon we should head to the Corner and meet the guys."

Up until then, the only member of the band I'd had direct contact with was Rusty. We stopped by our hotel to retrieve our car, then followed Rusty to the Corner Hotel. Even though I had spent years in wrestling locker rooms with famous people, I felt nervous about meeting the other members of Electric Mary. I hoped I would say the right thing and not make an ass of myself—something I'm very good at doing from time to time. Rusty unexpectedly invited us to the band's sound check, and we eagerly accepted. When we arrived at the Corner Hotel, I took out my camera. Upcoming events are painted on the side of the building in place of a marquee.

The white lettering on the black wall alerts the public to the upcoming schedule. Right smack dab in the middle, it read, "**ELECTRIC MARY — June 29.**" We made our way inside the back door and noticed a busy scene inside, with equipment being moved into place and lots of people milling around. Directly inside the door stood Pete Robinson, longtime guitar player for Electric Mary. Pete is tall and handsome, with long straight black hair and black glasses. He looks like a rock star and backs up his appearance by being as one of the greatest guitar players in the world. Rusty introduced us, and to my surprise, he knew who we were. He very graciously welcomed us to Australia.

He also asked I take it easy on the handshake.

"Not too tight mate," he quietly requested.

It was all I could do to refrain from screaming, "Peteeee Robinsuuuun!" like I'd seen Rusty do in YouTube videos during onstage band introductions.

We walked into the venue, still following Rusty, and met Brett Wood, another tall, handsome guy with a youthful look and laid-back way about him. Brett is also one of the greatest guitar players in the world. An Electric Mary hallmark is that Pete plays right-handed while Brett plays left-handed. What a pleasure to finally meet them both. Next, we met Pete Donegan, not a band member, but a longtime Electric Mary family member. Pete welcomed us to Australia and told us to let him know if we needed anything. Alex Raunjak walked up and introduced himself. If you look up "rocker" in the dictionary, you will find a photo of Alex with one hand in a fist raised overhead, and in the other hand, his well-traveled bass guitar with its chipped and faded paint. With his long black curly hair and intense look, you might not guess he was a new dad to a beautiful baby girl. Once he was done setting up his drums, we met Paul "Spyda" Marrett. Just like everyone else we encountered, Spyda welcomed us. Right away I noticed his Los Angeles Dodgers baseball cap, and I told him that next time, I would bring him a proper Boston Red Sox hat. The entire band made us feel at home and welcome.

Our introductions continued with Mahalia Swinfield. A tall, stunning woman whose job was to take care of everything behind the scenes that makes a rock show unfold. I was impressed with her take-charge attitude. She presented Betsy and me with Electric Mary all-access passes for the tour. I wore the pass around my neck day and night for the duration of my stay. Sound check began right around this time. The entire situation felt like a dream. I was still physically exhausted from travel, but also excited and ready to listen.

Rusty walked over and said, "I'm very glad the both of you are here, and now, not only do you get to see us, you get to *feel* us."

To kick off the sound check, they played one of the band's anthems, "Let Me Out." This song holds a special meaning for me. The words mirror how I felt while going through my divorce. Being in Oz, at the Corner Hotel, and hearing this song created in me a feeling of inner peace. That might sound like a contradiction—feeling peace during a loud rock 'n' roll sound check—but it was exactly what happened. I was standing in front of my favorite band, for the first time, during a private sound check. It doesn't get any better than that. And then, Rusty surprised me.

"Knuckles, come up here," he said.

Without hesitation, I walked to the side of the stage toward the stairs. As my foot hit the first step, the band broke into

"Gasoline & Guns," which I'd first heard on a Spotify playlist. It was the song that had introduced me to Electric Mary two years earlier while I was out riding my Harley-Davidson. The song was so powerful, I pulled the bike to the side of the road to look at my phone to find out who was playing. The rest, as they say, is history.

I walked up the stairs and stepped onstage with my favorite band. I did just as Rusty had requested. I felt it. I felt everything around me. It felt good. It felt powerful. I felt free. He began singing the opening lyrics, "Get on your knees and beg for this." Then he grabbed me around the neck and put the mike up to my mouth, and we sang the song together. The same song that had brought happiness back to my life a few years earlier. It felt surreal and natural at the same time. On the surface, the song may appear to convey a stereotypical macho message, but it has a much deeper meaning. It's thoughtful and honest, like all of Electric Mary's music. The reason the catalog of songs resonates so deeply with me is the lyrics. The songs deliver honest messages about relationships, marriage, divorce, success, failure, and the feelings associated with life on life's terms.

We all have secrets. As I grow older, they become fewer and fewer. Prior to writing this book, I had a doozy of a secret that I'd thought would accompany me to my grave. Before the life-changing experience of meeting my childhood hero, "Handsome" Jimmy Valiant, and now traveling to Oz to go on tour with Electric Mary, I'd had occasional suicidal thoughts. That was my personal deep secret. My mom's passing, my divorce, and everything in between had a domino effect. I could see two completely different paths before me. The path to the right was bright and colorful and full of life. The path to the left was dark. Being left-handed, I felt a pull to the left side, strongly at times. The thought of ending it all was not a regular occurrence. It seemed to have a mind of its own. It would address me in the morning when I woke up, before I'd even opened my eyes. It would come calling at night while I lay in bed, trying to fall asleep. I planned out a few scenarios to execute my dark secret. The one that seemed easiest was to swallow a bottle of sleeping pills.

My conversations with Jimmy Valiant helped me immensely, but I never told him I was having suicidal thoughts. Boogie has a way of accepting life on life's terms. He understands that life will keep going, no matter what he does. He possesses the ability to share his beliefs with others. My across-the-planet conversations with Rusty also helped. Still, it was his music. The music of Electric Mary, that truly saved my ass. From the very first time I heard that very first song, the music touched my soul, and it always will. Rusty knew about my suicidal thoughts because I never held back in our conversations and frequently asked for his advice. It was a deep connection between two madmen on opposite sides of the planet.

The time spent backstage prior to a music show is similar to the time spent in the locker room before a wrestling show. A long wait to walk through the curtain and do your thing. As the support acts took the stage, I grew more excited inside. I was unfamiliar with the opening bands and had no connection to them. We met more beautiful people from the Electric Mary family, including Eric "Chowie" Chow and his partner, Melania Felekidis. They welcomed us and went out of their way to hang out with us during the evening. They offered to let us follow them back to our hotel after the show. I quickly accepted the offer. After my ordeal behind the wheel the day before, the thought of following them home provided me immediate comfort. Chowie is a brilliant photographer. I was already familiar with his work prior to my trip to Australia. He is one of several people I was meeting in person for the first time but already had a connection with, thanks to social media. Chowie's fingerprints are all over this book, featuring several of his amazing photos.

Me with Chowie and Melania

Without warning, my lack of sleep hit me like a ton of bricks. My legs got weak. My vision was blurred. I was struggling to keep my eyes open. These symptoms reminded me of Marty McFly in *Back to the Future,* when he was onstage playing guitar with *Marvin Berry and the Starlighters* while his siblings started to disappear in the photo from the future. I was seriously concerned I might collapse. Aside from a three-hour nap the night before, I had been awake for about thirty hours. With a second band following the opening act about to play a full set before the Marys, I needed to find a way to get it together. I was about to introduce my favorite band and needed to be alert. I staggered back to the dressing room and fell on the couch next to Rusty, bumping directly into him. He noticed me swaying and laughed, asking if I was OK. I said I was fine.

He laughed louder and said, "No you're not, mate. You have jet lag."

I told him I would be fine and got up and wobbled outside for air. I immediately started to practice Ujjayi breathing from my yoga practice. In through the nose and out through the nose. I could hear my teacher, Philip, saying, "If you don't like the way you feel, pay attention to your breathing." It helps every time. I began to regain my composure. I walked around, continuing to breathe in through my nose and out through my nose. In my head, I began to rehearse my band introduction. I thought about how cool it was to have the opportunity to introduce my favorite band in their hometown of Melbourne, Australia. I had no intension of screwing it up. If I did, it was doubtful I would get another opportunity, and instead, be considered a one-and-done. I gave myself a couple of hard slaps across the face and walked back inside. The second band was nearing the end of their set, and then it would be time for the main event. I was kicking around different ideas for my intro. I'd introduced the Boston-based band Movin' On all over New England, so I had plenty of practice. In that moment, the introduction fell into place. I knew exactly what to say.

After a short break following the support bands, it was showtime. The crew closed a large curtain covering the entire stage in preparation for the headliner. I would be introducing the boys from the side of the stage because of the curtain being drawn. Mahalia asked if I was ready.

I said yes and asked her, "This is a special night, isn't it?"

"Yes, it is," she said. She smiled, gave me a hug, and told me to have fun.

The band members walked up the steps to the stage and took their positions behind the drawn curtain. The crowd was ready. I could feel them. Instinctively, I started to bounce back and forth on the balls of my feet like a fighter. The table was set. The pressure was off since I would be on the side of the stage, out of view from the audience. Mahalia gave me my cue, and without hesitation, I said:

> *If you wanted to see*
> *a rock 'n' roll show tonight,*
> *you have come to the right place.*
> *You have made*
> *the right fucking decision*
> *because it is now time for the main event.*
> *But you don't have to take my word for it.*
> *See for yourself.*
> *Please welcome*
> *the greatest show on Earth . . .*
> *ELECTRIC MARY!*

The crowd roared as the curtain opened. I put down the microphone and ran to the front of the stage, moving through a sea of fans to stand with Betsy. She embraced me, and the people around us started patting me on the head and shoulders.

Betsy said, "Everyone knows who we are. I told them you were introducing the band!" That explained why no one had been upset with me for pushing my way to the front of the stage.

The band opened with a short instrumental before bursting into "Let Me Out," one of the most underrated songs in rock 'n' roll history. I prepared myself to sing along. Once the band began playing, Rusty made his way to the stage to a loud ovation. Right on cue, we joined in with the opening lyrics: "Sat on my hands for as long as I can." As soon as the words came out of my mouth, the crowd began to sing along, drowning out everything—including Rusty. A huge smile filled his face as he stepped back from the microphone and welcomed the crowd to sing along. He was dressed in black from head to toe, with his shirt open, exposing his chest. Two necklaces hung down around his neck, and his long dark hair, no longer tied back in a ponytail, fell around his shoulders. The true king of Aussie rock 'n' roll was right where he belonged: onstage in front of his fans. The moment is forever etched in my memory.

Rusty

Electric Mary onstage in Melbourne, Australia

The second number of the evening was "Gimme Love," The first song from the 2019 album *Mother*. Followed by "No One Does It Better Than Me." They then went deep into the catalog, playing "Lies." Then "Gasoline & Guns," which, in my opinion, is the best rock song of all time. (I know "all time" covers the history of music, but that is my honest opinion.) They kept it coming with another new song, "Woman." The first six songs were delivered with an energy and emotion best experienced live. Another song, "Sorry Baby," from the new album came next, allowing Rusty to show off his vocal range. He surprised me at the end with an impromptu chorus of "All Right Now" by Free and "Shooting Star" by Bad Company—a moment in the show that held special meaning for me. I love legendary vocalist Paul Rodgers' music, and to witness Rusty singing those lyrics was a major bonus. Next, they played

"Sweet Mary C." This song is a tribute to Mary Campbell, the woman who'd inspired the name of the band and urged Rusty, as a musician, to follow his path and play the music he wanted to play. They mixed old songs with new, and the crowd recited every word of every song. It was awesome to be a part of it. Whenever I glanced over at Betsy, she was singing, smiling, and completely in the moment. The band continued to rock with another new song, "Hold On to What You Got," followed by the epic "Already Gone." This song highlights the incredible guitar work of Brett and Pete—left-handed and right-handed guitarists. And the next song they played was one of my very favorites, "Long Way From Home (Do Me)." This was the song playing from my motorcycle speakers as I drove down Alleghany Springs Road in Shawsville, Virginia, on my maiden voyage to Boogie's Wrestling Camp. After playing almost a dozen great songs, Rusty took a moment to address the crowd. He explained to everyone that two fans had traveled a great distance to be in attendance—all the way from Boston, Massachusetts, USA. He pointed the two of us out. This was a very unexpected moment.

A Marys welcome
(Photo courtesy of Chowie Photography)

Electric Mary in the zone

Rusty has impeccable timing. I'm not just saying this because he picked us up at the airport on time. After spending time with him, I realized he has a gift. He says the right thing at the right time on a regular basis. Without effort or prior planning, he expresses his feelings honestly and fully in the moment, especially onstage. The next song they played was "The Way You Make Me Feel." This is the song that mentions me, Knuckles Nelson. A wrestling character I'd put to rest twenty years ago had been brought back to life in a song by my favorite band. And now I was about to hear them play it live. Rusty told the crowd that the next song was about the man in attendance from Boston. He told me to raise my hand. Instead, I raised a scarf with "Electric Mary" written on one side and "Rock 'n' Roll the Way It Used to Taste" on the other. I proudly displayed the scarf, receiving a loud ovation from the crowd. I was also recreating a photo

Rusty had posed for once in which he'd held up a scarf in the same manner. I turned 360 degrees, making sure everyone at the Corner Hotel knew whom I was there to represent.

As I lowered the scarf, a woman made her way through the crowd and cried out, "Brendan! I'm Kim!"

I recognized her immediately as my Facebook friend Kim Bencic. Over the past few years, I had friended several people from Australia on Facebook, introducing myself to the Electric Mary fan base and family. I loved the way Kim decided to introduce herself *in the moment.* I felt incredibly in the moment myself. In yoga class, or in personal meditation, I try to stay as in the moment as possible. Inevitably, I drift off and need to try to re-center myself. But staying in the moment during this show was effortless.

The concert provided everything a rock show could possibly deliver. I felt fresh and alert the entire time—a sharp contrast from a few hours earlier, when I was out on my feet. The intensity and energy Electric Mary deliver onstage made it impossible for me to feel fatigued. It wasn't adrenaline. It was being present. Having no thoughts of the past or future enabled me to be exactly where I wanted to be in my mind and body.

Monkey see, monkey do

The final song of the set was "My Best Friend," a true, feel-good sing-along and one of Betsy's favorites. As soon as Pete started to play the opening riff, a positive vibe filled the room. Good feelings danced in the air. It was magical. The crowd, on cue, joined in to sing with Rusty, and away we went: "Ain't it funny how you think that your friendship's gonna last through everything . . . ." To be in Oz, at the Corner Hotel, watching the Marys play this number filled my heart with joy. I stayed in the moment, enjoying every second of it. Toward the end of the song, Rusty left the stage and handed it over to the band to finish up. Spyda gave the crowd a treat with a powerful drum solo. Alex, who seemed to never stop playing and moving about, reminded us what an incredible bass player he is. Then the left- and right-handed guitars had at it—one at a time, then both together, like a rock symphony. The song ended in true Electric Mary style, with a big finish, followed by a massive ovation from the hometown standing-room-only crowd. I stood there soaking it all in, with tears streaming down my face. I looked over at Betsy as she wiped away tears of her own.

The crowd wanted more, and so did I. The boys returned to the stage to another well-deserved ovation. I wondered what they might do for an encore. I'd asked Rusty several times to divulge the set list, but he'd been hush-hush about it. He'd quietly told me, "No, mate, you gotta wait." I fucking love that guy and his timing.

The boys returned to the stage after a short rest in the back. Then the unmistakable sound of "OIC" started to play, and the roof came off the Corner Hotel. When playing live, Rusty hits every note the same way he does on his albums, and this number was no exception. Toward the end of the song, Rusty delivered the final lyrics: "Pretty young thing, seen 'em all, step up here, and take your best shot." He then repeated the lines with great emotional intention before leaving the stage again and handing it over to the band to rip it up once and for all. The song continued with another solid instrumental. When it was over, Rusty returned to the stage, and he and the rest of the band members waved goodbye to the hometown crowd.

As they say, all good things must come to an end. The crowd was eager for another song, but the houselights came up. The show was over. Luckily for *us*, though, the night was just getting started. After the show, the scene included the band coming out to the merchandise area to sign vinyl, CDs, and T-shirts. The adoring faithful waited patiently in line, and everyone left happy. This band has always been fully aware of their responsibility to their fans. They take time to connect with them on a personal level. They make sure everyone gets an autograph and a photo.

The after-party was similar to a wrestling after-party. The band would not be sleeping anytime soon. It would take them a while to wind down from what they'd just unleashed on the audience. Once they had returned to the dressing room, their family members and friends made their way in to mingle. One of the highlights of the night was when two of Rusty's daughters (both with movie-star looks) walked in and hugged their dad. They told him how proud they were of him. I could see in his eyes that he was even prouder of them. For a moment, rock star took a back seat to proud father.

Betsy and I sat in the dressing room, enjoying the after-party. We conversed with everyone there. The friendly atmosphere was much needed for me. My battery felt fully recharged—for the moment, anyway. The band members spoke among themselves, reflecting on the evening's performance. The feedback appeared to be quite positive. That evening was nothing short of magical.

The set list and all-access passes from the show

The band liked my Electric Mary–tribute tattoo.

As promised, Chowie and Melania escorted us back to our hotel in St. Kilda. We turned into the hotel parking lot, beeping the horn (at least the horn was in the same place on the steering wheel as it was back home) and waving as they drove off into the night. We went up to the room and fell into the bed, neither of us speaking a word. I drifted off into a peaceful sleep, but I woke up in the early morning hours. Tears streamed down past my temples as I lay on my back. I was in a state of tranquility. Completely in the moment. One year earlier, I had traveled by motorcycle to Virginia to visit Jimmy Valiant, and the experience had changed my life. Now I was in Australia with Rusty and the life-changing evolution continued. I fell back to sleep in total bliss.

Sunday morning, we found ourselves on our own for the day. Our first order of business was to locate a yoga studio. We easily found one that was walking distance from the hotel. Ihana Yoga Studio is right in the heart of Acland Street on the second floor of a small shopping mall. For twenty-five dollars each, we were allowed to drop in for a class, which was taught by a pleasant yogi named Paul. His style felt similar to what I was used to, but the room was not heated. I enjoyed the class and found it to be a great start to our day of sightseeing.

We then decided to venture into the city of Melbourne to see the famous street art, and, of course, AC/DC Lane, a short street in the central business district of the city, dedicated to the world-famous Australian rock band. The paintings and sculptures of the legendary lead singer, Bon Scott, touched my heart. He has always been one of my favorite musicians, especially during my teenage years. The walkway displays artwork featuring many other musicians including Frank Zappa; Jimi Hendrix; the Rolling Stones; Rage Against the Machine; Led Zeppelin; and a personal favorite, Swan Song Records, the label of Bad Company and Led Zeppelin. It appears that the canvas is ever-changing. Artists were hard at work putting fresh paint on the wall as we explored the area. We navigated the city on foot. As it is for me with most cities, I'd had my fill by the end of the day. The following morning, we would be treated to a more personal tour.

Rusty joined us for breakfast at our hotel on Monday morning. He had cleared his schedule for us, and asked what we wanted to do. This would be our last day in St. Kilda. We were planning to go to Sydney to spend a few days there before the band arrived for their next gig, which would be at the Factory Theatre. I told Rusty that Betsy wanted to see some koala bears and kangaroos. Rusty rolled his eyes and without warning, moved behind me, applying a sleeper hold to my head and neck. This created a minor stir in the restaurant area, especially among the children in attendance. The kids observed the impromptu wrestling exhibition with wide eyes. Rusty released the hold and switched to a traditional standing headlock. By this time, the kids were laughing hard. He then suggested we visit the zoo in Sydney.

We told him about the time we'd spent in the city, and he offered to show us another side of Melbourne. He also offered to drive. I gladly accepted. Our first stop was Northside Harley-Davidson, a dealership featuring a motorcycle museum of unique old racing bikes. We toured both the dealership and the museum, buying a few shirts to add to my already overstocked Harley-Davidson T-shirt collection. I made a point to take a photo of every bike on display to send to my buddy and motorcycle mentor, Bob Quattrocchi, back in Rhode Island.

Next, we drove to Brunswick Street. This was the place we'd been looking for all along. A street lined with shops, restaurants, vintage clothing stores, and music venues. We parked the car and received a firsthand view of a day in Fitzroy. We walked and talked. Rusty explained the history of just about everything we strolled past. As we walked by storefront windows, people came outside, eager and excited to say hello to Rusty. We decided to have lunch at a lovely establishment called Naked for Satan. A multilevel building with a rooftop bar and restaurant called Naked in the Sky. Every seat offered a view of the city. Our rock 'n' roll fantasy continued.

A walk down Brunswick Street

Over lunch, Rusty told us about his band *before* Electric Mary. It was called Mr. Brown. I was familiar with the album *Four Foot Head,* and I'd found it so vastly unlike Electric Mary. I asked Rusty why it was so drastically different. He explained that he had a few sides to his musical personality. He is rock 'n' roll down to the blood flowing through his veins, but there is a pop side that he loves to this day. Rusty went on to explain that between 1992 and 2002, he'd been besotted with anything to do with the Beatles. For three of those years, he had listened exclusively to the Beatles and anything that resembled them. Then, around 2002, he'd started writing songs a little heavier, but with the Beatles still at the forefront of whatever he did. It was actually a friend of his, Stephen "Bambi" Daniel, who'd asked, out of the blue, why Rusty didn't write songs like the ones they'd grown up on. It was those very words that had led Rusty down the path to founding what would eventually become Electric Mary. It gave me goose bumps when Rusty said, "The Marys are the only band where the pieces continually fit in the puzzle for me." Rusty also decided to revisit the music he listened to in his youth. The band Deep Purple has always been his love. It's literally the rock 'n' roll that covers his skin. He went back to what he was doing at fourteen years old. He said it felt comfortable to wear that style again. He just needed a partner for his new direction, and in stepped Pete Robinson.

Rusty told us the fascinating story of meeting Mary Campbell, the manager of Jimi Hendrix's Electric Lady Studios in New York City, and how she'd had an immediate impact on him: He was in the States, on tour with guitarist Irwin Thomas, an American-born Australian singer-songwriter and former member of Electric Mary. Rusty was playing bass in his band. They did a few showcases for the album *The Evolution of Irwin Thomas*. One night, Rusty was asked if he wanted to take a tour of Jimi Hendrix's studio the following day, an offer he originally said no to because he was not thinking clearly at that moment. But when he woke up the following morning, he reconsidered, telling himself, *Of course I'm going!* He was greeted at the door by Mary Campbell, who had been managing the studio for the previous two decades. As they walked, Mary told him stories of the rich history of the studio. When they arrived at Live Room A, Mary said that this was where Lennon and Bowie had written "Fame." The hairs on the back of Rusty's neck stood at attention as he realized the historic significance of his surroundings. She pointed to the spot where the piano had stood for Stevie Wonder's album *Fulfillingness' First Finale* and where Guns N' Roses recorded "November Rain" years later. The name-dropping continued as she ran down some of the acts that had graced the studio over the years: the Who, the Kinks, Bad Company, Kiss, Radiohead, AC/DC, Foreigner, and the Rolling Stones. The list went on and on. Before Rusty departed the studio, Mary handed him her business card. She told him to stay in touch. She pointed to the card and said, "That's me, down at the bottom." It read, "Electric Mary." As he saw the words printed on the card, Rusty thought, *What a great name for a band.* In Rusty's own words, "And so it began."

It was such a pleasure to be sitting in a local eatery with my friend—a charismatic one-of-a-kind individual. Without realizing it, he had just provided me with yet another incredible memory to take home. After we finished lunch, the tour continued. We cruised the Melbourne Grand Prix course around Albert Park. Rusty's phone rang more that afternoon than mine does in a week. At one point, he received a call from one of his longtime mates. He put the call on speaker so we could hear. Rusty's friend gave him some feedback he'd heard from the Electric Mary show we had just attended. He told Rusty he'd heard the show was *grouse*. We sat in silence as he went on to say, "I heard there were some Americans in the crowd, and they were here having a look at you." Rusty looked over at me and smiled as he casually replied, "Yeah, man," never revealing we were in the car with him. We kept rolling down the road, listening to Ritchie Kotzen, the Bee Gees, and other artists. This was just another ride down a street Rusty had traveled routinely for years, but for me, it was quite special. Receiving a personal tour from Rusty was the best way to conclude our time in Melbourne. If I had simply attended the Electric Mary show and enjoyed a brief meet and greet with the band, this trip still would have qualified as the time of my life. But the personal interaction with Rusty made for a once-in-a-lifetime experience.

When we returned to the hotel, I thanked Rusty for his hospitality and told him that the concert the night before was the best show I had ever attended.

Rusty looked down and, in a humble tone, said, "Thank you, mate."

It was true. I have a long list of impressive concerts I've attended since the 1970s, and Electric Mary had catapulted to the top of that list the night I'd introduced them at the Corner Hotel in 2019.

The next day, we flew to Sydney. We stayed at a hotel next to the airport. We quickly learned to navigate public transportation, purchasing an Opal card, which allowed us to access trains, buses, and the ferry. We explored the city and made a stop at Taronga Zoo, where Betsy finally had her time with kangaroos and koala bears. At first, I had little interest in visiting the zoo, but it turned out to be one of the highlights of our stay in Sydney. It takes an entire day to properly explore it, and the experience ranked near the top of the list of fun activities during our "Magical Mystery Tour."

We located another yoga studio, where we decided to start our second day in the Emerald City. Modo Yoga is a beautiful space, offering everything I love about yoga. Our friendly teacher, Thy, led us in a challenging session of hot yoga.

After three days on our own, Electric Mary rolled into town. The Factory Theatre was to be the venue for the next gig. Rusty informed me we could ride to sound check with the band. In fact, our hotel sat right across the street from the band's hotel. We piled into the van with Brett, Spyda, and Rusty. I had no interest driving in a city of five million people. Once again, I felt free and eternally grateful for the VIP treatment. Once we arrived at the building, I started unloading equipment. In wrestling circles, carrying someone's gear is a sign of respect. I told each member of the band that I'd carry their gear anytime, a gesture they seemed to appreciate. Helping the band invade the venue made me feel more and more like Electric Mary family. When the doors opened, I met another friend from Facebook, Leanne Blundell. A tall blonde Australian rock 'n' roll girl. Her lovely personality was exactly as I'd come to know online. It was fun meeting her in person after our long-term social media correspondence, and we made plans to have dinner with her in Brisbane the following day.

Prior to the show, we met Virginia Lillye from the band Lillye. She seemed very mellow and unassuming, and confessed that she was feeling under the weather. However, once she took the stage, her demeanor changed into that of a strong, sexy rock goddess. Her vocal range sent chills down my spine. Her stage presence is undeniable. Lillye rocked the foundation of the Factory Theatre, setting the stage for the main event: Electric Mary.

  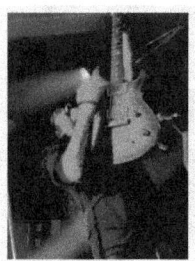 

Thank you, Rusty and the entire Electric Mary family, for the time of my life.

A standing-room-only crowd was there to see Australia's top rock 'n' roll band return to Sydney after a short absence. I must have delivered a satisfactory introduction at the Corner Hotel, because they let me do it again in Sydney. For the introduction, I once again stood on the side of the stage, hidden from the crowd. The show itself was amazing. The band picked up right where they'd left off in Melbourne. The crowd was into the show from beginning to end. They played the same set as in Melbourne. Rusty repeated his announcement about our having traveled from America to see our favorite band. The crowd reacted the same way, offering high fives and pats on the back. The only disappointing moment in the show came at the end of the night when, due to a time constraint, the Marys did not perform an encore. After the show, I got back to work loading equipment into the van as the boys signed vinyl records and took photos with the fans.

On the ride back to the hotel, I could see the trip coming to an end. It occurred to me there was only one gig left. I felt sad to think about this coming to an end, but more than anything else, I was grateful for the experience. I continued to stay present and in the moment as best I could.

The following morning, we caught an early flight to Brisbane for the third and final show. To our pleasant surprise, we were on the same flight as the band. I walked down the aisle—past the members of Electric Mary—wearing their T-shirt and holding up my all-access pass for all to see. To put it in wrestling terms, I was really *marking out* for these guys, and I loved every minute of it.

We landed in Brisbane and went directly to our hotel. Our friend Leanne offered to drive us to our scheduled dinner date before heading to the Zoo—the venue for our final night in Australia. At this "zoo," there would be no kangaroos or koala bears to cuddle, only rock 'n' rollers listening to rock 'n' roll the way it used to taste. Rusty told us to enjoy our dinner and catch up with him later. Leanne and her friend Evie, another Electric Mary faithful, graciously picked us up at the hotel, and we drove to the city of Brisbane. As we had just landed a few hours earlier, the city was a complete mystery to me. I had some knowledge of Melbourne, St. Kilda, and Sydney prior to my visit because I'd watched a lot of YouTube videos and have many Facebook friends from Melbourne.

Brisbane was a complete wild card. We soon learned the girls were not overly familiar with Brissie either. We found ourselves driving around an electric city (no pun intended) full of nightlife and culture. At every turn, we found the streets filled with fabulous people dressed to the nines. As nightfall arrived, we became mildly concerned in our attempt to find the venue. It seemed fitting the final show was being held at a place called the Zoo.

Then Electric Mary found us. Amid the hustle and bustle of the city, I heard a familiar sound: the unmistakable guitarwork of Pete Robinson.

As the four of us sat in traffic, I said, "Listen. Do you hear that?" We all fell silent. "It's 'Gasoline & Guns.' It's Electric Mary."

I thought we had missed sound check, but I was wrong. We were right in the middle of it. The entire moment felt surreal. We all erupted like teenagers, yelling and screaming. We found a parking garage and made our way to the upper levels, searching for an open space. Leanne had done a great job of getting us to the show.

Music filled the streets like a tidal wave coming onshore, flooding every inch of breathable air and consuming everything in its path. We got out of the car and stood in the parking garage (or *car park,* as it's called in Oz) just as they started to play "The Way You Make Me Feel." Right on cue, Rusty sang, "I'm gonna move you onto Knuckles, gonna see what he can do for me." We walked outside, and I looked up to see all the windows in the building wide open. I screamed, "RUSTY!" as we walked under the windows. This was a moment the four of us shared and will always remember.

Once I was inside the building, the show seemed to sneak up on me. In the back of my mind, I kept thinking that this was going to be the end of our rock 'n' roll fantasy for a while. I wanted to stay in the moment. I wanted to enjoy the show. Rusty had become a close friend of mine on this trip. I'd quickly embraced the idea of being around him on a regular basis, only to have reality return on this final night of the trip.

At one point before the show began, he looked at me and said, "I keep thinking I'm going to see you tomorrow."

I knew exactly how he felt.

Rusty was planning to head to another engagement after the show, so we would have to say our goodbyes in a few short hours. But before then, there was still the business of a rock 'n' roll show. I asked Rusty if I could introduce them *onstage* this time, instead of from the side and out of sight.

He looked at me with a straight face and said, "No."

Slightly annoyed, I asked, "Why not?"

He said, "Mate, you have a head like an old shoe."

I rolled my eyes and walked away. As I mentioned earlier, Rusty has a way with words.

When it came time for the band to take the stage, Rusty looked at me and said, "Do you really want to introduce us onstage?"

"Yes!" I replied.

He nodded, gesturing toward the rest of the band, already in position, and said, "Well, go ahead then." he said.

I walked up the stairs and onto the stage. From behind the microphone, I looked down at Betsy and Leanne and the rest of the crowd in attendance. In that moment, I was experiencing more gratitude than I'd ever felt before. I felt like I belonged with this group of people. We all love this band. It's not a *I'm kinda into them* feeling, it's an all-in emotional state. Pete Robinson gave me the nod to introduce the band, and I drew a complete blank. I couldn't remember anything I'd planned to say, and the guys were ready for me and my old-shoe head to get off the stage. Then this came out of my mouth:

> *I have traveled a long distance to be here tonight,*
> *from Boston, Massachusetts,*
> *because I love this fucking band!*
> *I have a question:*
> *Are you ready?*
> *Oh, maybe you didn't hear me. I said,*
> *ARE . . . YOU . . . READY?*
> *Because it is now time for*
> *the main event.*
> *You don't have to take my word for it;*
> *see for yourself.*
> *The main event is upon us.*
> *Please welcome*
> *Golden Robot recording artists*
> *ELECTRIC MARY!*

I walked off the stage to find Rusty standing at the foot of the stairs. We hugged, and I told him how much the entire experience meant to me. He didn't speak a word. He looked at me and put his hand on my face. Then he walked onstage. I made my way through the crowd to enjoy the show as a fan. Everyone in attendance stood and watched a phenomenal evening of music. I decided to video the final song of the set, "My Best Friend." While I recorded the song, I wished I'd captured more from the three gigs. The truth is, I'd been too busy enjoying the shows to hold a camera. They finished the song in a slightly different way than they had during the previous two performances—this time, with a bit more extended jamming. It was clear the lads were enjoying themselves. They left the stage to a thunderous ovation. I told the band prior to their taking the stage that if they did not perform an encore, the crowd would riot. They did not disappoint. They returned to perform "OIC" and, again, extended the song at the end.

We felt no rush to leave the building after the show. We hung out and spent our final hours with our Electric Mary family and friends. I enjoyed watching people spend time with the band members as they signed memorabilia for fans. Spending time with fans is very important in any industry. I learned to be as outgoing as possible with fans during my wrestling days because without them, all you really have is an empty venue.

I made so many friends in Australia. I became part of the Electric Mary family. I extended invitations to all of them to visit me in America. From the moment we landed in Melbourne all the way up to this moment, the adventure had surpassed anything I could have imagined. Betsy and I wanted to find the right time and the right words to say farewell, as everyone had shown us so much love. We spent a few minutes expressing our feelings with each individual member of the band. Betsy

OF THE ELECTRIC MARY PERSUASION

cried tears of joy as she hugged and kissed everyone goodbye. Make no mistake about it: this is Betsy's family too.

Then it was time for us to address Rusty.

He sat in a small group of family and friends. I felt very emotional as I approached him. We didn't say anything. Then we hugged and I told him I loved him. He told me the trip was meant to be. I knew we would see each other again someday.

Rusty hugged Betsy and said, "Love you, Miss Elizabeth."

Betsy turned to me as she wiped away tears, and whispered, "I don't want to leave." I knew exactly how she felt.

Then we turned and began to walk away. I managed to get about ten feet before turning back and calling to Rusty. He looked over, and I extended my arm with my hand in a fist, palm down, thumb out. He returned the gesture. We walked toward each other until our knuckles met. We both smiled. I hugged my brother from another mother one more time. We left the Zoo and stood on the sidewalk in Brisbane. The streets were mobbed with people. A much younger crowd was just coming out to begin their evening. We told Leanne we would take an Uber back to our hotel.

We would be coming home to America with plenty of keepsakes: A poster from the show in Sydney. An all-access pass. A drumstick signed by Spyda that read, "Knuckles, One in a Million," "One in a Million" being the title of an Electric Mary song. A beautiful Electric Mary scarf with which to keep warm during cold winter weather or to just show off. Plus, hundreds of photos. The best things I brought home from Australia, without a doubt, were the life experience and memories.

After returning home from any traveling experience, I always feel like a new person. Everyone back home is basically the same; they're still going about their daily routines. Travel expands the boundaries of my life. It provides me with a spiritual feeling that I try to maintain. Unfortunately, it usually falls away once I return to work.

This trip will remain in my heart always. The time I spent in Australia brought me a new level of awareness. At times it reminded me of the television show *Fringe*. Two universes in which many things are the same, yet completely different. That was the way Australia felt to me. Thank you, Rusty, Pete, Alex, Brett, and Spyda. You could never know how much you mean to me.

The following morning, we boarded a plane to LAX.

Sharing a moment with Rusty
(Photo courtesy of Johnny D Photography)

Pomp and Extenuating Circumstance

Living high small dreams
Stand up off your knees
You can have anything you want
If you believe
Open up, speak to me
Wipe away your history
It's been a long time, been a long time

Electric Mary, "It's Alright"

I RETURNED TO THE UNITED STATES JET-LAGGED TO THE max after two long flights. I'd had the experience of a lifetime. But as soon as I got home, I began to feel strange. And soon, my life would return to its usual state of emotional confusion. My little buddy, Friday, was happy to see me. Anytime I see my cat, he offers me a break from the mental health merry-go-round. But Friday's comfort only lasted a few moments. I had a feeling of great loss. Betsy had just left. *It's probably just codependency,* I thought. After all, if you look up the definition of codependent in the dictionary, you will find a photo of me waving back at you.

To compound matters further, without any warning, the thought of killing myself reentered my mind. The fact that this had happened so quickly dumbfounded me. I'd hoped my euphoric condition from the trip to Oz would last a bit longer before disappearing, like it always does after I travel. You would think I had some credit built up after the incredible adventure I'd just lived through. Unfortunately, my trip Down Under had not provided the answers to my questions. They remained in the category of *yet to be revealed.* I knew the answers must exist, but they kept eluding me.

My mind began to search for the next idea that might bring me some relief from my thoughts. Seeking out both my childhood hero and the singer from my favorite rock band would be difficult to top. I felt like I was sitting on a spaceship, looking out the window, hoping someone would just take me home. It would be one thing if I had never tried to find answers—if I had continued drinking and drugging my way through life. If I hadn't taken up yoga. If I hadn't read every self-help book under the fucking sun trying to understand what was wrong with me. But I *had* done the work. I'd tried and tried and searched and searched and traveled around the world—only to be right back in Rhode Island feeling suicidal. With no immediate solution in mind, I did the best I could and returned to day-to-day life. Keep in mind, ignoring these feelings is not a good idea. It's important to get help if you have suicidal thoughts, especially if you think you could actually go through with it.

A month after my trip to Oz, Electric Mary performed in Australia again before embarking on a world tour. Here in America, I was hard at work driving a bus in downtown Providence at 8:00 a.m. when my phone began to light up. My Electric Mary family had decided to let me know they were about to take the stage. In Melbourne, it was Friday night, and the venue, SS&A Albury, stood primed and ready to rock. First, Leanne Blundell sent a video of the preshow festivities, panning the camera around the room as everyone said a big hello. Next, Yvonne "Evie" Johnson went live, giving me and anyone else watching on Facebook the opportunity to witness Electric Mary doing what they do best: "Rock 'n' roll the way it used to taste." Some good old-fashioned, take-no-prisoners rock 'n' roll momentarily raised my spirits. Being *of the Electric Mary persuasion* has its privileges.

The next adventure on my summer itinerary was returning to Boogie's Wrestling Camp. I was planning to return one year to the day of my epic motorcycle trip to meet Jimmy Valiant. But an unexpected obstacle came up prior to the trip. I came down with pneumonia for the second time in two years. This illness felt just as crippling as it had the first time. I found myself bedridden and unable to work or practice yoga. My inner voice was telling me that this would probably be the way I'd check out of this world. It occurred to me that I wouldn't have to worry about flipping my own switch if pneumonia got me first. The sickness felt that intense. Eventually, I made a full recovery.

I felt a full-circle scenario unfolding with my upcoming visit to Virginia. So much had happened during the past year, and I was ready to return to BWC. I warned myself that going back to Virginia might not have the magical feeling the initial trip provided. I drove to Richmond to meet up with Jeff Katz. We were going to ride to BWC together. It would be a great opportunity for us to converse along the two-hundred-mile ride from Richmond to Boogieland. When I arrived in Richmond, he broke the news of a death in his family that would prevent him from coming with me to BWC. This development quickly changed the dynamics of my visit. I offered my condolences, understanding why Jeff had to back out, but I was also disappointed that we would not be spending the day together.

Sunday morning, before leaving Richmond, I returned to River City Diner, eager to see the waitress and staff from the previous year. My first visit to the diner was magical. This year, I found all new employees in the busy restaurant. I sat down to order breakfast, but it just didn't feel right. My self-warning that this visit to the diner probably wouldn't compare to last year's visit was right on the money. Trying to recreate last year's diner experience would not be possible. I scanned the menu and realized I had lost my appetite. I got up from the table and walked out of the diner. I never spoke a word and began the two-hundred-mile journey to BWC.

We celebrated Boogie's and Angel's birthdays as planned. Some new students, along with veterans, worked out in the ring for a solid four hours. After practice, a group of us gathered for the celebratory dinner at a local Chinese restaurant, including Brien Powell a.k.a. "Magnet Man"; his son, "Little Magnet"; Captain Joe; and, of course, Boogie and Angel. Boogie told me over dinner that he wanted to give me an honorary degree from BWC. I felt proud to accept his offer and made plans to return in the fall for graduation. After dinner, I drove through the night back to Rhode Island.

I had more events planned to help distract me from the sick thought returning to rear its ugly head. Even though I seemed to slide back down the mountain every time I made some progress climbing up, I realized that 2019 had still been a banner year for change and growth. I continued trying to keep my heart open for the future. The highlight of the summer was my brother Jeff's wedding. In August, he married the love of his life, Kindra. This wedding ranks as my favorite of all time. The ceremony required no dress code, a welcome decision for a humid summer day. In addition, there was an open bar—which I would have taken full advantage of in my drinking days. The menu included clam cakes and chowder (an Ocean State staple), barbecued steak, chicken, and corn on the cob, as well as corn bread and salad. The meal was topped off with dessert from a Ben and Jerry's ice cream station.

All of that took a back seat to the ceremony itself. I sat in the front row and watched my brother and his beautiful bride exchange wedding vows. Kindra looked both radiant and relaxed. Her sister, Naydeen, who was her maid of honor, stood by her side in a stunning dress, along with her two children and Jeff and Kindra's daughter. On the groom's side stood three handsome men. The groom, of course, and his best man, my brother Kevin, along with Jeff's son.

Family and friends gathered overlooking a lake to witness the emotional event. I will never forget the look in both of their eyes as they recited their sincere vows. The deep love shared between them was evident to everyone in attendance. I felt so much pride and love watching the ceremony. Having my entire family there was special. All my cousins and many close longtime family friends turned out in force. We all missed my mother, but knew she was smiling down on the celebration. This day was a reminder of what is most important in life.

Summer began to wind down, but I had one more weekend of rock 'n' roll on deck. On August 23, British rockers Bad Company were going to return to Rhode Island for the first time since 1979.

I had attended my first of many Paul Rodgers concerts over forty years prior to this upcoming show. I went to the show alone, as I'd been unable to find any friends interested in tagging along. That gig, in 1979, took place in the Providence Civic Center during a different era for concerts. People smoked pot freely in the arena back then. The restrooms were filled with scary-looking characters selling acid, THC, and mescaline. God only knows what they were *really* selling back then. A man sitting behind me smuggled in a couple of fine wines in his boots—in one, Boone's Farm Strawberry Hill, and in the other, Mad Dog 20/20. He shared his bounty with everyone around him. We all sipped from the same straw while smoking pot together. Security was nonexistent. Once the show got underway, all hell broke loose. Fans became rowdy inside the building. On the floor, in front of the stage, people began pushing and shoving, creating a sealike motion in the crowd. This chaos unfolded long before mosh pits became the fashion. Guitar player Mick Ralphs addressed the crowd, asking them to calm down. He said something to the effect of, "This isn't England, you know," implying that concert fans tended to get rowdy in his homeland. Paul Rodgers also pleaded with the crowd to tone it down. I watched highly intoxicated people falling to the floor and passing out. They couldn't possibly remember anything the next day. After the show, more chaos ensued in the streets of Providence. Fights broke out. Groups of completely wasted people vandalized property and automobiles. I had no interest in participating in what was going on around me. This was just prior to my entering the heavy-drinking and -drugging stage of my life. I recall being quite scared watching the zombie-like people wreak havoc. My agenda had been simply to see my favorite singer, Paul Rodgers, perform. Fortunately, I managed to avoid conflict with my fellow concertgoers. My father picked me up outside the building after the show. He was plenty disgusted with the scene unfolding in the city.

The following day, the then-mayor of Providence, Vincent "Buddy" Cianci Jr., declared this would be the last *acid rock* concert in his city. Acid rock? There was one glaring problem with Buddy's announcement: Bad Company does not fall into the category of acid rock. They have some of the most beautiful songs in classic-rock history. I doubt the band knew about the shenanigans that had unfolded after the show, having already left town for their next destination.

The surviving original members of Bad Company would not return to Rhode Island together as a band until 2019. Due to health issues, guitarist Mick Ralphs was unavailable for the tour. Howard Leese, a longtime member of Bad Company and Paul Rodgers's solo band, assumed the role of lead guitarist, along with Todd Ronning on bass and Simon Kirke on drums. It was rewarding for me to attend this show because of my allegiance to the band. I sat in the front row to witness rock 'n' roll royalty in action. This was my thirty-ninth Paul Rodgers concert since 1979.

From Bad Company, the Firm, and the Law to countless solo shows, a Bad Company reunion in 1999, and, of course, his time with Queen, Paul Rodgers had always put on a tremendous performance. He has the perfect voice. In fact, he's called "The Voice" by his loyal fans. Somehow, he seems to grow younger as time marches on.

It was a treat for me to hear the iconic tunes played live once again. Over the years, the crowd has morphed into part of the show, singing in unison to songs like "Shooting Star," "Can't Get Enough," "Rock 'n' Roll Fantasy," and, of course, the band's anthem, "Bad Company." At the end of the show, the thought crossed my mind that this could be the last time Paul Rodgers would tour. The realization made me stop in my tracks. Then I thought, *No way; he'll be back next year.* On and on we ride.

In September, I traveled back to Virginia to attend Boogie's Wrestling Camp's twenty-seventh graduation and receive my honorary degree. I no longer required navigation. I made a pit stop at the Dixie Caverns, which has become a tradition for me. Alongside the gift shop, there is a giant indoor flea market. I love my flea markets, and this one in particular is a goldmine.

As I walked inside, my friend and owner of the establishment, Billy, said "Knuckles Nelson!" from behind the counter. During each trip to Shawsville, I stop and buy something to support this local business—usually a Harley-Davidson sign or something else that catches my eye. Billy always offers a story about Boogie and asks that I say hello to him. Alleghany Springs Road is just a short drive from the caverns. I remembered that first trip to BWC, just one year earlier: Riding my Harley, taking the twists and turns at a low speed in the hot August heat. How the Electric Mary song "Long Way From Home (Do Me)" started to play through my speakers as I turned onto the rural road. How I stopped at the foot of the property, looking up at the complex before proceeding up the steep driveway to meet Boogie.

This year's visit found the road and driveway lined with cars and trucks. After finding a parking spot, I walked up the driveway and then the stairs. Well over a hundred people were milling about. I could hear wrestling practice taking place in the main building. A friendly vibe filled the air. I went inside and said hello to everyone. Angel appeared from the crowd and greeted us. I could see Boogie on the other side of the ring, holding court with his people, and I knew that in time, I would have my turn to say hello. In the meantime, I caught up with old and new family members, including head trainer Shawn Christian, Dee Moody, Brien Powell, Dennis Warren, Mike Mars, and world-renowned manager Captain Joe. In addition, I made the acquaintance of the first-ever BWC student, Frank "The Tank" Parker.

Jeff Katz had driven down from Richmond to attend the graduation ceremony. With Jeff in attendance, I felt like the whole family was there. Once Boogie moved closer, we greeted him. His warmth and love never seems to wane. He makes time for every single person in his space. At times, he appears tired but remains available for questions and listens to stories from people who ask him if he remembers meeting them for a brief moment twenty years ago. With his amazing memory, Boogie always remembers the meetings.

The day's lineup included the graduation ceremony, followed by a series of wrestling matches. For the first time in almost two decades, I wanted to wrestle. However, I quickly changed my mind. Instead, I asked Boogie if I could serve as a referee for one of the matches. He smiled and said, "Of course you can, brother." Boogie asked if I had seen the banner with my name on it for the class of 2019. I walked to one of the museum buildings, and to my surprise, they had put my real name, Brendan Higgins, on the banner. I loved it.

Boogie keeps a close eye on the time during hours of operation, making sure his scheduled events move along. He entered the ring with Angel to hand out the 2019 diplomas. One by one, students entered the ring to be recognized for their accomplishment of graduating from Boogie's Wrestling Camp. Once the diplomas were distributed, "Handsome" Jimmy Valiant, my childhood hero, stood in the ring with one final certificate to present. Boogie told everyone that I had traveled all the way from Rhode Island and then welcomed me to join him and the class of 2019 in the ring. I glanced over at Jeff Katz, and we shared a smile. I spontaneously decided to jump over the top rope to enter the squared circle, but I wasn't sure if I could actually do it. After all, it had been almost twenty years since I'd last attempted the jump. I stepped onto the ring apron and jumped over the top rope with ease. I embraced Boogie and told him I loved him. What had begun the day I met him in Rhode Island—when he extended his invitation to visit BWC—had continued right through that moment, forming a circle in my life that was now complete.

After the ceremony, it was time for some wrestling action. Boogie gave me the option to referee the match of my choosing. I like to go on first, so I picked the opening contest. "The Stache" came to the ring with his protégé Rex Keller—a large man who reminded me of Crusher Blackwell. His opponent was BJ Connor, a good-looking young athlete giving up size and strength in this contest. The match went well, with BJ chalking up a hard-fought victory. It felt good being back in the ring, and I enjoyed every second of the match. Several more matches rounded out the afternoon of wrestling. At 4:00 p.m., BWC closed after another successful day of interactive wrestling action. It's said that one never fully graduates from wrestling school, but on that day, I did.

They say you never fully graduate from wrestling school, but on this day, I did.

BWC Class of 2019

POMP AND EXTENUATING CIRCUMSTANCE

BWC4LIFE

The Universe Speaks

I got a little bit of something
You got a little bit of everything
You better dig a little deeper
Cause you're just not getting it
I got a little bit of you
You got a little bit of me
I want to paint a bigger picture
But you're just not listening

Electric Mary, "Long Way From Home (Do Me)"

After the BWC graduation ceremony, I returned to Rhode Island. Almost immediately, I sustained another emotional crash, but this one was unlike any I had experienced before. There was a definite progression of whatever this was. Just like after my return from Australia, the boom was lowered right away. I resumed with the amplified feelings of resentment, rage, dishonest behavior, isolation, overlapping thoughts, indecision, bad decisions, sex addiction, and the desire to end my own life. I had no idea where any of this emotional chaos was coming from. My mind raced constantly, and I had trouble making simple decisions. When I finally did make a decision, it was usually a bad one. I felt complete and utter despair. All this, I kept to myself, adding to an already solid level of confusion. After all the credible advice, wisdom, and experience that had been passed along to me by people I held in such high regard, from literally all over the world, how could this be happening? Especially considering that all that advice passed on to me had a proven and effective track record. I struggled to make sense of it all.

I began to make departure plans. A double meaning was attached to this secret plan. I wanted to die, and I kept it all to myself. I started to give away some of my possessions. I was not aware of it at the time, but this is a dangerous sign from someone contemplating suicide. I also wanted to move to a new location, and it didn't matter where. I just wanted to get away from myself. My will to live was being challenged, and I was losing.

I began stockpiling sleeping pills. I never took them to help me sleep, but I filled my prescription faithfully. I had a bottle of them, filled to the top, on my kitchen table, and I would just sit and stare at it, telling myself I didn't have the guts to finish the job. I would pick up the bottle, open the lid, and hold it up to my mouth, feeling the pills against my lips. Then I would consider how embarrassing it would be for my family if I decided to swallow the pills. I would look down at Friday and ask myself, *Who will take care of my cat if I'm dead?* All rational thoughts were long gone. For some reason, I never followed through with my plan. Perhaps the universe was not ready for me to die. Luckily for me, I also needed shoulder surgery. The reason I say "luckily" is that it allowed me the time to take a break from my job and busy routine. I knew I couldn't go on like this. Things needed to change.

Every single situation I'd thought had been corrected stood firmly, front and center, staring me right in the face. Each morning, I woke up angry. At night, I went to bed angry. I tossed and turned most nights, unable to sleep. Kind of ironic when you consider my fully stocked supply of sleeping pills. Because of the pain in my shoulder, I was limited in riding my motorcycle and practicing yoga, which eliminated the only relief mechanisms I had at my disposal. I was thoroughly convinced I was losing my mind. How could I have had so many recent incredible life experiences and interactions, and still feel worse than ever? I began to question everything. How could I have been so wrong to falsely believe I'd received answers to my questions?

One morning, I was having breakfast with a friend at Dave's Diner in Middleboro, Massachusetts. One minute, we were having a pleasant conversation, and the next, I was sobbing uncontrollably. I told my friend I thought I was losing my mind. I could see how concerned they were, but unfortunately, they couldn't help me.

I decided to return to the treadmill of meeting with another therapist. I had little confidence that anyone could help improve my current mental condition; after all, I felt like I had already tried *every conceivable idea known to man*. I felt fear in all directions. My biggest concern was losing my job and the security it provided. If I were unable to function, it would only be a matter of time before I would have to walk away from everything. At times, death felt like a way to stop the crazy cycle and the madness between my ears. Unless I figured out what was wrong with me, something tragic was going to happen.

I began meeting with a brand-spanking-new therapist, and we quickly established a good rapport. We met at his office overlooking Wayland Square on the East Side of Providence once a week. I started to feel like maybe—*finally*—this would be the necessary connection to help me feel better. Sounds familiar, right? We discussed various addictions: drinking, drugs, sex, food, and reckless spending. Like most therapists, this one claimed to have a proven track record in corrective techniques. I had no reason to doubt him except my own track record, which had led me to believe that no one could help me.

In one session, he suggested that I return to AA. I was attending meetings sporadically at the time, but really didn't have much of a connection with the program. The truth is, quitting drinking and drugging had been easy for me; I had given up that nonsense eons ago. What dogged me was all the mental health issues that remained a part of my personality after I'd stopped. So, I began attending meetings again in the Wickford area of North Kingstown. I did start to feel a little better after I had incorporated therapy and meetings back into my routine, but a giant hole still filled my entire being. I even went so far as to lie to myself that things were getting better when they were actually getting worse. Any feeling of inner peace or emotional well-being felt incomplete. It was quite annoying. As my surgery date grew closer, I found myself completely unaware that everything in my life was about to change. In fact, it would be my biggest personal realization since birth.

I had exhausted every conceivable solution that might have fixed the unsolved mystery within myself. I'd turned to every possible person my heart had led me to. I had pursued every avenue, old and new, to gain some sort of handle on my problems.

AND THEN I WOKE UP.

One afternoon, I was driving on Main Street in East Greenwich, Rhode Island—a road I'd traveled thousands of times in the past. I drove past a flower shop and turned to look at it as I went by. I knew the owner from my recovery meetings and had purchased numerous floral arrangements from him in the past. I kept driving, and what happened next can only be described as divine intervention. I swear, the car turned itself around. I drove back, parked the car, and walked inside the flower shop in a span of just a couple minutes. It had been several years since my last visit to the shop.

I could see my friend Bobby B. and his wife in the back of the store, behind the counter.

As I walked in, he said, "Hey, Bren, what's happening, brother?"

I stood in silence at the end of the counter. I was a completely defeated man. I was fried. I had no idea what to do next, but I was about to find out. Bobby is a handsome, charismatic man. He stood there looking down, working with some flowers in front of him. He looked back at me for a moment, waiting for a response to his question. When I began to mumble something about not being there to buy flowers, Bobby cut me off.

He said in a loud, confident tone, "Are you done? Have you had enough? Are you tired of living like this? Are you tired of feeling this way? Have you thought about killing yourself yet?"

I remained silent. I had no idea what was wrong with me, but he seemed to know exactly what it was. He asked me if I had a copy of the Big Book, referring to the book titled *Alcoholics Anonymous*.

I replied, "Yes, I must have it at home somewhere."

"Good," he said. "Go home and read the section called 'The Doctor's Opinion,' and come back tomorrow at 3:00 p.m."

That was it. The conversation was over. Luckily, I didn't have any questions. It felt like there was nothing left to say at the moment anyway. Without a word, I turned and walked out.

When I got home, I did exactly what he'd instructed me to do. "The Doctor's Opinion," held little meaning for me as I was reading it; it was just a bunch of words strung together. I had a hard time concentrating on the reading.

The next day, I returned to the flower shop. I had no confidence that Bobby could help me. Why would I? I'd already tried everything humanly possible. I never explained to Bobby what was wrong with me, or why I'd come to see him in the first place. None of that mattered. A much bigger picture was beginning to unfold, even though I had no idea what it was.

Bobby took over. He was specific. He never left any doubt in my mind about what we were about to do. He was going to take me through the Big Book. We got right to work. We sat across from each other at a dark wooden table with our books closed. My copy of the book was new. His copy looked like it had been through a war, and it probably had. We opened the book to the first page, and Bobby told me to start reading. The book was originally published in 1939. At the top of the page, written in capital letters, on top of the other, I read the words out loud:

ALCOHOLICS
ANONYMOUS

They were followed by this statement: "The Story of How Many Thousands of Men and Women Have Recovered from Alcoholism." I looked up from my book. Bobby had an ear-to-ear grin on his face, and he was nodding *yes*.

"Oh," I said, in a tone that indicated something had been right in front of my face all along. "Oh," I said again, much louder but with the same intention.

Bobby laughed and said, "Yeah, man, it's all in here."

Something inside me clicked into place. At that moment, a channel opened in my heart and soul. I suddenly realized that the answers to my emptiness *did* exist, and the formula was in this book. It was intense and calm and peaceful, all at the same time. I felt safe. I felt ready to proceed. And Bobby was more than ready to guide me through the book. I felt total trust in him. You see, what I was unaware of was that Bobby had taken many people through the book in the past, serving as a guide to locate the answers to questions, problems, and feelings that seekers are so desperately in need of. His passion to help others is one that is noble and an amazing sight to see.

Over the next month, I finally discovered what was wrong with me. I'd already known I was a drug addict and alcoholic, but it turned out I had several other issues to address. I'm a sex addict. I'm extremely codependent. I'm a compulsive eater. I have issues with anger and rage. I'm dishonest. I'm suicidal. I'm a selfish and self-centered prick. Other than that, I was doing OK. Most important of all, I am an alcoholic, and *that* was now going to become my focus.

Bobby became my AA Big Book Step Study sponsor. The amount of growth- and fact-based education was about to finally unlock the answers to my long-standing questions. First, I was introduced to the world of Big Book Step Study (BBSS). What I mean is, I found out there is another type of AA. Unfortunately, it took me seventeen years of thinking I had all the answers before I found it. My experience (if you want to call it that) was in "open" or "discussion" AA. My only reference point is my own personal experience. BBSS became my introduction to truth and reality. Instead of focusing on fellowship and keeping track of how long it had been since my last drink, BBSS showed me an alternative. I quickly learned to rely on God and the universe for guidance. Now that I was in BBSS AA, with a hardcore BBSS sponsor, it was time to get down to the business of recovery. Bobby was about to show me the blueprint for achieving emotional sobriety. This was, without a doubt, the missing piece of the puzzle. Prior to the day I walked into the flower shop, I hadn't seen Bobby in several years. Without realizing it, I took the first three of AA's Twelve Steps the moment I walked into the flower shop. Step One: *We admitted we were powerless over alcohol—that our lives had become unmanageable.* Step Two: *Came to believe that a Power greater than ourselves could restore us to sanity.* Step Three: *Made a decision to turn our will and our lives over to the care of God as we understood Him.* To put into words how I took the first three steps in succession is best described as a newfound willingness and openness to allow myself to have a new experience, as opposed to the same one I'd had throughout most of my life. It felt like a release of just about every belief I held near and dear to my heart, and man, did it happen fast. In addition, my taking the first three steps in quick succession allowed for the possibility of a personality change in my heart and soul. After that, I never looked back.

Bobby showed me exactly how to proceed with the process. He is direct. He has no time for tire kickers. If he catches even a glimpse of someone not being serious about wanting to recover, he will close the Big Book and show them the door. He has a word for these situations, and that word is "NEXT!" I did not fall into this category. He never had to chase me. I was never late for our meetings. I was always outside the flower shop, sitting in my car, fifteen minutes early for each session. I felt a new hope. Every emotional problem and character defect I mentioned earlier began to improve or disappear completely. It all happened in a matter of weeks. It would have been great to have moved right into this work seventeen years earlier, but I needed to emotionally punish myself for a long time before I finally became willing to change, in 2019. The best way to explain what happened is this: I'd spent my entire life playing God. The day I walked into the flower shop, I turned my will over to the care of God. It was that simple. I'd searched high and low, looking for answers to my questions. *How do you determine the next right thing to do in life? How do you know it's the right decision?* I had tried to figure it out myself, and I had tried to depend on other humans to answer the questions for me. Even though I had received the correct answers from people much wiser than me, the answers had to come from God for me to fill the hole in my soul.

Many times over the years, I had read the Big Book from cover to cover in regular AA meetings. It never resonated with me. And the day Bobby told me to dust off my copy and read from the beginning, I felt more of the same: It was just a bunch of words on paper. Nothing was getting in at all.

The following day, the two of us sat at a table, and my perception changed. We reread each word that I'd already read the night before. In a wonderful tone of voice, Bobby offered me a perspective I had never experienced before. Once the block from God and the universe was collapsed, it all made sense to me. The truth has a way of being ingested with ease when a person is finally ready to hear it. Bobby stopped our reading frequently and explained what we had just read. It was inspiring. I sat and asked questions, and he responded with a combination of his personal experiences, the truth, and uncensored reality. He explained that I was at the point of no return. He told me I could never go back to my old beliefs or way of thinking—or to the regular AA meetings I was attending. He told me that the way I'd felt when I'd walked through his door the previous day would only get worse, possibly resulting in a tragic ending, if I did not accept this new direction in life. I believed him. I could feel it inside. I needed no further proof.

Before my evolution in the flower shop, I'd never fully allowed myself to feel joy and happiness. I'd always considered it a warning that something bad was right around the corner. That is the very definition of living in fear. At the end of our first meeting together, Bobby took out a white legal pad. He told me the time had come for me to take a walk down memory lane. This was the beginning of some serious writing. It was time for Step Four: *Made a searching and fearless moral inventory of ourselves.* My writing would begin with my earliest childhood memories and continue all the way up to the present day. I was to leave nothing out. This was no simple task. I would be listing—from birth—where I had lived, where I'd gone to school, what sports I'd played, where I'd worked, and who had been there along the way. Then I would list my fears, my resentments, the people I had harmed, and the biggie: an inventory of my sexual partners. Like I said, it was no simple task.

In just a few hours of my sitting with Bobby, he became a trusted friend. I began to feel some relief in my head, and more importantly, I felt hope. This awakening was similar to what it would be like for me to move next door to Boogie and be able to see him whenever I wanted to. Like attending an eternal Electric Mary concert with Rusty. Like embarking on a motorcycle journey with Bob Quattrocchi to an incredible destination. Like engaging in a never-ending heart-to-heart talk with Jeff Katz. This time, I was embarking on a journey that would last a lifetime.

Every good feeling or realization I'd had could only be temporary until I turned my will over to God. Once I accepted the responsibility of doing this work, things fell into place quickly, though it required a lot of writing. That meant putting this book on the back burner indefinitely, which turned out to be a good decision. When you consider that what I had written up until this point had left me feeling just short of dead inside, with no real ending to the book except my wanting to kill myself, my taking a break from writing was a good idea. Suicide was not exactly the feel-good finish I was looking for.

During the days leading up to my unexpected visit to the flower shop, I'd found myself standing at the gates of Hell, a defeated man ready to die. Another gift from God was my looming surgery date. I needed to make my new writing assignment *priority one* because I would not be able to use my left hand after surgery on my left shoulder. That meant I needed to dedicate my time to writing my fourth step until it was done. The surgery also freed me up to do the work. I'm not sure I would have attempted it while working my regular job, twelve hours a day, six days a week. Instead, I might have continued doing the same thing over and over, expecting different results. You know, yoga, therapy, self-help books, the gym, sex, food, travel, and ineffective recovery meetings. Luckily for me, God had another plan, and I was ready to follow it.

While all this unfolded, I still wanted to change my living arrangement. I now trusted in God, so I asked the universe, "Where do you want me to live?" Shortly after that, I moved to a private ten-acre property in Saunderstown, Rhode Island. I asked God to help me find the right place to live, and He delivered. The owner of the property, a woman named Lisa, explained to me that this beautiful place was a good location to heal. She must have picked up on the fact that I did, in fact, need to heal. Without any type of credit or background check, she offered to let me move in, right there, on the spot. She told me she could tell I was the person she was looking for. With my new home base, I now had the perfect location to continue my soul-mining expedition.

I informed Betsy of my decision to give step work my complete attention. I asked her to understand that I needed to be on my own during the process. She was supportive and knew I needed to do this work. It was the key for me to grow as a man. Eventually, Betsy and I went our separate ways. The challenges of living in two different states, along with the personal overhaul I was undertaking, made it necessary for us to continue our journeys separately. Each day, Bobby assigned me a writing task. I wrote at home. I wrote at the library. I wrote in my car. I made a searching and fearless moral inventory of myself. At times I felt like I wanted to throw up due to some of the memories I recalled. My crazy, irresponsible past was being downloaded from the depths of my brain onto paper. I kept going. I knew this had to be done. I began to see the selfishness of my ways.

I could finally understand my real problem: I had turned my back on God at some point in my life. Probably at a young age. Some of my life experiences may suggest that my snubbing of God came early on in life. The writing process triggered memories from as far back as kindergarten and first grade. While attending St. Francis Elementary School in Warwick, Rhode Island, I was already demonstrating a rebellious side. My mother would dress me in a clean, pressed uniform and make sure my tie was straight before I went out the door. Once outside, I would remove the tie and discard it. Then I would unbutton the top button of my shirt. When the nuns would question me at school about why I was not wearing a tie, I would say, "My mother forgot to give me one." My parents must have spent a small fortune on clip-on ties. What a piece of work I was. I would sit in the classroom with my legs stretched out and crossed at the feet in the aisle alongside my desk. The nun teaching the class would tell me on a regular basis to keep my feet under my desk, but I would do as I pleased. One day, as she was reading to the class and walking backward along the aisle, she tripped over my feet, which sent her crashing to the floor. I'd been completely unaware she'd been walking behind me. I remember feeling awful and offering her assistance to her feet. Instead, she got up on her own, grabbed me from my seat, and hurried me down the hall to the principal's office. She escorted me inside to face the head nun and closed the door behind us. I remember feeling complete terror. I knew I was in serious trouble. The room was dark. The highest-ranking nun sat at her desk. On appearance alone, the two nuns scared the living shit out of me. Their outfits made me think of space aliens. The veils they wore only added to their out-of-this-world appearance. On top of the desk sat a table lamp that lit up the desk drawers. In what can only be described as a twisted Hallmark Channel moment, the principal opened the top drawer and presented me with a gold-toned metal ruler. She asked me if I wanted to know how it felt to be hit on the hand with it. For some reason—probably unadulterated fear—I said, "Yes."

She struck the back of my hand several times. I started to cry. Then they both got down to business. They pointed to a box in the corner of the room. About the size of a box a large window air conditioner might be packaged in. It was big enough to put a child in, and before I knew it, they ordered me to get inside the box. They told me they were shipping me to China for being a bad boy. Then they put the lid on top.

It's amazing how this memory returned in such vivid detail. From inside the box I told the Sisters I had an idea. I explained that it might be quicker to dig my way to China. I also told them I wanted to talk to my mother before they sent me on my journey. I asked how long it would take for me to get to China because I needed to go to the bathroom. After a brief stay in my mode of transportation to the Orient, they let me out of the box. They attempted to cheer me up as I laughed and cried at the same time, probably scarred for life at this point. Maybe I didn't turn my back on God for good that day, but I definitely turned my back on nuns forever. I would have more dealings with the nuns as time marched on. I don't think I ever told my parents about what had happened in the office that day. The sooner I crammed it down and forgot about it, the better.

Another time that might qualify is when I attacked another player on the field while playing Little League Baseball. The worst part was that he was my teammate, and my aggression toward him was a result of his having made an error at a crucial moment, almost costing us a victory. It's scary to think what I might have done if his blunder *had* cost us the game. My father had to look on as the coach carried me like a wild animal from the field. I screamed and cussed and kicked and swung my arms around the entire time. On a side note, my dad was standing with the mother of the teammate I had just pummeled at home plate. She was also my gym teacher at school. Even though a strong case could be made for this being the moment I turned my back on God, I think I can most definitely pinpoint the moment when I stopped trusting in God.

While I was in elementary school, I was recruited to become an altar boy. I'm not sure whose idea it was, but it definitely wasn't mine. I remember being told to show up to orientation in black pants and a white shirt. Of course, I did not comply. Everyone else in the room dressed accordingly, while I wore jeans and a T-shirt. I was already smoking pot at that point and had done so just prior to entering the room. A nun whose name eludes me took me out in the hallway and informed me they were cutting me from the team. Just like that, with no explanation. Although she did point out that I was not what they were looking for. I looked her in the eye and said, "That's OK, Sister Mary Elephant, because I never wanted to do this in the first place." ("Sister Mary Elephant" is a Cheech & Chong reference.) She then asked me if I had been smoking marijuana.

I replied, "It's none of your fucking business; you just fired me, remember?"

This ended my life in the church. I went outside and got high again. I was in total fear of facing my father, as I would have to break the bad news to him that I couldn't cut it as an altar boy. From that moment on (and possibly earlier in life), I assumed the role of God. For decades, I started the day like this: "Today the role of God will be played by Brendan Higgins." Then I would jump on my steamroller and proceed to steamroll everything and everyone in my path. It's no wonder I found myself living alone, on the verge of suicide. But the twelve-step process would help me to recognize my past behavior while also offering a path to change.

In October of 2019, I began writing my Fourth Step. One month and six days later, it was time to share it with the person of my choosing. I never considered anyone other than Bobby. It was now time for Step Five: *Admitted to God, to ourselves, and to another human being the exact nature of our wrongs.* The very personal experience of reading my life story to Bobby took place in the flower shop after business hours. The entire process took eight hours over a two-day period—five hours the first day and three hours the second day. On the first day, during the first half hour, the pace of the reading felt awkward. Then it shifted to another gear, and a yoga flow kicked in. It assumed a rhythm of its own. It was powerful. My understanding of what was wrong with me became crystal clear. It came to light while reading my Fifth Step aloud. My past was filled with my attempting to control everything around me. I dominated people. I allowed no room for any opinion except mine. I would scream and yell at people with my "expert" opinion and wouldn't allow them to respond at all. Once the internet burst onto the scene, I became well versed in typing my opinion without any consideration for others' feelings. I never once wrote a message and let it sit for a period of time before deciding to send it. I just pushed "send," and I pushed that button in earnest. I was a bully. I was a full-on asshole. I lived a selfish life with flawless execution. I thought I was better than everyone. No one could live up to my expectations. I was selfish and self-centered. I was playing God around the clock.

Thankfully, while reading my Fifth Step, I understood that I was now going to begin living a new, inspired life. I would no longer look to anything or anyone except God for help with my problems. I would have a new purpose in life: to follow God's will. The questions I needed answers to would still be asked—probably many more times in the future—but now, they would be directed to God. After completing my Fifth Step, I left the flower shop feeling free from the secrets that had haunted me my entire life. It had all been lifted from me. The process Bobby guided me through is the only thing that helped me to understand who I am and what was wrong with me. Everything else I had ever tried may have appeared to help for a short time, but it was always temporary. For years, I thought that quitting drinking and drugging would solve my litany of issues. The flaw with that theory was my thinking that drinking and drugging were the whole problem; they were just *part* of the problem. I had a much deeper problem, and I needed to come to terms with it. My real problem, without a doubt, was living a life disconnected from God. Turning my will over to God was, and continues to be, a sincere intention. The formula to achieve a conscious contact with God is working Steps One through Nine, and then living in Steps Ten, Eleven, and Twelve. It felt like a monumental undertaking. I had many questions for Bobby.

Shortly after completing my Fifth Step, I had shoulder surgery. The timing was impeccable. God gave me the extra time, just at the right time, to complete my Fourth Step writing and my Fifth Step reading before going under the knife. The surgery was a success; I was told in the recovery room that it was a best-case scenario. Just a few days after surgery, I returned to my regular AA meetings around Rhode Island with my arm in a sling. I was eager to tell my sober pals of the recent, amazing changes in my life. I began to share with them the twelve-step process that I had recently been through, which was known as the Hyannis Method. But my new outlook on recovery was not well-received. In fact, some people were so skeptical, one might say they were threatened by my enthusiasm. It probably didn't help that I walked into AA meetings and announced my discovery of a different AA that I described as a "much more effective method for treating all the issues we sit and bitch and complain about over and over again." I was disappointed by the less-than-enthusiastic reaction I was getting, and needed to consult with Bobby. I returned to the flower shop, very discouraged. I told Bobby about my recent experiences at the meetings. He sat me down and reminded me of our past conversation regarding how regular AA meetings would no longer charge my newfound spiritual batteries. He explained to me that the time had come for me to attend some more appropriately suited AA meetings. He told me it would require my driving to Massachusetts because the type of meetings we needed to go to were not available in Rhode Island. My questions continued to mount. I couldn't understand how an imaginary state line could affect the type of meetings being held. Bobby couldn't answer that question, but he strongly recommended going to Big Book Step Study meetings—and as usual, he suggested I go immediately.

 I attended my first BBSS meeting on a Friday night. From the moment the meeting started, I felt a sense of belonging. I experienced the same relief and joy I had been feeling over the last month while meeting with Bobby in the flower shop. I was no longer getting any positive feelings from attending regular AA meetings back in Rhode Island. Now I could see why. The BBSS meeting keeps its focus on the solution. This was mentioned at the beginning of the meeting: "If we are talking about the problem, we can't possibly be talking about the solution." That one statement alone made me want to jump out of my seat and scream, "Yes! That's right! Thank you!"

 For the entire ninety minutes, I related to every word spoken in the meeting. I realized very quickly that everyone who spoke at this meeting had been through the same process I had. Going through the Twelve Steps via the Hyannis Method, and living my life in the Steps, turned out to be the difference between BBSS and regular AA. In non-BBSS meetings, the Twelve Steps and the Big Book are rarely mentioned. From that moment on, BBSS meetings became my focus.

Since regular AA is all they have in Rhode Island, I continued to go to meetings around the area. It became increasingly difficult to relate to what I was hearing. The message felt incomplete. I would try to share my life-changing experience of having a BBSS sponsor and taking part in step work and BBSS meetings, but it fell on deaf ears. In one Rhode Island meeting, I raised my hand, and when called upon, I said, "Did you guys know there is another AA?" I explained to a room of about fifty people that BBSS meetings are conducted in a different manner, and we were not doing things "correctly." That, of course, was my own opinion and not true, since I have no idea what others experience and what work they do on their own. Even though I was spiritually wide-awake now, I was still inexperienced in transmitting the message properly. My enthusiasm was simply off the charts. I suggested that everyone go through the Hyannis Method so we could start having *real* AA meetings in Rhode Island. I was way off base and out of line in making such statements. Needless to say, my extreme feedback did not go over well at all. Especially with the old-timers, who are set in their ways and have been doing things outside of BBSS for years.

I told the group, "It's time to stop recovering, and actually recover."

One man went as far as to say, "It is not possible to recover!" as he slammed his fist on the table.

I quietly asked, "Well, how do you explain me then?"

I felt awful after local meetings and vented to Bobby on a regular basis. In sharp contrast, I felt alive and free during and after BBSS meetings. You can connect the dots. I stopped trying to convince anyone after a while. It was the same thing as walking into a bar and trying to convince someone to quit drinking. In time, I realized that different methods and ideas work differently for everyone. I began to realize that everyone holds on to what they believe is true for them, the same way I hold on to *my* truth. I became aware that some people are sicker than others. And I became aware of the fact that I was sicker than most people. I openly shared that fact because I no longer harbored secrets. I had nothing to prove. I was free. I had found the solution. Sharing my experience with BBSS felt necessary. I realized that instead of trying to convert people to my new path in life, it was better to let people believe what they want and be who they are and not let it affect me— just like my yoga teacher Philip had taught me years earlier. Besides, I still had plenty of work to do on myself. I was just a glorified rookie in BBSS, and some of the most important step work was still ahead of me.

The good news was, Bobby was going to continue guiding me through the process. I can't imagine what might have happened if I had not walked into the flower shop that day. I hope anyone struggling with any or all of the issues I struggled with will reach out to me or someone in BBSS to help guide them through the same process. Sitting in regular AA meetings, waiting for something magical to happen, or thinking the more time you have accumulated since your last drink is somehow going to help treat alcoholism is false hope. Step work is the answer.

There was a relatively easy transition from Step Six: *Were entirely ready to have God remove all these defects of character* to Step Seven: *Humbly asked him to remove our shortcomings* to Step Eight: *Made a list of all persons we had harmed, and became willing to make amends to them all.* Now it was time for Step Nine: *Made direct amends to such people wherever possible, except when to do so would injure them or others.* The idea of reaching out to people I had harmed felt like a step I might take a pass on. I was convinced that certain people, like my ex-wife, would not be interested in hearing from me. But I quickly learned that God was going to take it from there. Out of the blue, while I was literally in the process of writing my Fourth Step, I received a message from Jim Leavitt, a former student from my wrestling school and longtime independent pro wrestler. I had lost touch with Jim twenty years earlier. He wanted to thank me for everything I had done for him in the past. At first, I allowed my self-will to respond with a cold, generic answer. Then, after a short time of reflection, I asked God to help me find the words. I told "Big Gun," as he is known in the wrestling world, that I had missed the boat on being a good teacher to him and others. As I wrote the message, I realized I had several people from the wrestling world who I needed to make amends to. I went on to tell him that the day comes when a good teacher knows the student no longer needs him. I had fallen short in this area due to my addictions and selfish, self-centered lifestyle.

Then God struck again. I received another out-of-the-blue message, this one, from Jason DellaGatta a.k.a. Jason Rumble—another wrestler to whom I owed an apology. He invited me to an upcoming wrestling event that would celebrate the twenty-year anniversary of the passing of Tony Rumble. An opportunity presented itself to be in the same place at the same time with quite a few of my old wrestling buddies whom I hadn't seen in years. A wrestling show celebrating the life of our dear friend and mentor turned out to be the place where many old wounds would be healed. Jason promoted the show, reuniting the likes of Erich Sbraccia, Bull Montana, Luis Ortiz, Wagner Brown, Tre, Gino Martino, Rich Palladino, and Sheldon Goldberg, along with the guests of honor: Tony's wife, Ellen; his daughter Dawna; and his grandson, Hunter. We all gathered for the event in Wakefield, Massachusetts, to remember our dear friend. It was the perfect venue for me to bury the hatchet with everyone. I made a point to make amends to several people that night. The old wounds from years ago washed away with ease. Tony Rumble smiled down on the building as the wrestling family he created reunited once and for all.

It was especially healing for me to spend time with Sheldon Goldberg. Sheldon was one of my wrestling family members who unfortunately got caught in my crosshairs more than once. We may not have a lot in common, but two things we do share is our love for professional wrestling and our love for Tony Rumble. As soon as I saw Sheldon enter the building, I walked directly over to him and hugged him. We embraced for a moment, and when we separated, our eyes were full of tears. No words were necessary; all was forgiven. My harsh words in the past made me think I might need to go into detail as to why I was sorry, but in this case, we were friends again—instantly. Nothing needed to be rehashed. It was a beautiful moment.

One of the wrestlers performing that evening remains a personal favorite of mine, Brian Milonas. After his match, he stayed in the ring to thank us old-timers who came before him. He explained that Tony Rumble and the people who worked for Tony had made it possible for him to do what he loves. I was already a big fan of this kid, and his sincere gesture meant a lot to all of us at ringside.

NWA New England Reunion

With Sheldon Goldberg

With Brian Milonas

With Rich Palladino

After such a positive experience at the Tony Rumble Memorial Show, I was off and running. It was time to heal more old wounds. I knew I needed to contact more old friends and make long-overdue amends. Now that I was letting God run the show, another opportunity presented itself quickly. "Big Gun" was hanging up the tights after a twenty-year run of his own. I realized this was another golden opportunity to travel to my old stomping grounds in Newburyport, Massachusetts, and make things right. Another friend and former student from my wrestling school, Joe Moakley, had followed in my footsteps as a wrestler/promoter. His wrestling company, Atlantic Pro Wrestling, has a long history on the seacoast, picking up where I left off years earlier. I was extremely hard on Joe when he began running shows. I said some hurtful things about him and his promotion from my high horse after I used very unprofessional language in the ring while he had me at his show as a guest. I hadn't spoken to Joe for many years. I reached out to him, hoping to get a chance to apologize. He was happy to hear from me and expressed nothing but love after so many years had passed. Joe invited me to the upcoming wrestling show as a surprise guest-referee during the final match of "Big Gun." I loved the idea—and loved it even more when he told me it was going to be a secret for both the fans and "Big Gun."

At the show, I waited in my car until the retirement match. Only a few people knew I was in the parking lot. Joe eventually came outside to escort me through the locker room. Before we entered the building, I stopped Joe in the parking lot and told him I was sorry for the way I'd treated him years earlier. I reminded him how much more successful a promoter he was than me. I also told him I recalled he had an impressive dropkick back in the day.

He laughed and said, "I can't get up that high anymore."

I shook his hand and hugged him with my free arm. I told him I loved him and that I knew "Big Woody" was smiling down on us. When we walked inside the locker room, only a handful of people had any idea who I was. It was more of the same when I was introduced to the crowd and walked out to the ring. "Big Gun" seemed surprised to see me. I stood outside the ring and offered him a salute out of respect. And just like that, another broken relationship came full circle. I only wish Brian Webster, Gil Bonk, and "Big Woody" could have been there. After the show, I spent some time with my former students, "Big Gun," Derrick Mitchell, and Joe Moakley. It was like old times: all friends again. It felt great to be with the guys.

After righting some old wrongs, it was time to keep going with some more personal amends. One by one, I attempted to make appointments to meet with people from my past. Some accepted my invitation, and some passed on it. The entire process helped me to grow as a person. I asked God for help constantly. The decision to rely on God changed the course of my life.

I kept asking Bobby for guidance, and he consistently reminded me to talk to God. He said he didn't give financial, employment, or relationship advice. He did, however, continue to guide me through the steps. He explained to me that the amends process is ongoing. He suggested moving on to Step Ten: *Continued to take personal inventory, and when we were wrong, promptly admitted it;* Step Eleven: *Sought through prayer and meditation to improve our conscious contact with God as we understood Him, praying only for knowledge of His will for us and the power to carry that out;* and Step Twelve: *Having had a spiritual awakening as the result of these steps, we tried to carry this message to alcoholics, and to practice these principals in all our affairs.* So that's what I did. He suggested I pray in the morning and follow that with meditation. He suggested I read pages eighty-four through eighty-eight in the Big Book every single day. He also suggested I pray and meditate at night. I did all of it like my life depended on it. I came to believe that only two kinds of alcoholics exist in the world: those who have recovered and those who have yet to recover. I recovered.

The empty feeling improved in dramatic fashion. The key is to keep one's spiritual condition running like a well-oiled machine. Certain other long-standing problems I lived with, like sex addiction, improved dramatically. It was quite astonishing. My mind no longer raced. My temper subsided and rarely reared its head. My eating disorder seemed to hang around the longest. I stuffed my face with unhealthy choices, probably because I was running out of things to quit. My ego was running out of places to turn. My will now belonged to God. In time, my eating habits stabilized. Everything depended on my contact with God. As 2019 closed out, change continued to unfold in the world and in my personal life. Tom Brady left the New England Patriots, and everyone started talking about something called Corona virus.

One day, I received a phone call from a nurse employed by my health-care provider. Several months earlier, I had tried another round of therapy. The person on the other end of the line was following up on my progress. I told her that while I'd liked the therapist, I'd stopped going to see him. She asked why, and I told her the reason.

"No therapist alive can help me unless they direct me toward one specific thing."

"What is that?" she asked.

"God," I said. The line fell silent for a moment. "You probably don't understand what I am talking about," I said.

But then, in a sweet tone, she replied, "No. I get it." She thanked me for my time, and we hung up.

The more I depended on God for help, the more incredible reunions continued to unfold. In the spring of 2020, I was doing rewrites for this book. I found myself writing and thinking about my girlfriend from long ago, Shannon. I stopped writing for a moment, picked up my phone, and searched for her on Facebook. About a dozen or so women came up with the same name. They all had profile pictures, and I easily eliminated them one by one. Then, I came across a profile without a photo. Instead, it had this phrase: "If you can't beat fear, do it scared." Before I clicked on the photo, I knew it was her because that was the same thing she had told me many years earlier regarding my fears about attempting certain challenging wrestling maneuvers. It appeared she was still living in Massachusetts. She didn't have a big social media presence, so I couldn't tell much about her life from her profile. I decided to send her a message to let her know I was writing a book and that she was mentioned in it. My finger hovered over the send button for several moments as I contemplated the idea of sending the message at all. What if she was married and had a family? What if she had no interest in hearing from me at all? In the end, I decided to hit send. This was the message I sent her: "Do I say hello or not? OK, hi, Shannon." I sent the message and went to bed.

In the morning, I noticed she had responded. She wrote, "WOW!!!!! I'm psyched you FOUND ME!!!!" She included a photo of a necklace I had given her decades earlier, when we were dating. She told me it had moved around with her over the course of her adult life. She told me I'd been good to her when we were together, and I'd always been one of her favorite men. We started to write back and forth regularly, recalling our own personal memories of each other. This reunion found us both happy to be back in touch with each other. We quickly learned we had some things in common. Neither of us were married, neither of us had kids, and we both continued to love Harley-Davidson motorcycles. We'd gone for motorcycle rides years earlier, and we talked about the possibility of riding together again. She was living a happy life, and I was happy for her.

We eventually managed to get together in person. Shannon looked amazing. We quickly realized time had changed us both, to the point that we knew the idea of our getting back together was unrealistic. After I realized that Shannon and

I would not be riding together or keeping in touch, I began to ask God who the universe wanted me to be with. My self-will had attracted quality people into my life over the years, but I had never asked God, "Who do you want me with?" I included my question in every morning and evening prayer and meditation for a month or so.

Then one day while scrolling through Facebook, I read a post from a Facebook friend who was a stranger to me. (We all have them, right? Facebook friends we don't know offline.) Her name was Charlotte. She delivered a post in the form of a gentle reminder to everyone to take deep breaths. I decided to send her a message thanking her for her suggestion. It is not in my character to contact a stranger online, but I sent a message to Charlotte without hesitation. She responded that the reminder to breathe was for herself as well. This simple message exchange led to a day-and-night-long online conversation that rocked both of our worlds. We seemed to have a way of finishing each other's sentences. Our conversation flowed like a yoga class. It felt like the only thing missing was thunder and lightning with howling wind and heavy rain. It was awesome. I told her our conversation was much needed on my end.

She responded with, "The universe connects people for a reason. There's no mistakes, man."

I agreed with her and asked if she wanted to meet in person.

Without hesitation, she said, "Yes."

We both had no expectations surrounding the meeting, but we did want to meet. We offered each other a spiritual connection best described as *warrior to warrior.* I could see from her Facebook photos that she was a stunning Irish woman with beauty and intelligence. Style and strength also emanated from her photos.

The following morning I sent Charlotte a message. It was direct and to the point: "Would you like to meet this morning?"

Again, she responded with one word: "Yes."

She told me she had something to do, and then she could meet me. We needed a meeting place, and both of us simultaneously suggested India Point Park in Providence. This would not be the last time we had the same idea at the same moment.

Full of curiosity, I drove my motorcycle to meet this mystery woman. The entire situation was unexpected for both of us. However, we'd both felt a need to meet in person. It didn't feel like a date. It felt like a higher purpose was in play.

I arrived first. I sat on a stone wall in front of my bike, calm and at peace. There was no pressure or anything to prove. I was beaten down by past relationships and the damage I had caused in them. Charlotte pulled up in her car and got out with a giant smile on her face. She immediately gave me the hand sign with index finger and pinky finger extended. A rock 'n' roll sign for sure. She was dressed in jeans and an Army fatigue T-shirt. Her hair was long and dark. Her face, alive with emotion. I stood for a moment, trying to process why this was happening, and then I caught myself and promised I'd stay in the moment for the rest of whatever this meeting was. We'd had such a monumental conversation the night before, we embraced with a hug, the same as old friends would. The park is set on the water, with lots of people jogging and hanging out. We began to walk.

Before I could ask Charlotte which direction she wanted to go in, she said, "Come on, the universe is taking me this way."

Before long we were sitting in the sun on another stone wall, with the water about twenty feet below us. Our feet were hanging freely off the wall. We resumed our conversation from the previous night. We spoke about relationships and addiction and music and her son and a whole host of other topics. At one point, I put my arm around her, and her head tilted toward my shoulder. It was a moment in time we will never forget.

After baking in the sun, we decided to move under some trees to continue exploring whatever this was. Once we'd landed in our new spot, we realized my fatigue shorts matched her T-shirt. Almost as if we were both going into battle—except this turned out to be a peaceful gathering. I found Charlotte to be honest, and she gave off a vibe of zero bullshit. In other words, she was not giving any and most definitely was not taking any. As we sat and continued to get to know each other, a tall thin woman with short dark hair, wearing jeans and a red T-shirt, approached us. She knelt down and asked if she could say a prayer with us. Charlotte informed the woman that we had just met, but it didn't feel like she believed Charlotte. We told her it was fine if she wanted to pray. So she did. In fact, she proceeded to offer a marathon prayer. It brought Charlotte to tears. I don't think it was our unexpected guest's words as much as it was Charlotte's releasing something that no longer served her that caused the emotional response. I put my arm around my fellow warrior as the woman continued to pray.

I whispered to Charlotte, "Would you like me to ask her to stop?"

But Charlotte said, "No, let her go."

Once the woman finished, I asked if I could say a prayer as well. The woman seemed pleased with my request. I offered the Third Step Prayer: *God, I offer myself to Thee—to build with me and do with me as Thou wilt. Relieve me of the bondage of self, that I may better do Thy will. Take away my difficulties, that victory over them may bear witness to those I would help of Thy Power, Thy Love, and Thy Way of life.*

Once all prayers were spoken, the woman told us what a beautiful couple we were. Charlotte told her for a second time that we had just met. This time she believed Charlotte. She stood up, and before leaving, announced to both of us that she would be attending our wedding. Then she walked away. Charlotte looked at me with a look of shock on her face. *Did she really just say that?* After a while, we decided to walk in the general direction of our vehicles, but we landed back on the wall on which we'd originally sat. We felt a physical connection forming between us.

Charlotte said, "I can tell you want to kiss me."

It was true; I did want to kiss her.

Instead, I backed off and said, "When you are ready, you will let me know."

She seemed to like my decision. We knew we would see each other again, and that there was no rush. Eventually, we said goodbye, until next time. I watched her drive away with the same smile on her face she'd arrived with.

I looked at my phone for the first time after she'd left, and five hours had passed. I still can't define our first meeting. It felt like the universe had said, *These two are ready for each other,* and put us together. We met later that day and grew as close as two people can possibly get in such a short span of time. It turned out to be the beginning of a relationship we'd both been waiting a lifetime for.

Over the next month, we made the most out of every moment we spent together. We practiced yoga. We meditated together. We made fabulous dinners and enjoyed deep, meaningful conversations over them. I began to spend time with her son Hunter. We felt great chemistry together. Charlotte became my partner in every conceivable way. I stood in awe of her ability to bond with my cat, Friday. To the best of my knowledge, Charlotte is the only other human in thirteen years to ever pick up my cat and hold him. He comes to her whenever she calls him. When she picks him up, he purrs in her arms. I couldn't believe my eyes, as Friday is as antisocial as it gets. The signs were effortless for both of us to recognize.

We began to take long motorcycle rides together. Our chemistry on a Harley is intense. In this new era where gender lines are blurred, the two of us have no problem allowing me to be the male and her to be the female. Our chemistry drew attention everywhere we went. We received compliments over and over on how good we looked together. Our connection on two wheels felt like magic to me. We listened to loud, powerful music, like Electric Mary and Lana Del Rey. We rode along the coastline of the Atlantic Ocean every chance we could. The reason strangers commented on the way we looked together is so easy to explain: No matter how fucked up the world gets, people recognize love. They enjoy witnessing it. We welcomed the positive words. We had both paid our dues in the past.

I can only share with you what happened to me. This is my experience. I came to understand that I had been living in a fantasy world in my own head, where I played God all day every day. If someone told me something I didn't care for, or probably—more accurately—*couldn't* deal with, I would take their words into my mind and turn them into something I *could* deal with, and that version of the story would come out of my mouth. Then I would believe *my* version of the story. I had no idea I was doing it.

After the pattern of doing the same thing over and over and expecting different results ground on, I knew I had to get help.

Otherwise, I was going to die. I tried every conceivable remedy known to man and could only find temporary relief. My go-to solutions favorite included self-help. If that term was in the title of a book or DVD, I was quickly on board with whatever it was. After my journey through the steps with Bobby, I had a complete change of heart regarding self-help. I no longer want anything to do with things that have the word *self-help* in the title. I found the help I needed in talking to God. I began to trust and rely on it. I can talk to God anytime and anyplace. I do not need to be in a church or official place of worship to open a dialog with Him. I began to see how much time and effort I spent on my problems. Then, as fate would have it, I turned my attention toward the solution, and my will over to the care of God. My questions were valid:

How do you determine the next right thing to do in life? How do you know it's the right decision?

The answers are equally valid. I keep myself spiritually fit. I start my day by asking God what is needed of me before my feet hit the floor. I continue to ask for guidance to carry out God's will throughout the day. I practice yoga and meditate with the same intention. I'd practiced yoga for half a decade and never once invited God into my practice. Now, I ask God to join me on the mat every time I unroll it. I invite God to go motorcycle riding with me. God definitely rides a Harley. I ask God to join me and my passengers each time I get behind the wheel of a bus to keep me alert at all times and to allow me to be of service to all. I review each day before I retire to make sure I've carried out God's will to the best of my ability. I keep in close contact with friends like Bob Quattrocchi and

Jeff Katz. I continue to listen to Electric Mary at a high volume on a regular basis. I talk to Rusty often. I make regular visits to Boogie's Wrestling Camp to be with family.

I ask God to allow me to have new experiences, unlike those in my past. I make myself available to help anyone who is struggling with drugs, alcohol, and all the other issues from which I was able to achieve freedom. I stand ready to take others through the same process that Bobby B. escorted me. I ask God to show me how to be the best possible addition to the lives of Charlotte and her son Hunter.

My journey is only now beginning. Each day is filled with excitement and hope. I look forward to the next task God is going to assign me. The idea of returning to my old way of living, or, more importantly, my old way of thinking, is of no interest to me. Why would I want to navigate away from such a peaceful course? To live my life free of fear and remorse is the reward. I no longer worry about money or concern myself with thoughts of material things. If I follow God's will, my questions will always be answered with ease.

The Big Book

THE UNIVERSE SPEAKS

THE BEGINNING

Acknowledgments

Thank you to the following individuals:

My family: Robert J. Higgins, Barbara J. Branch Higgins, Kevin R. Higgins, Jeffrey M. Higgins, Kindra Fortson-Higgins, Cole Fortson-Higgins, Vaeh Fortson-Higgins

My friends: Heidi Jaillet, Harrison Katz, Joseph Katz, Julia Katz, Elizabeth Gingras, Carol LaRosa, Clinton Perry, Walter Schwab, Irene Tomkinson, Shawn Tomkinson, Kathy Wingfield, Kelly Adams, Brian Warburton, John Manocchio Sr., David Tellier, Astrid Howe, John Harding, Gilbert Bonk, Brian A. Day, Erich Sbraccia, Patrick J. Doyle, Bull Montana, Brian Webster, Derrick Mitchell, Astroman, Dylan Kage, Mike Hollow, Richard Byrne, Killer Kowalski, Scott Taylor, Ed Hunt, Steve Bradley, Jim Cornette, Kevin Sullivan, Tony Garea, Silvano Sousa, Shunsuke Yamaguchi, Wally Yamaguchi, Bill Irwin, Barry Darsow, Jim McCarthy, Matt Bloom, Sheldon Goldberg, Jason DellaGatta, Joe Moakley, Jim Leavitt, Harold Nabhan, Ron "Zombie" Celentano, Dakota Cowell, Bob Evans, Nick Steel, Brian Breiger, William Kennedy Sr., Billy Kennedy, Kevin Kennedy, David Thilbeault,

Peter Salemi, Philip J. Urso, Renee Armen Deslauriers, Lori Defusco Pagliaroni, Jess Gumkowski, Masha Besedin, Gale Pelham, Britta Koeppel, Ava Koeppel, Tabitha Lord, Jo-Ann Alquist Langseth, Tracey Buffum, Jessica Patricio, Pete Robinson, Brett Wood, Alex Raunjak, Paul "Spyda" Marrett, Pete Donagen, Chowie, Mahalia Swinfield, Melania Felekidis, Leanne Blundell, Kim Bencic, Bobby Venuto, Bill Upham, Paul Myers, Mark Silva, Wayne Carreiro, David McCarron, Jes Swisher, Shannon Dooling, Lisa Giusti, Lisa Widmaier DeCeglie, Rene Moyen, Dawn Alarie, Bailey, Alexa, and Friday

I also want to thank the following people:

Tony Rumble: For opening doors I never could have opened myself. For all the advice you provided over the years, especially the advice I did not want to hear. For the opportunity to be a member of "The Brotherhood." Most of all, for your friendship.

Jeffrey A. Katz: My best friend. For consistently being there. For giving meaning to the letters "MBF."

Elwood "Big Woody" Apt: For all the great times. The road trips. The trips to Fenway. The incredible meals. For being a true friend. Such a *know-it-all!* I miss you and Duncan.

Robert Quattrocchi: My first wrestling opponent from grade school. For letting me ride your Harley-Davidson as a teenager. For passing along Frankenglide to me. For teaching me to be a better biker and a better man. For never holding back your honest opinion. For all the long talks in the garage. Thanks, "Rep."

Joe Gliottone: My godfather from the Hill. The older

brother I never had and always needed. For the open door to your home then and now. For the advice you continue to offer. For always picking up the phone.

Kerri Stowik: My photographer. For helping me think outside the box. For asking, "Do you think you can climb out on those rocks?" kerristowik.com

Nancy Case: *Fluffy Kennedy.* My editor. Where to begin? For the incredible ability to encourage me to dig deeper and deeper and deeper. For never holding back your opinion. For the countless suggestions you made that vastly improved this book. For reminding me that the process of writing a book takes time. For providing brilliant editing. For having the most awesome cat in the universe. www.wordfashioning.com

To everyone at Redwood Publishing: Avery, the expert proofreading and detailed detective work was great. Sara, you had the best ideas to improve my book. You made the whole process fun. You also kept every promise you made to me before we embarked on this journey. That in itself is noble. www.redwooddigitalpublishing.com

Angel Valiant: For keeping the line of communication to Boogie open 24/7. For treating me like family from the moment we met.

Charlotte O'Dell Starr: For providing true love. The universe knew it was time for us to merge together. You and Hunter are my family. I love you both.

Rusty Brown: My brother from another mother. For offering friendship, kindness, and support to a stranger on the other side of the planet. For welcoming me to the Electric Mary family. For making the most incredibly healing, kick-ass, take-no-prisoners music I've ever heard in my entire life. For the countless great conversations. For touching my soul when you sing. Love you, brotha. electricmary.com

Bobby B.: For guiding me to the truth. God took me by the arm one day, led me to you and said, "Here, Bobby, see what you can do with this one." Nicely done, brother. I love you. bbstepstudy.com

Boogie: My childhood hero. For welcoming me to the BCW family. For being the person who showed me the true meaning of forgiveness. For spending so much time with me and never asking for anything in return. For believing in me. For sharing your life experience. Woo . . . Mercy Daddy! jimmyvaliant.weebly.com

Thank you, God, for helping me push my pen.

2018 Boogieland Motorcycle Playlist

Gasoline & Guns	Electric Mary
Why Do You Tell Lies	Robin Lane and the Chartbusters
Five Bullets	Anders Osborne
Love Has Taken Its Toll	Saraya
Let Me Out	Electric Mary
Drag Me Down	Jennifer Nettles Band
Beat the Devil's Tattoo	Black Rebel Motorcycle Club
Mr. Rock & Roll	Jim Breuer and the Loud & Rowdy
Open My Eyes	Rival Sons
Sweet Mary C	Electric Mary
One in a Million	Electric Mary
No One Does It Better Than Me	Electric Mary
Monkey Business	Skid Row
Lies (LIVE)	Electric Mary
Stained (LIVE)	Electric Mary
OIC (LIVE)	Electric Mary
With Our Love	Paul Rodgers
We All Go Down	Electric Mary
Bad Girl's Lament	Jennifer Nettles Band
Slave	Electric Mary
Crashdown	Electric Mary

Woman	Electric Mary
Precious and Grace (LIVE)	ZZ Top
Arrested for Driving While Blind	ZZ Top
Keep It Close	Bones Owens
Only Friend	The Temperance Movement
Lipstick Wonder Woman	Tyler Bryant & The Shakedown
Tennessee Mojo	The Cadillac Three
Mississippi King	Five Horse Johnson
Victoria	The Kinks
Badass	Black Robot
El Camino	Hogjaw
Blackwater Swagger	Blackwater Conspiracy
Luv Me	Electric Mary
Peace Sells	Megadeth
So Cruel	Electric Mary
Let It All Out	Ram Jam
Lights Out	UFO
No One Does It Better Than Me (LIVE)	Electric Mary
No More No More	Aerosmith
Mr. Blues	Stone Machine
Down Mississippi Way	Elias T. Hoth
Brendan's Dead	Brendan Higgins Band
Adam's Apple	Aerosmith
Come to Poppa	Bob Seger
Travellin' Man	Rambler
Rattlesnake Trail	Smokey Fingers
Make It	Aerosmith
Lord of the Thighs	Aerosmith
Boogie King	Screamin' Cheetah Wheelies
Born With a Broken Heart	Dirty York
The Charm	Devil's Hollow
Sweet Southern Sound	Moon Dog Mane
Can't You See	Black Stone Cherry

Long Way From Home (Do Me)	Electric Mary
Busted	Electric Mary
Hey Now	Electric Mary
Gasoline & Guns (LIVE)	Electric Mary
Stars	Electric Mary
Oxygen Thief	Electric Mary
Right Down to the Bone	Electric Mary
All Coming Down	Electric Mary
Man on the Silver Mountain	Rainbow
Since You Been Gone	Rainbow
Run to The Hills	Iron Maiden
Too Bad	Bad Company
Leaving You (LIVE)	Bad Company
Laying Down the Law	The Law
Make or Break	The Firm
Shooting Star	Bad Company
Rock 'n' Roll Fantasy (LIVE)	Bad Company
Shift	Jennifer Nettles Band
El Camino	Jennifer Nettles Band
Perfect Strangers	Deep Purple
Too Hot to Handle	UFO
Electric Phase	UFO
Stone Cold Crazy	Queen
Southern Native	Blackfoot
White Man's Land	Blackfoot
Hey Joe (LIVE)	Bad Company
Long Way From Home (Do Me) (LIVE)	Electric Mary
My Best Friend (LIVE)	Electric Mary
Miss Misery	Electric Mary
Heard It on the X (LIVE)	ZZ Top
Nicotine (LIVE)	Electric Mary
Already Gone (LIVE)	Electric Mary
Sweet Mary C (LIVE)	Electric Mary

Home in My Hand	Foghat
Fool for the City	Foghat
Stranger in My Home Town	Foghat
Selling Jesus	Skunk Anansie
The Seeker	The Who
Let Me Out (LIVE)	Electric Mary
The Boy From New York City	Manhattan Transfer

To contact Brendan directly, please reach out to him at:

bhigginsauthor@gmail.com

You can follow him at the below:

www.yogibiker.net

Facebook: @FromtheWrestlingRingtotheYogaMat

Instagram: @waking_up_book

www.ingramcontent.com/pod-product-compliance
Lightning Source LLC
Chambersburg PA
CBHW050310120526
44592CB00014B/1851